TRUE LOVE CAST OUT ALL EVIL

JOHN AND ROBIN DICKSON SERIES IN TEXAS MUSIC
Sponsored by the Center for Texas Music History,
Texas State University
Jason Mellard, General Editor

TRUE LOVE CAST OUT ALL EVIL

The Songwriting Legacy of
ROKY ERICKSON

Brian T. Atkinson

Forewords by BILLY GIBBONS and HENRY ROLLINS

TEXAS A&M UNIVERSITY PRESS   COLLEGE STATION

This paper meets the requirements of
ANSI/NISO Z39.48-1992 (Permanence of Paper).
Binding materials have been chosen for durability.

Manufactured in the United States of America

Library of Congress Cataloging-in-Publication Data
Names: Atkinson, Brian T., editor. | Gibbons, Billy F., 1949– writer of
foreword. | Rollins, Henry, 1961– writer of foreword.
Title: True love cast out all evil: the songwriting legacy of Roky Erickson /
[edited by] Brian T. Atkinson; forewords by Billy Gibbons and Henry Rollins.
Other titles: John and Robin Dickson series in Texas music.
Description: First edition. | College Station: Texas A&M University Press,
[2021] | Series: John and Robin Dickson series in Texas music | Includes
discographies and index.
Identifiers: LCCN 2021030134 (print) | LCCN 2021030135 (ebook) |
ISBN 9781648430435 (cloth) | ISBN 9781648430442 (ebook)
Subjects: LCSH: Erickson, Roky. | Rock musicians—Texas—Biography. | Rock
musicians—United States—interviews. | Psychedelic rock music—United States—
History and criticism. | 13th Floor Elevators (Musical group) | Bleib Alien (Musical
group) | BISAC: MUSIC / Genres & Styles / Rock | MUSIC / Individual
Composer & Musician | LCGFT: Biographies. | Interviews.
Classification: LCC ML420.E733 T78 2021 (print) | LCC ML420.E733 (ebook)
| DDC 782.42166092 [B]—dc23
LC record available at https://lccn.loc.gov/2021030134
LC ebook record available at https://lccn.loc.gov/2021030135

To

JANE

for reasons known to her

People need the tormented artist archetype because it satisfies some belief that crazy people are touched by God and somehow are clear signals from the Great Mystery. That goes for the candle on Michelangelo's forehead, Van Gogh's ear, Townes Van Zandt's fucking saxophone—and I contribute to that mythos in most of what I say [in my interview in this book]. No one wants to hear the story about Roky Erickson crying in the dark on his porch in the middle of the night. Everyone wants to hear the story about Roky carrying around a beetle in his pocket because the insect actually is an emissary from an advanced alien race. I just want to admit that I was complicit in romanticizing the scam that mentally ill art is better, which doesn't help the health of artists in general or Roky as a specific example. We all want the story of magnificent madness, but not the story of the terrible sadness.[1]

—*Jon Dee Graham, July 2020*

CONTENTS

PART II. The Interpreter

FOREWORD

Billy Gibbons

THE 13TH FLOOR ELEVATORS SHOWED UP ALL OF A SUDDEN IN Houston and embraced the term "psychedelic" to describe what they were doing. They had a runaway insane message and mission. No one had seen anything like it. The Elevators were having an impact on the whole Texas music scene. We were acknowledging their impact [by saying], "Well, gee, elevators go up. We should be [Gibbons's first band before ZZ Top] the Moving Sidewalks because that goes forward."[2] Roky Erickson came to mean many things to many admirers and will continue to resonate with a legacy of remarkable style, talent, and poetic and artistic tales from beyond.[3] Roky [was] one of the out-and-out wildest rock singers. The talent behind his voice is the mystery factor that no one could touch. He stands alone to this day and is revered as an artist because he had the gift of a wonderful voice. Every musician had such respect for this crazy thing that the Elevators were coming up with. They were the big heroes. There was no way they couldn't make it.[4]

FOREWORD

Henry Rollins

ROKY COULD REALLY SING. WHENEVER I WROTE SONGS THAT dealt with horror—not something in a film but real-life things that truly alter and ruin the act of living—I would think of Roky songs like "If You Have Ghosts" and "I Think of Demons." Roky was a deep well. Many people have enough going on as is and don't have the time or inclination to "go there," which Roky's music requires. He was startlingly good and a genuine original. You will not come across a talent like him again ever. Roky Erickson is as much an American treasure as Woody Guthrie.[5]

PREFACE

TRUE LOVE CAST OUT ALL EVIL: THE SONGWRITING LEGACY OF Roky Erickson touches on but does not thoroughly dissect Erickson's early years in his youthful band the Spades and the revolutionary psychedelic rockers the 13th Floor Elevators. Paul Drummond's expansive *Eye Mind: The Saga of Roky Erickson and the 13th Floor Elevators, the Pioneers of Psychedelic Sound* (Process Media, 2007) and *13th Floor Elevators: A Visual History* (Anthology Editions, 2020) cover that ground with enough detail. Additionally, countless books examine the San Francisco–based psychedelic rock movement during the late sixties in general. Ben Graham's *A Gathering of Promises: The Battle for Texas's Psychedelic Music, from the 13th Floor Elevators to the Black Angels and Beyond* (Zero Books, 2005) offers a solid foundation focusing specifically on the Lone Star State's vast psychedelic music scene.

This book instead spotlights Erickson's sporadic but sensational solo career from the early seventies through his late-career peak *True Love Cast out All Evil* and beyond. The following interviews reveal that Erickson's last fifty years in music mined territory as influential—if spectacularly underappreciated—as his work with the iconic Elevators. Special note: longtime author and journalist Joe Nick Patoski's generosity allowed permission to reprint in these pages the key interview he, Doug Hanners, Kirby McDaniel, and Deron Bissett conducted with Roky Erickson over two sessions in 1975. Segments from that interview appear in this book as the prologue as well as in Erickson's own chapters. Those contributions proved invaluable in my research. They were originally published in the first *Not Fade Away* fanzine that year.

My fingerprints on the primary source material within these pages are minimal. I cut and pasted sections of an interview to improve clarity and flow and edited out peripheral words and phrases when necessary. I cut redundancies and added material if an interviewee left out a word, song title, or reference. Readers can assume that I never deliberately changed words said by an interviewee except to correct factual errors or add clarity. Those interview passages are bracketed. Also, a few interviews offered compelling anecdotes but simply did not fit the book's natural rhythm and flow. I have included those transcriptions in the end notes. Finally, as a nod to Roky Erickson's poetry collections written while incarcerated in Rusk State Hospital in the late sixties and early seventies, I titled the two section introductions "Openers I" and "Openers II." Both Erickson poetry books shed significant light into one of modern music's most compelling minds.

ACKNOWLEDGMENTS

THANK YOU FIRST AND FOREMOST TO LONGTIME AUSTIN-based singer-songwriter and music industry renaissance man Troy Campbell for suggesting a book about Roky Erickson several years ago. Troy's book vision was significantly different than *True Love Cast out All Evil* ended up turning out, but I never would have considered the subject if he hadn't brought up the idea. As always, very special thanks to the John and Robin Dickson Series in Texas Music, Thom Lemmons and everyone at Texas A&M University Press, and Dickson Series editor Jason Mellard and former Dickson Series editor Gary Hartman for making this idea a reality. Special thanks to Jenni Finlay, my partner in all my crimes in life and work. Great gratitude to my parents, Ted and Ruthanne Atkinson, who have supported even my wildest ideas all these years. Additionally, big thanks to Mike Alvarez, Bill Bentley, Mikel Erickson, Clementine Hall, Freddie Krc, Casey Monahan, Joe Nick Patoski, Toby St. John, and so many others who encouraged this book and opened doors.

Biggest thank-you to all the singer-songwriters, players, and industry veterans who offered their time to talk about Roky Erickson. A few I wished to interview remained unavailable despite several requests, but nearly everyone jumped at the chance. Finally, thanks to the friends who constantly encourage and tolerate me as these books take shape: Scott Beckwith, Janet Berger, Ginger Bloomer and Nancy Friedel, Mary Keating Bruton, Lefty and Lil Finlay (and their late, great sister, Banjo),

Chris Fullerton and Lindsay Preston, Mike and Michelle Grimes, David Holmes and Mary Miken Holmes, Kipling McFarland, Jennifer Menchen, Dolores O'Riordan, Tamara Saviano, Troy Schoenfelder, Sean Tracey, and Marianna Whitney. Many thanks to everyone who has supported our Squeaky String Productions, Eight 30 Records, Catfish Concerts, Barefoot Recording, and Red Burgundy Films.

TRUE LOVE CAST OUT ALL EVIL

PART I

The Psychedelic Sounds of the
13th Floor Elevators

SELECTED TIMELINE FOR THE 13TH FLOOR ELEVATORS

1947

Roky Erickson is born on July 15, 1947, in Dallas, Texas.

1949

The Erickson family moves to Austin, Texas.

1965

Erickson quits Travis High School during his senior year.
Erickson forms the Spades with best friend John Kearney.
They record "We Sell Soul" and "You're Gonna Miss Me" at TNT
    Studio in San Antonio.
"You're Gonna Miss Me" patents Erickson's screaming singing style.
Erickson's songwriting credit reads "Emil Schwartze."
Erickson leaves the Spades and joins the 13th Floor Elevators.

1966

The Elevators release *The Psychedelic Sounds of the 13th Floor Elevators.*
Erickson cowrites "Roller Coaster," "Splash 1," "Reverberation,"
    "Don't Fall Down," and "Fire Engine."
"You're Gonna Miss Me" becomes the Elevators' only charting single.
Future psychedelic rock legend Janis Joplin reportedly wants to join
    the Elevators.

The Elevators frequently perform at the Avalon Ballroom and the
    Fillmore in San Francisco.
The psychedelic rock movement develops an epicenter in
    San Francisco's Haight-Ashbury district.
The Elevators perform "You're Gonna Miss Me" on Dick Clark's
    American Bandstand.

1967

Jefferson Airplane, Janis Joplin, the Grateful Dead, Jimi Hendrix, and
    others rise toward fame.
The legendary Monterey Pop Festival launches a cultural revolution.
The Elevators release their high-water mark album *Easter Everywhere*.
The album features six Erickson cowrites including "Slip inside This
    House" and "I Had to Tell You."

1969

The Elevators fizzle with their third album, *Bull of the Woods*.
Erickson pleads insanity after being arrested on drug charges.
Authorities place Erickson under psychiatric care at Rusk State
    Hospital in Rusk, Texas.
The 13th Floor Elevators disband.
Erickson begins receiving electroshock and Thorazine treatments at
    Rusk while occasionally on LSD.
He is diagnosed with paranoid schizophrenia and undergoes
    treatments at Rusk for three years.
Meanwhile, Erickson fills notebooks with lyrics, poems, and
    elaborate drawings.

PROLOGUE

Roky Erickson

I STARTED PLAYING [THE CIVIL WAR BALLAD] "AURA LEE" AND [Elvis Presley's] "Love Me Tender" on guitar when I was thirteen. Then I got into Bo Diddley and Little Richard. "You know what I like?" [Richard] would say. "I like to hear my voice. Listen. I like the way that sounds." His singing had so much influence on me. James Brown is my favorite performer. He blows my mind. I like Elmore James, Blind Willie McTell, B. B. King, Bob Dylan, Mick Jagger, Keith Richards, Eric Clapton and the Bluesbreakers, and "Changes" by David Bowie. [His] words have many levels.

I was playing with the Spades at the Jade Room [in Austin, Texas] when these four cats came in. They had auras around their heads. I said, "I wonder who they are." They came up and said, "Listen, man, we're with a group called the Lingsmen. We want to put together a super group called the 13th Floor Elevators." They [had] this image of playing hard rock and roll music. "We want you to be our singer," they said. "We'll do all the music." Then they played for me over at their house and blew my mind. I quit the Spades, which was a hard thing to do. You have personal involvement and don't want to hurt anybody. [Spades band member] John [Kearney] was a real good friend. You don't wanna be cruel: "Listen, man, forget you. I've got another band out here."

Joining the Elevators was like leaving home. Real emotional. Their records were a little heavy and wild. I liked Tommy's idea for the [percussive electrified] jug. We were known as the first psychedelic band. [Our]

5

music would make you lay back and envision things like Dylan does. We liked Dylan, but we wanted to put out a rock and roll band. Dylan was one single person, [and] we thought we could put out more sound if we did the whole thing as a band. We made a point to be in a place when we played so that we could hear things to play for the audience. Say somebody wasn't able to get high—well, he would get high with our music. He could have his consciousness or his cortex opened just by our music. We believe you need access to the cortex, which allows you to open up into the many psychic things in your mind like ESP.

The Elevators [started playing at] the New Orleans Club, the Jade Room, La Maison [Ballroom] in Houston, and then did two shows on Dick Clark's [*American Bandstand*]. This was a real funny [moment]. We asked Dick, "Would you ask us who's the head of the band?" He comes up and says, "Who's the head of your band?" "Well, we're all heads." This was on nationwide television. We [had already been] on television in Dallas, but we didn't have much luck there. We were on television in San Antonio and in Houston [on the *Larry Kane Show*]. Then we played with the Byrds in Fort Worth at Will Rogers [Coliseum]. [We were] poor and driving an old car. The carbon monoxide was leaking into it, and the devil—or God—looks down. "Hey man," he says. "I can't handle it anymore." We got a ride to the concert. Everything was all right.

Then we went out to San Francisco and played the Avalon Ballroom. We had a pretty wild all-Texas show one time with three groups: Sir Doug [Sahm], Big Brother and the Holding Company with Janis Joplin, and the 13th Floor Elevators. All three groups got pretty far out. Doug jammed his blues. He's really good when he gets going. Janis Joplin blew my mind. She got so famous, but she was a real person to her good friends. She wasn't one who went, "Get away from me. I've got all these things to do." She blew your mind just as much offstage as she did onstage. I'm sorry she died. We did some benefits together and loved her. She needed to get her own name more than just a member of the Elevators. She had to be Janis Joplin. I had to be Roky Erickson.[1]

—Roky Erickson, 1975

OPENERS I

13th Floor Elevators

ROKY ERICKSON SANG LIKE SERPENTS SHADED HIS SHADOWS. After all, the mystical and mythical Austin-based singer-songwriter and psychedelic drug enthusiast, a creative cyclone who fronted the pioneering 13th Floor Elevators throughout the late sixties, delivered from deepest depths. "Roky's voice was undeniable," Butthole Surfers drummer King Coffey says. "He screamed and yelled like great Texas blues singers—freaky, rocking, weird. People argue that Janis Joplin took her style from him. His voice was the perfect storm. Roky was a visionary singer and songwriter, a total home run."[1] "Roky Erickson opened the door," echoes legendary outlaw country singer-songwriter Ray Wylie Hubbard. "He was the first one through. He showed the way. Bands today still strive for what he brought to music."[2] Erickson, who was born in Dallas, Texas, on July 15, 1947, and died in Austin on May 31, 2019, achieved enlightenment early on.

Transcendence came with a price.

Erickson's kaleidoscopic journey began as the 13th Floor Elevators— cult legends who exploded with regional success but crumbled unceremoniously into relative obscurity—helped launch the psychedelic rock genre with their debut *The Psychedelic Sounds of the 13th Floor Elevators* (1966). Their legacy cemented with the masterwork *Easter Everywhere* a year later. Then the band imploded, and their lackluster final album, *Bull of the Woods*, fizzled with the sixties. Erickson soon was arrested on drug charges and disappeared into state psychiatric care. His reality immediately distorted from electroshock therapy and Thorazine treatments. Erickson remained locked away under high scrutiny and maximum security for three years. "Roky came back a different guy after he was incarcerated and put away at the nervous hospital in Rusk [Texas]," childhood friend Mike Pankratz says. "Sometimes he would know me, but he knew me less than before."[3]

VERSE

You're Gonna Miss Me

MIKE "MIGUEL" PANKRATZ

We were best friends. The local pot-smoking Beatnik scene was pretty small for our age group in Austin, and we didn't take long to meet everybody. Roky and I spent many nights at his house. His parents were way bohemian. Their house was wacky. Nobody ever put anything away or did the dishes. Calling them liberal would be an understatement. His father was an architect, and his mother was a fairly high-style artist. The worst thing Roky could say about somebody was that they were boozers. He had a hard time growing up with alcoholic parents, but we had less adult supervision at his house than anywhere else. Roky had total freedom on one hand, but on the other he had total freedom at that age. Roky paid a price for how his parents were, but that sure made him a reader and a thinker. We started playing music together in ninth grade.

We would take wine and cigarettes down to Campbell's Hole here in Austin and drink and talk about music and philosophy and read poetry to each other until daylight. We had a pretty Huck Finn–like situation. I came from bohemian parents myself. We were born into this liberal scene, which is why Roky and I got along so well. We weren't restricted by any odd thought process or religion. We were a couple free hippies who knew how to get around in the world. We both were reading Allen Ginsberg and other New York hip dogs. Our friend [and Erickson's bandmate in his first group, the Spades] John Kearney's older brother Mek was an absolute genius with a Rhodes Scholar brain. He turned us on to books by the great philosophers and told us about eating peyote and seeing the face of God in the eighth grade. He would make that sound amazingly real to us. That became our reality.

Roky's song "You're Gonna Miss Me" was straight out of the Little Richard handbook. Roky was absolutely dedicated to Little Richard and had his scream down. I think the Spades played three shows total over the school year. We must have practiced daily for two months for the very first one we did. Roky played piano. The show was two hours long and at a teen dance night for our school down at the YWCA on the University of Texas campus. I'm pretty sure we played everything Little Richard had recorded that night as well as Buddy Holly and Ritchie Valens songs. We used to study [Bob Dylan's 1963 album] *The Freewheelin' Bob Dylan*, which came out that year. We also knew Austin's great folk scene. I could go to the Chequered Flag underage as a player. All they would do is not let you drink. I met Joan Baez, Buffy Sainte-Marie, and Lightnin' Hopkins there.

I went in another direction during our tenth-grade year. Blues was all I wanted to hear after a while. I ended up playing in an all-black band in East Austin. Roky met the other people and players in his life. The Beatles played Ed Sullivan a year later. Everything changed. Every guy in town who knew three chords started a band. Roky was running with [future 13th Floor Elevators bandmate] Tommy Hall and other older guys from the University of Texas when he was in tenth and eleventh grade. I didn't know those guys at the time. [Golden Dawn lead singer] George Kinney was in our crowd. I was the only white guy playing in a soul band by 1965. Roky definitely had discovered acid by then. The curtains were pulled away once Roky met Tommy.

I could tell that Roky was a lifer with music during our first month rehearsing with the Spades. Music was all he wanted to do. We would go straight from school to his house to rehearse. We would have long talks about how to play things musically. We had decided that there was no way to compromise. I don't think Roky ever had a tendency to do anything other than music. He was too good. He understood the mathematics about music without having to go to school. He and Tommy could figure out arrangements, passing chords, and other stuff you learn in school. The Elevators were a great band. You could tell they rehearsed all the time. They had a real deep following here in Austin.

I hadn't seen Roky in a while by twelfth grade. I walked into school one morning, and he had grown his hair all out and was wearing beads and a long trench coat. He had a one-pound coffee can full of weed. Roky and I didn't graduate. I got a GED in the military after I got drafted and spent two years in the service and one in Vietnam. Everybody I knew in Austin was playing in a band when I got back. Roky had started the 13th Floor Elevators, who were hands down the best white band in Austin. They were playing a brand-new kind of music and inventing a name for it. I often saw them play. Roky and I would see each other around, but we never played together again. The Elevators went to San Francisco and stayed awhile. There were whole neighborhoods with Texans in San Francisco. I was out there once visiting for a month before I met anyone not from Austin and Houston. San Franciscans loved our accent. They thought we were southern cowboys who didn't know the rules.[1]

Mike "Miguel" Pankratz has been a gigging musician around Central Texas for more than half a century. He currently performs with Stop the Truck and the Mau-Mau Chaplains. His daughter Lisa Pankratz is an acclaimed drummer for roots-rock icon Dave Alvin and several others.

MIKEL ERICKSON

We grew up in a two-bedroom home in Austin. The house was being built in 1947 while my parents were still living in Dallas, which is where Roky was born in July that year. I was born when we moved into the Austin house in 1949. Our brother Donnie came in 1951. Dad called Roky, Donnie, and me the Three Musketeers. The Three Musketeers took over both bedrooms. Our parents slept on a Murphy bed in the living room. Our dad worked all the time because Roky started playing music around eleven, twelve years old. Dad had no peace at home. He would come home from work and find teenagers playing music and beating on drums because the house was always open for any neighbor kids to come in, eat, and play in the yard. Our mother would let us have pool parties all the time because no one else had a pool. Our father had built a test swimming pool in the backyard while working for the Perry Company.

Our mother was a soprano opera singer and piano player, but she didn't work. Our father was the breadwinner as an architect in Austin and paid for a couple forty-fives of her singing. There was constant music like opera and *Porgy and Bess* in our house because she loved it. Roky and I both took piano lessons from Mrs. Ward down the street during that time. Roky also played cornet at Porter Junior High School and picked up the harmonica around the same time as the guitar. Our parents had bought him a guitar and amplifier from Sears and Roebuck as he got into Chuck Berry and Bo Diddley. Roky was involved with several bands in high school.

Roky's band the Spades with his friend John Kearney got hooked up with Zero Records in San Antonio and cut "You're Gonna Miss Me" for the first time in history. Roky put his name down as Emil Schwartze [as the songwriter] on the single. They were playing around Austin and had a residency at the Jade Room when they were on Zero Records in 1966. The Spades became so popular you couldn't even get into the place. I was their doorman. The Spades had become popular not so much for the music as Roky's singing. The Spades were stiff and dressed up in their uniforms. They were pretty much what you would call geeks nowadays. Then you had Roky [screaming], "Owwww."

I had seen the Lingsmen play a couple times at the Dunes Club in Port Aransas when I had hitchhiked down there with Pat Pankratz, who was Mike Pankratz's brother. "There are these guys," I told Roky, "and they're really cool." Then Tommy Hall, Stacy Sutherland, John Ike Walton, and Benny Thurman walked into the Jade Room five weeks later and had a talk with Roky. The Elevators were meant to be. Everything was hitting on the right notes. They moved their equipment over to Tommy Hall's house by the University of Texas around Thirty-Third Street. The Elevators were playing music late one night at Tommy's when the cops came to the door. They wanted them to shut down the music, so I went over and told them to shut it down. Tommy Hall was saying, "Don't worry about it. It's your trip, not mine."

I moved to Fifth Street on Austin's west side to live with Charlie Prichard from the Conqueroo in 1965. Then Charlie moved out, and Roky moved in. My place was a safe harbor. The apartment was a small one upstairs. You went up some stairs and took a right at the top of the stairs. Then you were into the hallway. You would go into the front bedroom if you took a right. That room overlooked Fifth Street. If you took a left, you would go down the hall and take a right into the kitchen or a left into the bathroom. Then the second bedroom was all the way down at the end of the hall, which was Roky's room and had a door that would open back up into the kitchen. I worked down the street at the foreign car clinic and would walk home and find Roky and Tommy sitting at the little dining room table writing. They wrote some of *Easter Everywhere* sitting at that table. Tommy was domineering but knew what he wanted to say.

The Elevators were thunderous onstage. You cannot understand the feeling if you never saw them live. Sandy Lockett had put together an amazing sound system that filled every place they played. He was a genius who was born to work in electronics. Sandy had Stacy running through a mixing tape, which gave him an echo sound that was hard to produce. They do that now with wah-wah pedals. You could feel the music and Roky's voice. Roky sang and screamed in tune. I was their roadie and would drive Tommy's AMC Rambler around from the gigs. I saw a lot of cool shit for a fifteen-year-old, but things got really serious with the cops. I would pull up somewhere, and they immediately would surround the Rambler and our white van. They would take everything out and unscrew it immediately. Crazy. [The band] would leave, and I would be stuck somewhere in Houston with the cops. Things really started to change. Chaos.

I still call the [Elevators'] song ["I Had to Tell You"] "Chaos." The song goes, "Chaos all around me / with its fevered clinging / but I can hear you singing / in the corners of my brain." The song was written at Clementine Hall's parents' ranch. She was like the mother hen who would keep everyone focused and on track. Roky and Clementine were sitting in the yard by a big tree and collaborating. Roky started playing this rhythm guitar and Clementine started singing along. Roky would add a verse, and it went on and on. That song was written in two takes as I remember. I don't remember anyone else being there besides the three of us.

That moment watching them write that song was so pleasant and easy, almost like being reborn. Seeing Roky and Clementine together that day was one of the high points of my life. There was no care in the world. These two individuals were talking about chaos and things in the world that surrounded them, but what they were hearing was keeping them sane. They were saying, "I can hear you now." Roky and Clementine just matched. I felt that they had a lot of feelings for each other back then and even to this day. They were kindred spirits, which was completely different from Tommy—or anybody, really—and Roky. Clementine and Roky had a different vibe.[2]

Mikel Erickson is Roky Erickson's younger brother. He lives in Austin, Texas.

CLEMENTINE HALL

My husband, Tommy Hall, and I met the other Lingsmen in Port Aransas. There was a very small community who smoked marijuana so we spotted each other very quickly. We found out they were musicians. They needed a singer but hadn't met Roky yet. Then we came back to Austin. [Texas folklorist and musician] Tary Owens said, "There's this phenomenal kid you have to see." He talked us into going to the Jade Room. Tommy and I looked at each other the moment Roky started performing and said, "He's the one. The guys will go crazy when they hear him. He's perfect." Roky was only nineteen years old, but he was strikingly beautiful, exceptionally bright, and bubbly. He had a wonderful voice and would scan the audience so intensely that every single person thought he was singing directly to them. Roky was so genuine. Nothing phony. He made eye contact. There was an electrical charge. Absolute charisma. Very sweet and very childlike guy.

We rushed back down to Padre Island and told the other guys they had to come up and see him. They flipped when they saw him perform. Tommy, Roky, and the Lingsmen took LSD and jammed all night long. They mostly played instrumental stuff but also songs they were familiar with on the radio. They bonded instantly. I did a lot of cooking and tidying up at that time. I had two very small boys, so I was the only one who was always straight. I only took LSD or smoked marijuana when the two children went back to the ranch with my father. My father worked in Austin on the weekdays, and I was in school there during the week. I would turn on with the Elevators on the weekends.

Roky was extremely extraordinary. He was worried about his best friend John Kearney, who was the drummer in the Spades, if he were to abandon them for the Elevators. Tommy and I went over and explained the situation to John. "We don't want to break up your friendship," we said. "I knew sooner or later something was gonna take Roky away," John said. "He's way out of our league." We had a house where the entire floor was a playroom for the children. I told him we could make that into a suite for him and his girlfriend Susie. Roky was over at the house all day every day rehearsing. "You can still keep seeing Roky," I said, "and you and your girlfriend don't have to keep meeting in cars and other people's apartments." John said he was sad at losing Roky as a fellow musician, but he was delighted to be a part of our family. That took away the only objection Roky had. John and Susie moved into the flat above. We furnished it. They married not long after, and Susie and I became very close friends. "I understand we'll be living upstairs," was the first thing she said. "How would you like to have a nanny for your kids?"[3]

Clementine Hall was married to 13th Floor Elevators lyricist and electric jug player Tommy Hall in the late sixties as the band launched its career. She and Roky Erickson cowrote the popular Elevators songs "Splash 1" and "I Had to Tell You." Hall currently lives in Napa Valley, California.

RAY WYLIE HUBBARD

The Elevators were groundbreaking. They played at Arlington State College when I was going there around 1966. The Beatles had hit, but the United States was still very conservative at the time. You would still very much be seeing short hair, desert boots, and corduroy jackets with elbow patches at colleges. The full-tilt hippies hadn't hit yet. I remember they had set up a stage about three feet off the ground in a hall, and the show was sponsored by a sorority. The Elevators came in from Austin with their entourage like Woodstock people coming in. My mouth was open the whole time. I had never seen anything like this. Roky took the Beatles, the Rolling Stones, Herman's Hermits, and Buffalo Springfield and raised the bar. He brought something new and went to a place where nobody else had gone with the psychedelic rock.

The Elevators weren't wearing matching outfits when they came in. They sauntered up onstage and started playing with this energy and vibe that I'd never felt. The whole audience was like, "What is this?" They were like the Blues Brothers at Bob's Country Bunker. We were mesmerized.

The sorority girls had to be in their dorms by curfew at ten o'clock, but the Elevators started late and were going late. Everybody was milling around. Then teachers had a confrontation [with the band] at the side of the stage. Roky said, "Well, they're telling us to quit because there's a curfew." "Boo," the crowd went. "No. No. Let them play." They played one more song, and the professors pulled the plug. They made a big deal. They went, "Awww." The night was exciting, incredible, intense, and still vivid today, which is how cool it was. Roky would close his eyes when he sang and was so into the music. You could tell nothing else mattered but the music. Roky had definite charisma. The lyrics to "You're Gonna Miss Me" were a blues, but the song had the energy and power of Robert Johnson at the crossroads.

I saw the Elevators on the television show *Something Else*, which was like the local *American Bandstand* in Dallas with Ron Shipman hosting. They were so badass cool when "You're Gonna Miss Me" came out. There hadn't been anything like that on the radio. You had Elvis and the Ventures before the Beatles so it wasn't bland, but you also had Fabians and Bobby Riedels. Then the Beatles and Stones hit, and the music was so fresh. The Elevators were so different from everyone. The lyrics were so vivid and impressive. The Elevators set the bar with rock music the way Townes Van Zandt did in folk music. You aspire to be them. Those guys were hip. They knew what was going on and were aware. They had inner knowledge and were the enlightened torchbearers. Then Roky's drug bust happened and [started] a very turbulent time. Longhairs would have to put their hair up under their hat in Texas. I heard that Roky had gone into an institution. You felt compassion knowing what he had been through [when he was released from the institution]. You could empathize with him. He was always gracious. You could tell he had a gentle compassion.[4]

Ray Wylie Hubbard has transformed from court jester of seventies outlaw country music in Texas into the state's most sage and sober mystical songwriter. The Messenger: The Songwriting Legacy of Ray Wylie Hubbard *(Texas A&M University Press, 2019) tells his story as a musician.*

BILL BENTLEY

The Elevators were playing a club in Houston called La Maison in early 1966. I already might have heard "You're Gonna Miss Me" on the radio because I felt the need to see them. The band hadn't come onstage yet when I got there, but I was fascinated because the jug was on an amp and John Ike Walton had this monstrously cool silver sparkle drum kit. The Elevators had this otherworldly presence when they came out. They were probably on LSD because they did that pretty constantly when they played, but they looked at the audience differently than anyone I had seen. They had this regal sense about them. This was a whole other way of being on a rock and roll stage. Taking LSD takes you to another world within this world. Roky and Tommy had really studied what the psychedelic experience could do to you, and that's the way they lived. They were coming from another level of existence, and we could elevate ourselves to the plane they were on once we took LSD and would go see them. You could feel that they were above us in terms of where their mental states were.

The music completely tore the top of my head off. I had never heard anything like it. I had seen the Stones and every band that came through Houston, but there was something so powerful about the Elevators, like they had some other mission than playing. They created a life force. Tommy was the [primary] lyricist on the songs besides "You're Gonna Miss Me," so I got deeply fascinated by the lyrics as well as the music itself. They had almost like a cannonball approach delivery. I could tell right away that Tommy was writing from a very philosophical area that nobody else in music was writing about then. The Beatles and Stones couldn't touch his lyrics like in "Rollercoaster," "Reverberation," and "Fire Engine." They're very intricate songs about how rock and roll can be used to share ideas.

The Elevators created the original live rock and roll scene in Austin. They weren't all that social in the San Francisco scene, but they were hooked into Chet Helms. Texans hang out with Texans. I moved out to Los Angeles in 1980 and don't think I hung out with anyone from California for ten years. Why bother? Texans are more fun. The Elevators were pretty much over by 1968. They went to San Francisco in late August 1966 and played the Fillmore Auditorium. The Great Society opened. Roky played at the Avalon in San Francisco four or five times. Buffalo Spring-field opened for the Elevators one time because they already had had a hit with "You're Gonna Miss Me" in the Bay Area in 1966.

I've been listening to *Easter Everywhere* for fifty-two years now, and the other night was the first time I ever noticed that there is no jug on the Dylan song [the album's fifth track, "Baby Blue"]. Isn't that interesting? There's jug on every other song. I wonder if Tommy had such a reverence for Dylan that he didn't think it fit. Tommy has this theory that [Bob Dylan's] "Frankie Lee and Judas Priest" is an answer song to the Eleva-tors' "Slip inside This House." There are five or six similar lyrics where he swears Dylan was writing back to him, like "It's not a house, it's a home." I read somewhere that Dylan thought their version of "Baby Blue" was the best cover of his song ever. The Elevators' version is incredible. I think it's better than Dylan's.

I loved Roky so much. Seeing him as a fifteen-year-old opened up the whole world. These were Texas guys who weren't too much older than me. I was stuck in Houston, which was a very uptight, right-wing city in the sixties, and they showed me it was possible to think outside the usual limits and maybe create a life for yourself even if it was only mentally. Houston was a rough place in the sixties for hippies. I got busted for one joint in 1968 and was given a felony narcotic charge with a sentence of five to life. Luckily, I bribed the judge and just got probation. It was re-ally scary. I was eighteen and gonna go to Huntsville for one joint. The Elevators gave us hope that there was another world. You never forget it when someone gives you that hope.[5]

Bill Bentley produced Where the Pyramid Meets the Eye: A Tribute to Roky Erickson *in 1990 and was as executive producer for* I Have Always Been Here Before: The Roky Erickson Anthology *(Shout! Factory) and* May the Circle Remain Unbroken: A Tribute to Roky Erickson. *He lives in Studio City, California.*

"CRAZY" CARL HICKERSON

Roky Erickson and the 13th Floor Elevators were like a tidal wave. Most bands didn't play Austin after they got big, but the Elevators still did.

Everybody was tripping on acid. Actually, I met Roky the night I discovered LSD. I exchanged about a hundred fifty peyote buttons outside the New Orleans Club that night in 1966. Roky was the main source of the purchase. I remember staring into his eyes for five minutes. Then I went home and took [the drugs] and found out that the dose was way too much. Roky was always with at least four other people when he was walking down the street. Seeing him always was an event. "You're Gonna Miss Me" was such a big hit for the Elevators. That song was number one around Austin forever. Everybody was talking.

I believe all the marijuana coming into the country from Mexico got chopped up in San Antonio before 1966. Then marijuana started getting chopped up here in Austin. You could always tell when the weed was really good because there would be more money on the [University of Texas] Drag. Roky was perfect for this town because Austin is an imaginary city. You have to believe in all the major industries here for them to exist. Think about it: you have the government, which is only there because you believe in it. Same with education. Roky was one of the few real Austinites. He was untouchable before I even knew him. "Wow," you would say. "That's Roky." Everybody knew that he was this great musician. I can't imagine a more informative musician.[6]

"Crazy" Carl Hickerson helped define the Texas capital city's "Keep Austin Weird" mantra by spending forty years twirling flowers downtown. He is the subject of the documentary film Crazy Carl and His Man Boobs: An Austin Love Story *(Beef and Pie Films, 2014).*

ROKY ERICKSON (PART I)

[The term] "psychedelic" [implies] that you're getting away from being addicted—like if someone takes one snort of heroin, and then they don't take any more [because] they experienced it. I'm concerned about finding geniuses like Lenny Bruce dead in their room. Oh, man, it just tears you up. All you can do is wad up your magazine. That's bad. One thing I'm not pleased about is they got me in [the mental institution] and said, "Son, we looked at your head, and you've taken over three hundred LSD trips. You may have a regression where you're seeing things again." "Why, he may have a flashback and might go crazy again." Then they put their arm on my shoulder and said, "Son, we would have to put you back in here again." Why don't you guys go bury yourselves?

I've always had the quest for something that would raise my consciousness. Maybe it's the fact that I've been in the flow of things, but I think people should be able to talk about it. Some people probably think I'm a nut. So nothing interesting or really far out gets said because everybody's so afraid to say anything. People need to say more about what they're afraid to say, so things will be discovered. Science [is] being able to accept that there's something beyond and there are beings on other worlds that are our friends. [They] are maybe thirty thousand years ahead of us intellectually.

Maybe we're all aliens. Maybe they came down here, colonized, and lived on earth. Then they split and left everybody living here. Maybe we had to look like cavemen because we were living with dinosaurs. You had to be rough to exist in the environment. Maybe cavemen were smarter than you think. "I'm gonna have to be here, so I'll form my body in this way." Maybe they were aliens. They could be real flexible. I could come in looking like Roky and then look like somebody else. Then maybe cavemen could form their shape to be real big. They have lots of hair because of the cold and everything around during the Ice Age.[7]

POWELL ST. JOHN

Then Janis Joplin showed up one day.[8] She had studied American roots music in much greater depth than I had, knew many more songs, and performed them with great power and authority.[9] We saw her coming into the Chuck Wagon in the University of Texas student union with Dave Moriarty. She had long, straight hair with a long black dress. I said, "I gotta meet that one." Janis had exotic looks. She showed up at [the notorious Austin apartment commune] the Ghetto that evening and heard us playing. She said, "Can I join in?" She didn't have a guitar but started singing. What a blues voice. We were all gobsmacked. Janis became the third Waller Creek Boy. We played together maybe two years. Janis was a real hit.[10] Few have heard Janis sing Appalachian mountain ballads, but she was the equal of anyone performing that music at the time.[11] "I know an old man who runs a bar in town," I said. "His name is [Threadgill's No.

1 owner] Kenneth Threadgill. You should meet him." They had a daddy and daughter relationship. Then the rest of her story happened.

Electric music was appealing. I thought the sheer volume I could achieve electrically would compel people to listen to my message whether they wanted to hear it or not.[12] So, I had reason for wanting to play amplified music, but the main reason was my friend Tommy Hall. He came up with the novel idea to put together a first-class rock and roll band in 1965. The message would be: "Expand your mind through the use of LSD," which sounded crazy but intriguing to me given Austin's buttoned-down, conservative atmosphere. The nonconformist and social deviant community was skeptical about the whole idea at first [as well as] Tommy's ability to pull it off.[13] I found Tommy a real source of information about music. For instance, he introduced me to James Brown, Wilson Pickett, and others I had not heard before.

Tommy was from Memphis and probably had a better perspective. He was an encyclopedia of musical knowledge, and I was trying to learn as much as I could. I used to go over to his place and play records.[14] Tommy and his wife, Clementine, took me to the Jade Room to hear a group of high school students that had a band named the Spades. Roky Erickson was a supertalented, dynamic, highly energetic performer. I must say I was impressed.[15] That's how I came to write some material for the Elevators. Tommy and I wrote songs, and he had me present them [to the Elevators]. All their practices were closed off. Tommy engineered it that way. "We're gonna come out any day now," he would say. "You'll be knocked out when we debut."

People considered Tommy a huckster. They didn't take him seriously, but there was electricity all through the audience when the Elevators hit the stage for their debut at the Jade Room. Crazy.[16] [Roky] was electrifying. There was no doubt that this [teenage kid] was a genuine prodigy. He was born with all the chops. Suddenly Tommy's dream of putting together a band didn't seem so farfetched at all.[17] Everyone around town knew Roky could sing. The results were electric. Nobody doubted Tommy Hall after that. The Elevators were a really crack band, a fusion of guitar genius Stacy Sutherland and Roky Erickson, and the haunting lyrics [written by] Tommy and Clementine Hall.[18] They created original material contributing to the message that proselytizes for the use of psychedelics. Ultimately, the Elevators worked up six of my songs. The results were spectacular.[19]

There were always teenage girls in the front row looking gaga at Roky. I thought, These girls don't understand anything. They don't appreciate things like they should. They think they like Roky, but they don't know him or anything like that so I wrote the song "You Don't Know." Then I wrote a song about a psychedelic experience epiphany I had on LSD called "Kingdom of Heaven." I wanted to tell people about LSD, but the drug was not legal. I couched the lyrics in terms that would be familiar to most Christians who actually read the Bible. That was the natural way for me to do it with my Christian background. I never practiced any religion, but I knew the terms that religious people used.

The Elevators' rehearsals were an eye opener for me because in those days I naively believed that a band made up of experienced individuals would not have disagreements and would not behave like ordinary human beings. I believed everything would take place on a higher level. Well, they did behave like ordinary human beings. They did have disagreements. John Ike and Roky mixed it up quite a bit. That revelation led me to begin considering the band members individually rather than as some nebulous superbeing. What I saw was a group of highly skilled musicians working as a unit. John Ike, Benny [Thurman], and Stacy [Sutherland] formed the basic unit. They were already a seasoned band and used to one another. Roky the phenom vocalist was added to this as well as Tommy the jug virtuoso and constant looming presence.[20]

The establishment was up in arms when drugs hit town in the sixties. The Austin Police Department, the university police, and the FBI were working to fight the menace. They [thought] if they could bust a few of the ringleaders and make an example of them then the rank and file would fold and the issue would be settled. University students were high on the list of suspected druggies, especially the scruffy nonconforming types. The authorities were most afraid that some Dallas oilman's daughter would get involved in a drug-related incident and cause great embarrassment to the university and Austin as a whole, not to mention the loss of endowment money that would follow.[21]

Singer-songwriter Powell St. John was a member of the Austin, Texas–based group Conqueroo in the sixties and wrote several songs for the 13th

Floor Elevators. The band included St. John's "You Don't Know (How Young You Are)" on their debut, The Psychedelic Sounds of the 13th Floor Elevators.

CLEMENTINE HALL

Susie and I would do housework and watch the kids together. I stayed upstairs with her the first time she turned on with acid. Then I took her downstairs when she was finally stable. I made sure she had a good trip. We were intimate friends from then on and had so many friends. We would go across the border, get marijuana, and give it to our friends—or sell to them if they wanted more than a little. I cooked everything back then. I would make ravioli from scratch with a Bolognese sauce. Tommy and I adored any cuisines from other countries. We went to this Italian villa restaurant where I would observe, taste, and figure out how to replicate the dishes. My mother was the world's worst cook, but she traveled. She was so beautiful and elegant that she would go talk chefs into giving her recipes that they wouldn't even give to gourmet magazines. So, I had access to fabulous cookbooks.

I think the Elevators took my cooking for granted. They were young guys about the age of the frat boys all around. Roky loved me like a mother. In fact, he kept telling me I looked just like his mother. Then I met her. He was right. I looked like she probably did when she was younger, but I instantly saw something horrible going on. We called it "smother love" back then and "spousification" later. You take your child and make him into your husband because you're not sleeping with your husband. Her first baby became her "little husband." She owned him. Roky absolutely worshiped his mother and needed a mother figure. He would not get out of bed until somebody handed him a glass of orange juice when he was living at our house. I had to squeeze the oranges and take him the orange juice. He was used to being spoiled like that.

I remember vividly the night I named the Elevators. I was reading in bed when Tommy came in. He was in the living room getting stoned with the other Elevators. "We need a name," he said. "I suggested I check with you since you're good at naming things." "Well, you want to be like the rhythm and blues band names," I said. "They have such good one-word names like the Temptations and the Shirelles. Why don't you call yourselves the Elevators?" He checked. "They love it, but it's too short. They need more." "How about the 13th Floor Elevators?" There wasn't a building anywhere in the United States back then with a thirteenth floor because people were superstitious about the number. Of course, thirteen was my lucky number. Also, thirteen is the letter "m" for marijuana. "Why not the 13th Floor Elevators? You elevate people to a place that nobody else goes to that doesn't exist anywhere else." He went back out and came back a little later. "That's it," he said. "They said yes." The name did sound very psychedelic but also hokey.

We didn't listen to any psychedelic music back then because there wasn't any. We might find a piece of music from Africa or Afghanistan that sounded psychedelic. Tommy had a huge record collection. People were always borrowing from him because he had so many. Tommy was interested in every kind of music and educated me. I was already educated with classical because my family wouldn't let me listen to pop music. Tommy educated me about African music and tried to educate me about jazz music. I never liked it but was addicted to old blues. I first heard live blues and went, "Where has this been all my life?" Roky had to stop borrowing records because he would bring them back looking like somebody had run over them with golf cleats. He probably got stoned and stepped on them. Tommy was the kind who would carefully lift up a record with his middle finger in the hole and his right thumb on the edge so his fingers wouldn't touch any grooves.

Tommy and I were really good friends with Janis Joplin. I remember the first time Janis turned on. This was before Tommy even came into my life. Janis lay on the floor beside me, and we really delved deep into each other's personalities and attitudes. Then she never wanted to turn on again. Janis and I laughed and laughed. You would do the same with the Elevators. Laugh and laugh. They were witty. We all purchased Astro Matic sunglasses one time, which I have never seen since. The sunglasses had a golden cast and made everything you looked at seem like Disneyland. The colors were so brilliant. They made us feel like being on LSD without being on LSD. They knocked our socks off when we were on LSD and wore them.

We would walk around the neighborhood and act like little kids laughing and having an incredibly fine time. "Oh," my son would say. "Are you going out on a jingle-jangle morning again?" That stuck with us. Even a trip to the store on a jingle-jangle morning would be especially fun with Roky. He would act out stuff he had seen. Roky was an incredible raconteur who said many things that were very wise. He was like Mork from another planet and could drop a few words in the middle of a scuffle, and everyone would laugh. Worked every time. I saw him do that all his life. Tommy would say, "Here come Roky's safety devices."

My favorite story happened when we were all at the Ghetto, which was very cheap university housing with a courtyard in the middle. Everyone but the Elevators lived there. Our friend Powell St. John, who wrote music for us, and Janis Joplin lived there. People like that were all in the courtyard smoking dope. We were in rocking chairs and started talking about the great things we were gonna do in our lives. We were young college students. Roky said, "I'll be a famous musician." Stacy said, "Me too. I'll be a famous guitarist." Tommy said, "I'll be a famous lyricist or poet." Powell said, "I'll either become a famous artist or musician." "You guys are crazy," someone said. "You're idiots. Don't you know that in twenty years you'll be sitting in this same damn hellhole talking about the great things you'll do with flies gathering all around you?" We all went dumb suddenly and felt stupid. "Ma'am," Roky said immediately. "That's not gonna happen. We are all gonna do something special. We don't want to hear your fly theories." We instantly got back our enthusiasm.

Roky brought in his guitar the first time we wrote together. He knew I was articulate. "I have this tune," he said. "I have the first line, 'I've seen your face before / I've known you all my life,'" which was a line I said to him when we first met in my living room. He said, "I feel exactly the same way. We don't have to say anything." We were very attuned to each other emotionally. So, that became the first line of "Splash 1." The refrain is "Now I'm home to stay." I wrote the lyrics very quickly, and Roky played it. The second one was "I Had to Tell You." I don't know why I didn't want to name it from a line in the song. I guess the same reason we were using a psychedelic name for the group: we wanted something different. I was in Roky's brain for that song with what I only learned later, which is that Roky was gonna experience being surrounded by craziness and chaos. I thought that whole one up except for the very last line, "Don't you even think about it, I'm feeling fine." Roky would say that. Roky wrote so many melodies that we had to throw some away. Tommy wrote so many lyrics that there weren't enough melodies.

Roky would sit on the second bed and Tommy would sit on the floor cross-legged like a Native American when we were on weekend tours. I would be trying to sleep in the remaining bed. Tommy would wake me up and say, "This isn't quite right." Tommy would always drag me in when he was writing even if it was the middle of the night. He would use me as his human thesaurus. "What's a better way to say this?" I'd tell him and go back to sleep. I could give him several rhymes when he couldn't find one. I think in rhymes and images and alternate ways of saying similar things. I would tell him to change this part to that and see how it all ties together. I was an English major. Tommy could write the most complicated poetry, but I became his tutor. Roky wrote totally different and beautiful lyrics from Tommy.

Roky was very innocent, magical, and had extreme wit. You don't see that combination often. You were the only person Roky knew if you were in his company, which was never a put-on before he started having serious emotional and mental problems. You literally were the apple of his eye. He was naturally charismatic. It was said once about Oscar Wilde that he had the sharpest wit but he never drew blood. His would be fighting words if anyone but someone like Oscar Wilde or Roky Erickson said them. Roky could tell you an [uncomfortable] truth, and you would laugh and go, "Oh, I didn't realize." You wouldn't be hurt. You'd trusted innocence and would realize the words weren't intended to hurt you. That's a quality precious few people possess. Roky was so kindhearted. People would push him around and take his artistic choices because of that. He would protect everyone else on this planet beside himself.

Tommy took all the Elevators to a soul food restaurant one time in Houston. We were the only white people in the restaurant. They put all these tables together so we could eat all this incredibly scrumptious food. This guy comes over and says, "You know, you look like the twelve disciples." We all had long hair, wore odd clothes, and were discussing philosophy and religion. This man was intelligent. "Also," he said, "I feel like each of you has a role in life." He pointed to Tommy. "He's the sage in your group." Then he pointed to Stacy. "He's the dark angel," he said. "People think he's mean because he always has a hard look on his face, but he's very tenderhearted." He pointed to Roky. "He's the child." Then he looked at me. "You," he said. "You are the queen." He was right, but that was our problem. Roky was a child and needed a father. Tommy was a sage and wanted a disciple. Their relationship was shaky because they didn't meet each other's needs.

Tommy and I were divorced in 1973. I stayed in San Francisco. He stayed in Texas. We had been living separate lives for a long time. The only time we connected is when he had me fly down to make *Easter Everywhere*. Tommy, Roky, and Stacy were absolutely adamant that I had to come and do the one song I did. Tommy had been in San Francisco just long enough to impregnate me earlier, and I had a miscarriage when I arrived. I was in a rather shaky situation but will never forget recording "I Had to Tell You." Everyone else was somewhere, so it was just Roky and me in the studio. We laid down the acoustic track with Roky playing harmonica and a gentle guitar. We were both sitting on stools in an almost completely dark room. We just saw a light shining on the technician. It was one of the most intimate, beautiful experiences I've ever had. We hadn't practiced but didn't have to do many takes. His melodies were exquisite. Magical.[22]

SANDY LOCKETT

Tommy Hall is a very, very smart autodidact. He had all the advantages and drawbacks of such people, but he was working on a frontier that not many people were at that time. He felt that music was one way to work at it seriously. He was right. He was a very peculiar person and a pharmacology major in college who was interested in what drugs do to people. He became more and more interested in that and eventually it came to the point where that was all he was interested in except music. He was quite interested in what might happen if you swallowed something odd. He and all his friends were trying to make sense of it. Tommy had this idea about how drugs altered the world, not just the person perceiving the world. The world. This is an important difference, and he really meant it.

[Tommy] loved his wife, which was fortunate because she was able to keep together the machine that he contrived to do this job. Most members of the band needed support of one sort or another. Tommy was not situated to do that, but Clementine was in such a way to either do that or find someone who would. It worked very good. What Tommy was doing was being a poet and trying to find his medium. People who deal with words are not like people who deal with music. That may have been one

of his difficulties. You can find out what someone is trying to say if you
listen to words in their songs. He was saying such obvious, simple things
as "leave your body behind." They can be interpreted literally. What he
wrote down was what was on his mind.

They were doing nothing but playing music, getting stoned, and behav-
ing themselves when the local cops decided they had to have an example
made. So, they did. They came there and found themselves a square tin
of marijuana and drug them all down and said, "Oh, you terrible people."
Stacy was a hell of a guitar player and a haunted man. He realized that
the devil was after him. I'm not sure why he concluded that, but he did.
He would sit there and play the guitar and the devil was two steps behind him all the way. He wasn't sure whether that was because he was
consorting with the wrong people or that he hadn't prayed that night or
because he was fooling around with fancy women, but he knew the devil
was after him.

Tommy did not blow into the jug as one blows into a trumpet or tuba.
He hooted. His wife called him the fastest tongue in the West. He used
the jug as a resonant chamber for the falsetto range of his voice. We tried
glass and plastic ones. We ended up with a kerosene jug, which was a
one-and-a-half-gallon galvanized kerosene jug with a strange handle on
it. That seemed to resonate with his voice properly. John Ike was terribly
important to the dynamic because he was such a mean son of a bitch.
He'd kick his drums if the foot pedal didn't work. That no-bullshit energy was very important to the whole situation. Every band from Austin
had to go to California because after a while they run out of money. You
could get money in California. I don't think there's any doubt [that the
Elevators were the first psychedelic band]. There was nobody playing
anything else like that.[23]

*Sandy Lockett and his business partners owned the iconic Vulcan Gas
Company in Austin from 1967 to 1970. Lockett was well known for his
work as sound man for the 13th Floor Elevators and others during the era.*

JOHN IKE WALTON

Drugs were a problem for the other [Elevators]. They were always putting
pressure on me to get high with them, and I got tired of being bugged. I

saw the paranoia consciousness [drugs were] bringing about. I was staring at a forty-five automatic in the face out the back door to the gig [one
night]. There was a cop at the back door. They busted me because there
were some seeds and stems that somebody had left on the floorboard of
the bus. They charged the bus with possession and confiscated it. We
had to go to court. Stacy and Tommy got two years' probation. Roky got
off because they put the wrong address on the search warrant. Then we
met Leland Rogers.

We played about three months in Austin before we went to California.
Then we came back to Austin after California, recorded our first album,
and played here in Texas. The crowds were bigger after we had gone to
California. The sessions took a long time and were very tiring. So, by the
time we got through the song we were exhausted. We cut our first album
in eight hours. We drove in from California and arrived in Dallas at three
in the morning. They opened the doors as soon as we got there and said,
"Come on in." They didn't even give us a break. I think I got $350 from
International Artists one time. That's all. I tried to get Stacy to stop [do-
ing drugs], but the [Elevators] just argued with me. I think it's terrible
the way he died. He was a good friend. I'm sorry I lost him.[24]

*John Ike Walton was the drummer for the 13th Floor Elevators. He lives in
Kerrville, Texas.*

FRANK DAVIS

I produced every record that was on International Artists in Houston:
the Elevators, Power Plant, Red Krayola.[25] Man, I would run so fast
from Leland Rogers and those lawyers. Ima Hogg paid one a hundred
thousand dollars to be a dark horse and run for mayor to shave votes.
They were just sleaze lawyers. They stole their own equipment, declared
bankruptcy, and ran off with the tapes. They sold the tapes to [Charly Re-
cords] in England. They reproduced them, but nobody got a cent. Leland
Rogers was supposed to be the producer for those tapes, but he didn't do
jack shit. He just got stoned, would go in the next room, and pass out.

The albums we did spelled disaster for every group involved including
the Elevators. Total bullshit. They were totally helpless and had been isolated. Their last album took almost a year, and they couldn't go anywhere.

They would go buy off FBI people and hire them to hang around, keep the drugs flowing, and be bodyguards. The pressure of the music they were writing was very great. Then they dispersed in depression when International Artists dissolved. They found out they were totally screwed, were never paid for anything, and they didn't own a thing they [had recorded for the label]. They each went off into their own demise. Roky, the one I would have voted least likely to succeed, did succeed.[26]

Frank Davis produced several records for International Artists, which released the 13th Floor Elevators albums The Psychedelic Sounds of the 13th Floor Elevators *and* Easter Everywhere.

DANA GAINES ERICKSON

The bad drugs started seeping into our lives. Roky started doing heroin. He gave me thirteen dollars one night and said, "Go get me a syringe with some heroin." I said, "I'm not gonna go do this." "Please," he said. "Go do this." "Oh," this chick Christine said. "I know where you can get it." This huge soul brother answers the door [when we got to the dealer's house]. "My friend here," she says. "Her boyfriend wants a syringe with some heroin and she's got thirteen dollars." That's not enough to get heroin. "That's okay," I say. "We'll just go." The guy closes the door behind us. I look over and this chick [I'm with] is passing out. He just shot her up. She's gone. I'm there alone. So, one man takes my arm, and the other shoots me up. I start going up real fast. I'm telling this man standing in front of me, "I love you so much."

Then I just start throwing up and crying. I was scared. I heard one of them say to the other, "She's OD'd." I remember these two men walking me in a circle for hours. Walking me. Walking me. [This man had] put my life in danger, but he saved it. He handed me a needle with some heroin and said, "I'm walking you home." He was so Christ-like. I go in, and Roky goes, "What took you so long?" A few days later I can't stand up because I'm sweating so bad. George Kinney and Roky walk into my apartment. "I'm taking Roky back to Austin," George says. "He's sick." "I know he's sick," I said. "He's got serum hepatitis. I've got it, too." We'd gotten it from that syringe. So, he went back to Austin. That's pretty much when all the heartache with the law started.[27]

Dana Gaines Erickson was married to Roky Erickson. She currently lives in Austin, Texas.

ROKY ERICKSON

We were in San Francisco's [Haight-Ashbury district] when it was right and going through some good changes. [Janis Joplin's band] Big Brother [and the Holding Company] were like a party from home at [legendary counterculture figure Chet Helms's hippie commune] the Family Dog. We got to see Moby Grape and Quicksilver there. [People say the Elevators were at their best during their first year] because we were more free. We would do things with feedback, and as the years progressed, we'd say, "Hey, don't do that, don't do this." The whole thing is like talking about something that you would suppress. I would get onstage and start experimenting, but it was curbed by the members. The whole idea of creating new experimental vibrations was forgotten later on. Bands will play something so fantastic but don't believe that it really happened. Then they'll forget it. That's what happened with us. We [forgot] what a sound we had, lost faith, and got blasé. We didn't have enough screaming feedback [anymore] and broke up. We didn't have that something extra special [anymore]. That was my gripe.[28]

EVELYN ERICKSON

Roky came home from San Antonio in 1968. He was supposed to play a whole week and was exhausted. He was in the backyard speaking gibberish and covered in sores. He said, "I'm unclean." I remember telling him to get in the tub. [The doctor] told me that he would be a vegetable the rest of his life. Schizophrenia is a broad term that covers a whole manifestation of unusual behavior. I thought name calling went out with the dark ages. He couldn't have any phone calls or visits [while he was at Hedgecroft Hospital and Rehabilitation Center in Houston]. Tommy Hall heard about it and took the hinges off the door and Roky escaped. They hitchhiked to California. Roky had a nervous breakdown the second time he was arrested when he had come home from California. He and a friend were arrested for possession and pleading insanity was probably the best thing. They put him in the state hospital. He was the only one at Rusk for a drug offense. It was wall-to-wall murderers.[29]

Evelyn Erickson was Roky Erickson's mother.

BILLY MILLER

I saw Roky Erickson perform at the Action Club [in Austin] the night they came and took him away to Rusk. He was beginning a new era with a band that was trying to be as far out as possible, but there was this notorious deputy sheriff in the audience looking for him. The cop was bad news and [probably] went out of his way for the privilege to serve the arrest warrant to Roky. There was an announcer onstage who kept saying he would be right back after a set break. Meanwhile, I was trying to lay low so the narcs wouldn't see me, but a riot was happening in the parking lot where a police car was torn up. I finally worked up the nerve to go outside and saw Roky in the car with the narcs. He was still wearing his white top hat in the car as I watched them drive him away. Roky's break would end up lasting three years. The last line he sung in public was "It's all over now, baby blue."[30]

Billy Miller played autoharp with the 13th Floor Elevators and occasionally on Roky Erickson's solo work. He's the creative force behind the band Cold Sun.

CHORUS

Goodbye Sweet Dreams

ROKY ERICKSON

I was driving along, and the cop said I had some marijuana with me. I [thought], What can I do? I lied because I was going to jail. I knew it. They were gonna come down hard on me because I was doing such controversial things. Other people were letting me do it. The cops said, "We're gonna make an example of him. We're not gonna have all these people grooving on what he's doing. We've gotta stop it now because he's a threat to the police." They had put me in [Hedgecroft] mental hospital. I ran away. Then when I came back to Austin to do a show, a policeman comes down and says, "Hi, man. I used to be a good friend of your father. You used to ride horses on my land. All we wanna do is ask you some questions. Just come down and answer the questions."

They put me in a cell as soon as I got down there. I didn't hear from them for a week. The club didn't know where I was. They had said, "Listen, if you get arrested, make your phone call to the club," [but] I wasn't able to make that connection. I was shafted, run over. I flew to Austin. This friend took me to the place that used to be the Action Club, and police were waiting for me. [I was put in Rusk] four, five years ago. Those were the longest three years of my life. I thought I'd never get out. You've [already] thought everything you could think in a million years by the end of one day, and you're tired of it. I was going to jail [otherwise], so I said, "Hey, man, I'm seeing things on the wall. I'm hearing voices. I'm

crazy. Put me away." They said, "All right, he's crazy."[1] I felt like a male
Jane Eyre in Rusk Concentration Camp, which would explain where my
memory has gone. "Roky, what's the date?" "Why do I have the need to
know any date? I'm never gonna get out." I would just forget it and say,
"Roky, you're in here forever. You might as well not remember any kind
of success you've had or that you're a talented rock and roll singer. Forget
it. Just forget it, man. You don't have a chance."[2]

I was such a good actor for three years. You gotta be careful when you
put your mind to it. You can really convince people. I'm sitting there at
the end of three years, and they say, "So you're still hearing voices?" "No,
man," I said. "I'm not hearing voices. I lied." They said, "Yeah, sure you
lied." It's obvious now I lied, but they were just mean as could be. I got
beat up once by an attendant at Rusk. People are victims of police and
bad record companies. They were like, "Here comes this guy with long
hair and a top hat." "Oh, boy," they said. "We got him." It would have been
just as bad if I was wearing a tuxedo. They cut my hair completely bald
and put me in khakis. You get up and clean up the place at six o'clock for
three years. Terrible, man. I got my GED and a couple college credits,
but that was the only interesting thing the whole time. A couple groovy
guys managed to get me out to be in a rock and roll band with some of the
patients. We were called the Missing Links, but I couldn't perform. I tried
to scream there, [but] I would be under so much tension that I couldn't.
I'll scream now as good as ever when I get onstage again.

[My wife, Dana,] came up to visit me every two weeks. We had from
eight a.m. until four [p.m. to visit]. She would bring me a carton of cigarettes, a television, and a twelve-string guitar, but you wouldn't wanna
watch television by the time you got it set up and passed all the regula-
tions. You couldn't be inspired with the guitar. I wouldn't do my own
material in this band. I'd do others because I had such a pessimistic
attitude that the [band members] couldn't learn this, they couldn't learn
that, or they wouldn't know what I'm talking about. You were there with
people who were in there for vicious murder, and they said, "All right,
here's the guy with the vicious murder [charge], and here's Roky. They're
equal. They're in here for the same thing. They're crazy."[3]

Roky Erickson, Austin, Texas, during the eighties.

PHOTO BY CASEY MONAHAN.

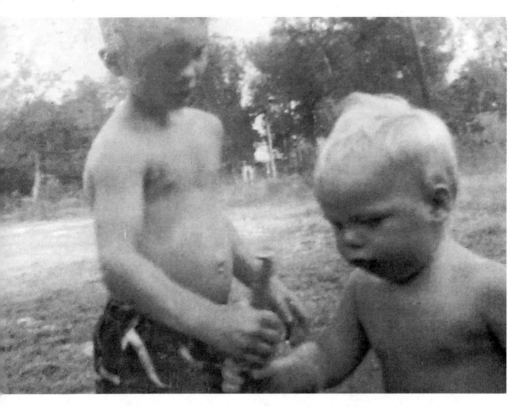

Roky Erickson (*left*), Mikel Erickson, Austin, Texas, midfifties.
COURTESY MIKEL ERICKSON ARCHIVES.

Roky Erickson on truck at home, Austin, Texas, midfifties.
COURTESY MIKEL ERICKSON ARCHIVES.

Jimmy Bird

Ronnie Bowen

Gary Briscoe

Dannie Brownlow

Harry Buckholts

Jack Carson

Dennie Conner

Sidney Cox

Frank Dillard

Ronny Eitze

Roky Erickson

John Fenner

Roky Erickson high school yearbook photo.
Erickson is pictured in the third row, second from right.

The Spades performing at the Jade Room, Austin, Texas, during
the early sixties. Roky Erickson is pictured at far left.

COURTESY MIKEL ERICKSON ARCHIVES.

Left to right: Unknown, Roky Erickson, and his mother,
Evelyn Erickson, Austin, Texas, in the midsixties.

Roky Erickson performing with the 13th Floor Elevators.

Roky Erickson performing in the late sixties.
COURTESY MIKEL ERICKSON ARCHIVES.

Roky Erickson (*center*) performing with the 13th Floor Elevators.
COURTESY MIKEL ERICKSON ARCHIVES.

Roky Erickson and Dana Gaines Erickson, date and location unknown.

Roky Erickson (*right*) with elevator operators taking him
to the 13th floor, date and location unknown.

Left to right: Roky Erickson, Dana Gaines Erickson, and Mikel Erickson at Mikel Erickson's home in Austin, Texas, during the 2000s.

Inside Rusk State Hospital today, Rusk, Texas.
Photo by Cristin Parker, *Cherokeean Herald*.

Cover of Roky Erickson's poetry collection *Openers I*,
published by Pyramid Press, Austin, Texas, 1972.

PHOTO BY BRIAN T. ATKINSON. *OPENERS I* COURTESY
MIKEL ERICKSON ARCHIVES.

TRUE LOVE CAST OUT ALL EVIL

PEACE, LOVE, SHADISTY AND GRACE
MERCY AND JUSTICE, THROUGHOUT EVERY RACE

TRUE LOVE CAST OUT ALL EVIL
TRUE LOVE CAST OUT ALL EVIL
TRUE LOVE CAST OUT ALL EVIL
RIGHT NOW RIGHT NOW

LOVE HAS IT'S TIME, ALL THE TIME, ALL THE
    TIME, ALL THE TIME
WE ARE MEANT TO LOVE ONE ANOTHER
ALL IN HARMONY, RHYME
AND SOMETIMES WORD RHYME

TRUE LOVE CAST OUT ALL EVIL
TRUE LOVE CAST OUT ALL EVIL
TRUE LOVE CAST OUT ALL EVIL
RIGHT NOW RIGHT NOW

LIVING IS A NECESSITY
PLEASE DO NOT DIE
LIVING THE GOOD LIFE, WITH GOD YOU ABIDE

TRUE LOVE CAST OUT ALL EVIL
TRUE LOVE CAST OUT ALL EVIL
TRUE LOVE CAST OUT ALL EVIL
RIGHT NOW RIGHT NOW

GOOD STANDARDS ARE SET, NEVER LEFT
GOOD STANDARDS BY AND WHAT OF
LOVE, LOVE, ONLY LOVE

TRUE LOVE CAST OUT ALL EVIL
TRUE LOVE CAST OUT ALL EVIL
TRUE LOVE CAST OUT ALL EVIL
RIGHT NOW RIGHT NOW

"True Love Cast out All Evil," by Roky Erickson,
Openers I, first edition, 1972.

PHOTO BY BRIAN T. ATKINSON. *OPENERS I* COURTESY
MIKEL ERICKSON ARCHIVES.

FOR

WITHOUT ONE THERE WOULD BE AN EMPTY
  EMPTY SPACE
WITH ONE I CAN SEE ONES OWN FACE

NOT FOR A LITTLE WHILE
NOT FOR A DAY
BUT FOREVER, FOREVER, FOREVER
ONE SHOWS ONE THE WAY

ONE IS NOT A STYLE
ONE IS NOT A FAD
ONE IS NOT A TREND
JUST, - THE THOUGHT OF ONE MAKES ME SMILE
AND ONE TELLS ONE WE WILL NEVER END

NOT FOR A LITTLE WHILE
NOT FOR A DAY
BUT FOREVER, FOREVER, FOREVER
ONE SHOWS ONE THE WAY

ONE IS NOT A LOSS
ONE IS A GAIN
WITH ONE ONE HAS
THE PLEASURE OF APPRECIATES AS OF KNOWING
  ONES NAME

NOT FOR A LITTLE WHILE
NOT FOR A DAY
BUT FOREVER, FOREVER, FOREVER
  ONE SHOWS ONE THE WAY

"For," by Roky Erickson, *Openers I.* "For" was retitled "Forever"
and included on Roky Erickson and Okkervil River's
superb album *True Love Cast out All Evil.*

PHOTO BY BRIAN T. ATKINSON. *OPENERS I* COURTESY

MIKEL ERICKSON ARCHIVES.

48

SWEET HONEY PIE

NO BAD PLACES
ONE HAS NO USES FOR ABUSES
NOT BECAUSE IT DOESN'T BRING DISGRACES
ONE DOESN'T HAVE TO PROVE ONE DOESN'T USE THEM

NO BAD PLACES
THEY CAN TAKE A PERMANANT VACATION
ONE DOESN'T WANT TO FALL ON OTHERS
EVEN THE SLIGHTEST OF THEIR NEGATIVE VIBRATION

SWEET HONEY PIE
SWEET HONEY PIE AND MANNA
SWEET HONEY PIE
IN CHRIST'S LOVE ABOUND

SWEET HONEY PIE
SWEET HONEY PIE AND MANNA
SWEET HONEY PIE
IN CHRIST'S LOVE ABOUND

STAYING AWAY FROM CRIME NOT JUST PART OF THE
  TIME
NOT BECAUSE AS FAR AS NO CRIME IS CONCERNED
THE FREEDOM BELLS ALWAYS CHIME
AND NOT JUST PART OF THE TIME

THERE IS A CATEGORY OF NO STIPULATIONS
FOR GOOD RELEASATIONS
NEVER TAKING A VACATION
THIS IS THE SENSATION

SWEET HONEY PIE
SWEET HONEY PIE AND MANNA
SWEET HONEY PIE
IN CHRIST'S LOVE ABOUND

SWEET HONEY PIE
SWEET HONEY PIE AND MANNA
SWEET HONEY PIE
IN CHRIST'S LOVE ABOUND

"Sweet Honey Pie," by Roky Erickson, *Openers I.* "Sweet Honey Pie" was included as a ghost track on the expanded edition of Roky Erickson and Okkervil River's *True Love Cast out All Evil.*

PHOTO BY BRIAN T. ATKINSON. *OPENERS I* COURTESY
MIKEL ERICKSON ARCHIVES.

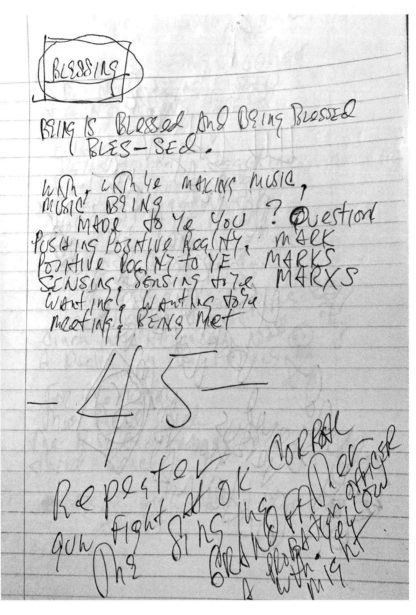

"Blessing," by Roky Erickson, handwritten lyrics
from Erickson's personal notebook.

ITS A CLEAR NIGHT
Con ye fell FOR LOVE In a flying
maCHINE
That doesn't HAVE a tAKe
off pull
when It HAS parted
started to FLy hearted
                    missing
to tell to tell   still missing
off so well off so well
one must be Relative to God
he must be ones heavenly
FATHER

without God A personl
couldn't even Do most
things once
with God ye can Do the
some thing AGAIN and
AGAIN

Why Doing the same
thing all the time

there are two wheels
the little deals
with No spokes on the wheel

All the time all the time

"Clear Night for Love," alternate handwritten lyrics
from Erickson's personal notebook.

PHOTO BY BRIAN T. ATKINSON. COURTESY CASEY MONAHAN.

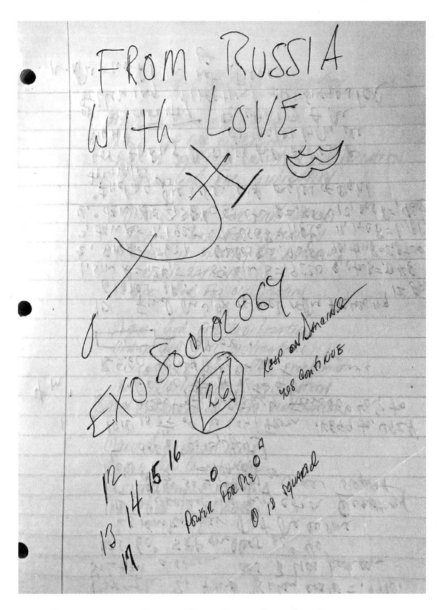

"From Russia with Love," by Roky Erickson, handwritten notes
from Erickson's personal notebook.

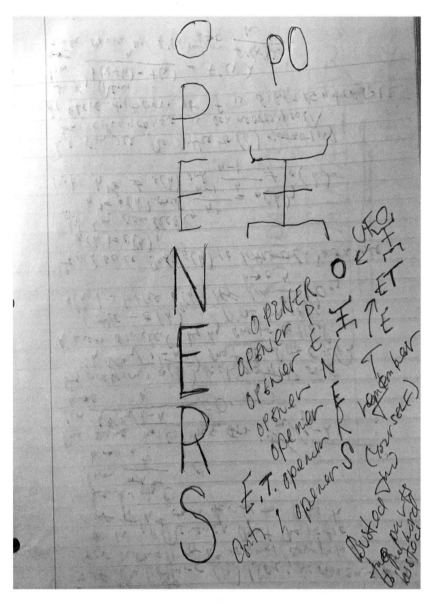

"Openers," by Roky Erickson, handwritten lyrics
from Erickson's personal notebook.

"I Love the Living You," by Roky Erickson, handwritten lyrics
from Erickson's personal notebook.

PHOTO BY BRIAN T. ATKINSON. COURTESY CASEY MONAHAN.

SAFE

SAFE IS WIThOUT TheM MORE

The reverends around me
have found me
I hear them on the radio—
I Don't mind
And it doEsn't Astound
ME
    Jesus I am behind

He and his way
never are A MAZE
From Faith
only A timely remembrance
of BEFORE
And I Can SEE NO enl
in his WAY

Christ hAs (AnY) ALWAYS InvitAtion
salvation
Through
HIS IS The WAY OF SALVAtion
Through Jesus Love Finds the
STATION

"Safe," by Roky Erickson, handwritten lyrics
from Erickson's personal notebook.

PHOTO BY BRIAN T. ATKINSON. COURTESY CASEY MONAHAN.

"May the Circle Remain Unbroken," by Roky Erickson,
handwritten lyrics from Erickson's personal notebook.

PHOTO BY BRIAN T. ATKINSON. COURTESY CASEY MONAHAN.

"Save Me," by Roky Erickson, handwritten lyrics
from Erickson's personal notebook.

PHOTO BY BRIAN T. ATKINSON. COURTESY CASEY MONAHAN.

"A Death in the Family," by Roky Erickson, handwritten lyrics
from Erickson's personal notebook.

PHOTO BY BRIAN T. ATKINSON. COURTESY CASEY MONAHAN.

AND

Through Jesus Evil
Love Shuns

Love is care
Love should be everywhere
Love is a good desire
Love can't and can't put out
a fire

Love can open doors
Carefully who have seen it
before
Love can turn up the sound
not disturbing those
Asleep sound

Jesus
Loves Good will power
Allower
is ours only love has power

49   13
× 2 → You continue
still missing
I want to register

"AND," by Roky Erickson, handwritten lyrics
from Erickson's personal notebook.

PHOTO BY BRIAN T. ATKINSON. COURTESY CASEY MONAHAN.

59

When ye but delighted you

? ? ?-65- 11--
11-- 11-- 11-- 33 6

Good standards are set nouerlost
Good standards br are whator
Love love only love

true love cast out all eul
right now right now

8 Hawk
-5?-
14--

Unforced Peace

Unforced Peace

6 six -60- two times
7--
An Ancient Enemy
the old house

Wake me Gently
WARNING 2b 3 25 7
-64- 10--

"Unforced Peace," alternate original version, by Roky Erickson,
handwritten lyrics from Erickson's personal notebook.

PHOTO BY BRIAN T. ATKINSON. COURTESY CASEY MONAHAN.

Show poster from Roky Erickson's eighth annual Ice Cream Social (featuring Okkervil River) at Threadgill's World Headquarters, Austin, Texas, March 18, 2010.

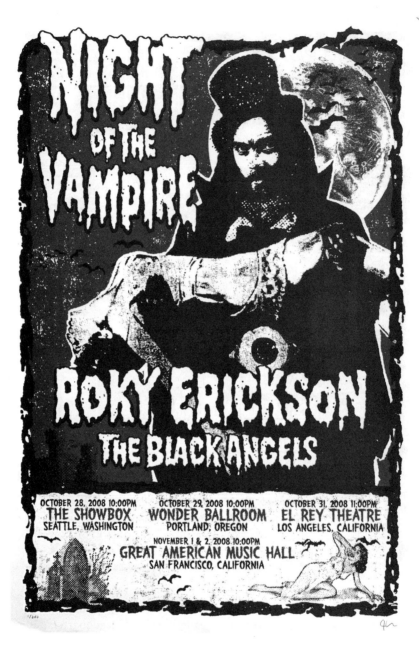

Show poster from Roky Erickson's Halloween tour, October 2008.

PHOTO BY BRIAN T. ATKINSON. COURTESY TROY CAMPBELL.

Show poster from Roky Erickson's Ice Cream Social, Threadgill's World Headquarters, Austin, Texas, March 19, 2009.

Show poster from Roky Erickson's Ice Cream Social, Threadgill's
World Headquarters, Austin, Texas, March 15, 2010.

Show poster from Roky Erickson's Psychedelic Ice Cream Social,
Threadgill's World Headquarters, Austin, Texas, March 13, 2008.

Autographed tour poster from Roky Erickson's
Sweden tour, December 2007.

PHOTO BY BRIAN T. ATKINSON. COURTESY TROY CAMPBELL.

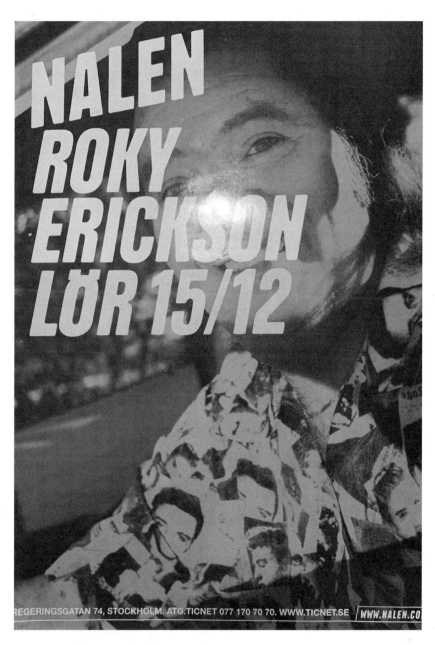

Roky Erickson solo poster.

"13th Floor Elevators" ice cream, Amy's Ice Cream, Austin, Texas.

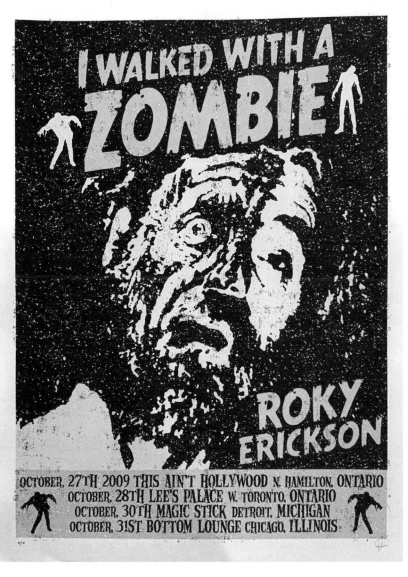

Show poster from Roky Erickson's Halloween tour, October 2009.

Mojo Nixon mistakenly identified as Roky Erickson during
South by Southwest, Austin, Texas, *USA Today.*

PART II

The Interpreter

SELECTED TIMELINE FOR ROKY ERICKSON'S SOLO CAREER

1972

Roky Erickson is released from Rusk State Hospital.

Erickson exhibits more erratic behavior.

Pyramid Publishing Company releases Erickson's poetry collection *Openers*.

1974

Erickson forms Bleib Alien.

Doug Sahm launches Erickson's solo career with the single "Two-Headed Dog" b/w "Starry Eyes."

1977

Erickson releases his full-length solo debut, *Bermuda / The Interpreter*.

1979

Erickson renames his band the Aliens.

Creedence Clearwater Revival bassist Stu Cook produces fifteen Erickson tracks.

Erickson and the Nervebreakers' show at the Palladium is later released as *Live in Dallas 1979*.

1980S

The Explosives become Erickson's most celebrated backing band.
They release *Roky Erickson and the Aliens* (CBS Records) and *The Evil One* (415 Records).
Erickson declares himself an alien as his mental health further declines.
Erickson releases the singular *Don't Slander Me*.
Gremlins Have Pictures, Casting the Runes, and *Live at the Ritz 1987* follow.
Erickson is arrested for mail theft, but charges are dropped.

1990S

Bill Bentley's *Where the Pyramid Meets the Eye: A Tribute to Roky Erickson* is released.
Demon Angel: A Day and Night with Roky Erickson, Halloween 1984 is released.
Erickson releases *All That May Do My Rhyme* on King Coffey's Trance Syndicate Records.
A second poetry book from his Rusk writings called *Openers II* is released.
Erickson releases *Never Say Goodbye*.

2000S

Medication stabilizes Erickson's mental health. He begins a career resurgence.
Don't Knock the Rok!, I Have Always Been Here Before, and *Halloween* are released.
Erickson plays European festivals for the first time and receives great acclaim.
He founds the annual Roky Erickson's Ice Cream Social during South by Southwest.
Erickson is featured on "Devil Rides" on Mogwai's *Batcat* EP.
The Black Angels' Alex Maas helps found Psych Fest in Austin in 2008.
Erickson performs Elevators songs for the first time in decades on tour with the Black Angels.

2010

Will Sheff and Okkervil River arrange Erickson's Rusk poems as songs.
Erickson and Okkervil River release his masterwork *True Love Cast out
  All Evil* (ANTI- Records).

2015

Psych Fest is renamed Levitation Festival in honor of the 13th Floor
  Elevators song.
The surviving Elevators members reunite and perform at the festival.

2019

Erickson dies on May 31, 2019, in Austin, Texas.

OPENERS II

Roky Erickson's Solo Career

ROKY ERICKSON EMERGED EQUAL MEASURES FRAGILE MAN and ferocious songwriter. The Rusk years opened fantastical new worlds—some heavenly, many more horrific—fast and freely. "[Being institutionalized] was pretty rough for him," Rusk State Hospital psychiatrist Bob Priest says in the Keven McAlester documentary *You're Gonna Miss Me*. "Roky would have a yellow legal pad most of the time. He would be sitting in the hallway somewhere writing music, real weak and slumped down. At least it took his mind off where he was."[1] The depth and weight Erickson developed lyrically—writing feverishly about ghosts and goblins, horrors and haunts, madmen and monsters, every creature from aliens to zombies—surveyed previously unforeseen territory. "Roky could pull something like a crazy fish from Marianas Trench," says Will Sheff, whose band Okkervil River helped shape Erickson's late-career high-water mark *True Love Cast out All Evil*. "Either his schizophrenia, his childlike nature, or the psychedelic experience allowed his kinesthetic quality to open to gibberish and insanity. His writing was a special gift and curse."[2]

The combination sparked wildly erratic behavior. Erickson spouted seemingly endless and senseless soliloquies about the gory and grotesque. He used the Bible anagram Bleib Alien as his new band name. Nonetheless, heart and humor backed most messages. "The Roky Erickson songs I worked on were horror themed but with a wink," says Creedence Clearwater Revival bassist Stu Cook, who produced Erickson in the late seventies. "Roky's poetry is really unique and clear on several levels, and he had a tremendous straight-faced sense of humor. My god, he could get you going."[3] "Roky was a very funny guy," confirms Shawn Sahm, whose legendary father, Doug Sahm, helped launch Erickson's solo career. "There was a thunderstorm one night at the house, and Roky clapped his hands when the thunder came to a crescendo. We were kids. We thought Roky was making thunder."

Many music critics misunderstood—or simply didn't care for—his vibrant vision. They believed his cultural impact came and went with the Elevators. "Erickson was an entirely different man when he emerged [from Rusk]," the *Guardian* wrote. "Plenty of music emerged in the subsequent years, often inspired by horror movies, sometimes very good, but never equaling those extraordinary Elevators records. There's little point pretending that Erickson's solo recordings or his work with backing bands the Explosives and the Aliens—whatever their merits—will be his legacy. His contribution to rock history is narrow—in effect, a brief couple of years from late 1965 to the end of 1967—but it is deep."[4] In fact, Erickson was only beginning to build his benefaction.

Diversity mapped the journey. Erickson effortlessly eased between hard rock ("Can't Be Brought Down," "Don't Shake Me Lucifer") and folk ("Forever," "You Don't Love Me Yet"), horror rock ("Creature with the Atom Brain," "Bloody Hammer") and pop ("Starry Eyes," "Goodbye Sweet Dreams") throughout the seventies and eighties. His nonlinear lyrics and distinct delivery became instantly recognizable. "Here I sit a skeleton at my organ," he howls on "Burn the Flames." "The candles in my candelabra burn hellishly hellish hell and the laughter unending echoes." Erickson shined brightest on early high-water marks like 1977's *Bermuda / The Interpreter*, the breakthrough *The Evil One* in 1980, and 1986's rock powerhouse *Don't Slander Me*. Additionally, his absolutely sublime swan song (2010's Okkervil River collaboration *True Love Cast out All Evil*) guided a new generation toward his music. His approach resonated deeply. "There was something very innocent about [what he does], and it's just flying out of him," Sonic Youth's Thurston Moore says. "It doesn't seem very calculated even though he was conceptual with his themes. He seemed really free."[5]

Erickson's creative independence opened widely his heart. He frequently doubled down on potential ("Clear Night for Love," "Realize

You're My Sweet Brown Angel Eyes") with pride ("Starry Eyes," "Sweet Honey Pie," "You Drive Me Crazy"). Earthy imagery tied both together. "They tell you that your opening line has to be a good hook," says longtime friend Clementine Hall. "Roky's best opening line ever was, 'You don't love me / You don't love me yet' [from "You Don't Love Me Yet" on 1995's *All That May Do My Rhyme*]. That says everything. Roky had no doubt that he would receive love. He didn't know that he could keep it forever—he had lost and grieved several girlfriends while I was around him—but he did believe that if he were around someone he didn't know it would be just minutes before they would become good friends."

Erickson discovered legions in indie rock circles. "I started listening to Roky's solo albums in 1977," former Half Japanese front man Jad Fair says. "Roky sounded so great. His guitar, songwriting, and vocal delivery were all right on. His songs struck a chord because I've always liked horror movies, and I thought he was one of the best lyricists around. Also, I'm very much in favor of positive, romantic songs like 'Starry Eyes' and 'Clear Night for Love.' They're so straight ahead like T-Rex songs, and everything works. I'm a huge fan."[6] "Roky Erickson," echoes Foo Fighters lead singer Dave Grohl, who performed Erickson's "Two-Headed Dog" for the television program *Austin City Limits*' fortieth anniversary, "is one of Austin's greatest heroes."[7]

The collection *Where the Pyramid Meets the Eye: A Tribute to Roky Erickson*—featuring the Butthole Surfers, R.E.M., Primal Scream, ZZ Top, and many more—spotlights his impact. "I came to know Roky's music deeper when we recorded 'If I Have Ghosts' for *Where the Pyramid Meets the Eye*," iconic British songwriter John Wesley Harding says. "'If I Had Ghosts' was the best song we ever recorded. The record was fantastic and really opened up Roky Erickson's music to people of my generation." "Roky is the hero of Texas rock and roll in the sixties, but he was just hanging out with people by the eighties," says *Where the Pyramid Meets the Eye* producer Bill Bentley. "He degenerated physically. I went out to his government assistance house out by the airport with the ten radios and televisions on, which was hard to watch. We were talking about how we could help, and the only thing we came up with was the tribute record. I want his legacy to live on."

Time undoubtedly will strengthen his consequence. Erickson simply saw beyond his days. "My music is real advanced," Erickson once told an interviewer. "It will take people maybe six years to understand the first level. Then it will take them even longer to grasp how it will keep going. 'Two-Headed Dog' is one. I controlled the people playing on that record. They were possessed by the devil when I opened my mouth to sing. The music started roaring like a growling demon from hell."[8] "Roky was the ultimate rock and roll wild man," Sheff says. "He was very willing to leap out into the unknown and was able to reveal a deeper meaning as a songwriter. Roky became the patron saint of these long-haired, weird, wild dreamer people. He was a singular creature who was gone too soon but left his mark in a really indelible way. He could jump into the cosmos and bring back something you've never seen before."[9]

VERSE

Two-Headed Dog

MIKEL ERICKSON

Roky's life would have been very different if he had not gone to Rusk. The courts [initially] had sent him for evaluation to the state hospital off Thirty-Fourth Street here in Austin in order to prepare him for a court hearing. Attorney [Jack] McClellen had told Roky to plead crazy, go to the state hospital, get this over with, and then go back in front of the courts. Roky could have gotten everything dismissed, but his friends [insisted on breaking him out]. The state hospital was pretty loose compared to Rusk. There were no fences. The building was bordered by Guadalupe Street and Lamar Boulevard, and you could just walk off the premises. Roky's friends would come take him out, but I kept telling them to leave him alone. "Wait two months," I said. "He will be out." Everything would have been cool, but they didn't listen. I found him out past Mount Bonnell a half dozen times when he got out. Roky would always be there high or doing something.

I usually would take him back to our mother's house to bring him down. Then I would take him back [to the hospital] the next morning when he was off the trip. Sometimes it was mandatory that I bring him back. People were calling me the gestapo, a narc, the police for trying to keep Roky in the state hospital. They said I wasn't very cool and told me to leave Roky alone. I kept saying that the authorities would get pissed off [that he was escaping the state hospital] and really put the screws to him.

I said they would send him away, which is what happened. Roky Erickson all of a sudden was being sent to Rusk State Hospital. They already had been doing the shock treatments and Thorazine in the state hospitals, but they were [more difficult] on Roky in Rusk.

I visited four or five times. Roky seemed comfortable. Sometimes he would play music for us. We would discuss things other times. I don't know what all happened to Roky when he was in there, but he wasn't raped. I talked with him about that. His music was a pleasure to the other inmates and set him apart from the others, but I know he was confronted a couple times. I wasn't aware that he was ever beaten up. I don't remember any bruising, but there were other [scars] you couldn't see. He kept writing music when he was there. He wrote most poems in *Openers I* in Rusk.

You normally can't get out of Rusk, which was an older building, a really sick place. People who were committed for being insane are put away for life in there. They're murderers, child molesters, rapists, the hardest-core mental people. Walking in there felt exactly like walking into a federal prison. You drive up and see three heavy strands of barbed wire around it. Guards were walking between the barbed and razor wire. You would check in but could not check out. Then they search you, take away your purse and belongings, and take you down this long corridor and into a courtyard where there are picnic tables. I was told by the powers-that-be that you could only appeal once a year to try to get someone out of Rusk. Almost no one had been released after being committed at that time.

I started putting together some funds and approached the people at the law firm about getting Roky out. Jon Howard was the main participant. "I want to get Roky out of Rusk," I said. "What will it take?" They said, "Money." I started by taking them ten thousand dollars in a brown paper bag filled with twenty-dollar bills. I think it cost about twelve or fifteen thousand total for their expenses. They would never take any more money after that. Their expenses were flying in Dr. Alexander from New York and another psychiatrist from San Francisco numerous times to do evaluations and to get to know the court systems. There only were psychologists at Rusk, so we hired the most brilliant psychiatrists there were. They gave their summary of Roky, which was professional

psychiatrists thinking he should be released. They said it was more detrimental to keep him in there.

We had a court hearing. Our mother was really worried that Roky
would go back to his habits if he wasn't released into somebody's custody.
The attorneys recommended that my mother take over custody of Roky
for a while. He was released into her hands. She was a very religious
Episcopal lady, so we had Charles Sumners and other pastors at Roky's
hearing. There were no hippies at the courthouse that day. Everyone
testifying on Roky's behalf were God-fearing, upstanding people. They
were saying he wasn't harmful to anybody or himself. The lawyers were
revolutionaries. Look up Jim Simons and what he has done in Arizona
and New Mexico. They were winning cases on Indian rights. They were
lawyers of the time.

Roky wrote this letter to our mother when he was in Rusk. Roky tells
her in this letter that he really wants to go overseas to study yoga, which
made sense. I remember sitting at a table in Rusk with Roky and George,
and Roky said he would really love to study yoga after he got out. Rusk
was a real turning point in Roky's life, though. He made an about-face.
You would ask him to do certain things after Rusk, and he would say, "Do
you think that would be good to do? Well, if that's best, let's do it." Roky
knew what he was doing, but he was putting up a defense. He was letting
people do things for him. One thing we did was *Openers I*. George came
up with the idea to make a book with lyrics from the songs Roky was
writing to help him financially. I said, "That's a great idea, George. Let's
go for it." Everyone says George had to smuggle Roky's notebooks out of
Rusk, but they let him take them. George set up Pyramid Productions in
1972. Then George's wife, Terri, and I put in five thousand dollars each,
and we did the book for ten thousand dollars. I later bought all the books
back when George and Terri divorced.[1]

CLEMENTINE HALL

Roky was put away in Rusk with murderous people. What a miracle that
he had such a great spirit that he could be in there and still come out
a loving person. Sandy Lockett and Tommy [figuratively] busted the
door open and got Roky out one time when he was in the state hospital.
Roky immediately went into an underground [network] with friends, a

chain link across the United States, bringing him to San Francisco. Roky moved in with me. I had a flat on Cole Street in the Haight-Ashbury, but Tommy remained in Texas. My flat had two bedrooms. I gave him my son Roland's bedroom and set up a nice cot in the hallway for Roland. He didn't care. The only time he was ever on his bed was to sleep. Roland was so hyper and always doing something. I took care of Roky, which was lovely, but he was not himself. He was somewhere else. I had trouble communicating with him. I didn't think he was dangerous even though I was a woman alone who had a seven-year-old boy.

Roky and Roland were both really batty—and I do mean batty—about horror movies. They found some guy who would drive them to any horror movie during the seventies. The guy couldn't stand those movies, so he would drop them off and pick them up and take them home. Roland was eight, and this lasted through when he was eleven. Roky was about those ages mentally. Roland resembled [the A. A. Milne character] Christopher Robin. He was very awestruck, innocent, loving. They were like a pair of little kids going to see the most horrific things on the screen together, which was hilarious because they're both so sweet tempered. Roky was always like Peter Pan. I always felt really comfortable with Roky staying with us until he crossed the bridge.

"My teeth are talking to me," he said. "The Russians are leaving messages on my teeth. The Russians told me I have to kill Jackie Kennedy." I tensed up a little. He was looking somewhere else then looked back at me. "Clementine," he said. "You look just like Jackie Kennedy." Well, I didn't look remotely like her. "Maybe they mean for me to kill you." I started immediately calling around to other friends the moment he said that to see who he could stay with that could protect themselves. It had to be a guy. A man and his wife took Roky in somewhere in the suburbs in San Francisco. My daughter Laura and I went to visit Roky one time. His hair was in total mats. He wouldn't let anybody touch it. His teeth were getting blackened. We were worried. He squinted his eyes like he did when he was happy and played "Two-Headed Dog." I thought, Oh, he's going through a dark phase.

I don't believe in schizophrenia. Roky received shock treatments starting from almost the minute he arrived at Rusk. That wouldn't have meant very much to me had my mother not gone through shock treatments. My mother never came back from them. She had shock treatment because she had had a horrible thing happen to her while we were away from my parents' ranch in Texas. There was a wild sow and her babies that our uncle left there. They were on our land with our lovely and safe pigs. The pigs didn't even have a pen. My mother had built them a shallow swimming pool so they could have clean water. We all knew you don't touch a piglet anywhere near the mother. The mother will attack. My mother went to stop the pigs and a little piglet squealed. The wild sow ran at my mother, knocked her down, and started eating her arm.

My mother spent six months at the army hospital. She found a doctor who gave her tons of painkillers, and they got her hooked on morphine. She became addicted. Then she was sent to a mental hospital and a doctor in Washington, DC, because that's where we used to live. Daddy had connections there. She died at age fifty-two, so she was fairly young when she went to the hospital. They did shock treatments that got her out of the addiction, but she was otherwise gone. She didn't know any of us. She was a bright woman and one of the most spiritual people I have ever known. Tommy and she used to have long, amicable conversations about religion even though she was an Episcopalian and he was a searcher looking into all religions. "I'm on the same trip you're on," she would say, "but I'm using different ritual items. We're looking for the same thing."

You would become hypnotic and anything people say around you gets internalized if you were on LSD and doing electroshock treatments at the same time. I can very easily jump from there to Roky thinking the Russians were telling him to kill someone through his teeth. It's entirely possible that the shock treatments partially caused how he went way off the rails. Roky was gone mentally when he was living with us and hearing from the Russians. I had several friends from Austin come up during that time. I hadn't met them at the time, but they were the ones who brought Roky out to San Francisco after he was busted out of the last mental institution. They were lovely people who all crashed at my house for a while.

One was a younger, heavyset woman called the Guacamole Queen. We instantly bonded. "Let's go down to the beach with Roky," she said. "It's freezing cold down there," I said. "Yep," she said. "That's even better. We can hold Roky between us. Let the waves pound on him." We held Roky there for about half an hour, and he was totally himself after the first time we did that. "I'm cold," he would say. "I'm wet." Suddenly, Roky came back in his eyes. He was himself for a couple hours. Then he slipped back into the strange fantasy world. We did the same thing a couple days later. He was himself again, but you can't keep up doing that forever without getting pneumonia. We saw the old Roky temporarily, but then he always went back. I had known Roky in fantasy worlds before, but they were always really nice ones. This one was scaring even him. Roky was such a lovely person and spirit. Saying he was meant to kill Jackie Kennedy was so unlike the Roky I knew. I was so upset letting him go.[2]

ROKY ERICKSON

I'm getting better. I have eighty-five songs written now. [My band Bleib Alien] plays space sounds influenced by the thrill and fun of going to a horror movie and being scared. Bleib Alien [is] brand new in the psychedelic sense. [We] will talk about the demon rising into the clouds and inferring the cloud-filled room of smoke. So, I have eighty-five brand-new songs ready to go [as I start my solo career]. One of them is called "I Have Always Been Here Before." Another is called "The Wind and More." You know, something else blows through when the wind stops. [They're] songs that make you think about psychic things beyond, ghosts, goblins, and gremlins waiting behind your door. Fun things.[3]

JOE NICK PATOSKI

[Legendary Texas singer-songwriter] Doug Sahm and Roky Erickson were fellow travelers who both were in San Francisco in 1966 and 1967. Doug would split the bill with the Elevators at the Avalon Ballroom. He was doing some pretty psychedelic shit around [Sir Douglas Quintet + 2's 1968 album] *Honkey Blues*, which was so out there it didn't sell very well. *Honkey Blues* was too weird even for San Francisco, but Doug was right in step with the Elevators. They also were doing gigs together at [Chet Helms's hippie commune and music venue] the Family Dog. Helms was the anti–[Fillmore Auditorium owner] Bill Graham. Graham was from New York and all about making money. Chet Helms was more about grooving, taking acid, and going to hear bands. Doug and Roky were right in the middle of that.

Doug had reinvented himself by then. He was big shit in Austin. He and Willie Nelson were contemporaries and peers. Willie did *Red Headed*

Stranger in 1975, the same year that Doug put all his energies into producing—well, allegedly producing—Roky Erickson's "Two-Headed Dog" / "Starry Eyes" single. Doug did it out of respect. He knew Roky's value and his role in psychedelic music. Also, Doug got popped for pot like Roky but somehow was put on probation in San Francisco. He was the one who got away. Roky got popped for pot, and the only way he could get out of it was declaring himself insane. Rusk fucked him up. Doug knew the consequences. He felt an obligation to help Roky. Doug always loved him. Roky had the voice. He wailed like no one else.

Doug had the benefit of some Soap Creek [Saloon] regulars who had a little pocket change. "Sure, we'll back you on this project. Go make a single." "Two-Headed Dog" and "Starry Eyes" wasn't a ten-thousand-dollar single, but that's what relaunched Roky Erickson's career and put him on the map as a solo lead singer. I went over to the studio one day [during the recording sessions]. My memory of the studio was everyone was getting really high on weed. I saw Billy Miller running around the studio with his autoharp chasing Roky. Chaos. Guys running around the studio. I think Roky felt comfortable in the chaos. The autoharp was the new funky instrument like the jug had been for the Elevators.

They were on a block of time and had used most of it fucking around. Then in the last hour and a half, it was like, "Hey, guys. We have to get something recorded." "Two-Headed Dog" with "Starry Eyes" is a really wonderfully imperfect record that's marred by Doug's use of the phase shifter. His music was drenched in this sound effect, and you couldn't really hear his guitar. It was a very weird, horrible feedback and wah-wah sound. You can hear that guitar on the Roky single, and it does not flatter his voice or the ensemble.

The period leading up to his first post-Rusk recordings like "Two-Headed Dog" and "Starry Eyes" was chaotic but fairly grounded in some respects compared to 1979 and 1980. There was a great deal of interest in England and through the United States then. Roky was ready to come back and with a really well-produced album, but he was getting really torn down by then. I'm assuming he was off whatever medication he was on or the effects of electroshock therapy were finally sinking in. His behavior was getting erratic. Roky was sitting in with Doug all the time during that period and went on the road with him. They played out in Los Angeles, and Roky followed Doug to San Francisco, which is where

Craig Luckin takes over. Craig was the guy with the good weed. He had the wherewithal and the personnel to get good players together with Roky to start recording in San Francisco. Stu Cook and Doug Clifford from Creedence were recording with Doug on [his 1974 album] *Groover's Paradise.*

These were legitimate musicians living in San Francisco with the indulgence of studio time. Roky was involved with lots of recording then, but he was spacing out. Things were not well. Maybe it was being in San Francisco. Maybe it was being around enablers who were letting him indulge in things he shouldn't. The fact is, all this runs up against what would become the epic album, but they had to do tracks in Austin and come get him out of the nuthouse to get it down. Doug sheltered him. He had a place to stay and hang out with Craig Luckin. He wouldn't talk to me for the film or the liners. John X. Reid was his minder. John was responsible for him in the seventies in San Francisco. Tommy Hall is in San Francisco at the same time, but he had very little interaction with Roky.

The Evil One comes out in 1980, but it was too weird for Epic Records. Roky was beyond Syd Barrett as far as the British were concerned, but 1980 was the year of Roky Erickson. The release of *The Evil One* was the biggest commercial push Roky had received over the course of his career in music. Fan interest was at an all-time high. Roky Erickson was in demand. Everyone wanted a piece of him—only he didn't have a band. The Aliens, his support group for the past five years, had split, deciding to go on their own and play around San Francisco at Mabuhay Gardens and the Back Door, as well as the Keystone in Berkeley. Meanwhile, Roky played with several different bands as the punk rock explosion had finally enveloped the Lone Star State.[4] We were in Paris in 1983 and had Joe King Carrasco signed to New Rose Records. New Rose had signed the Cramps. We were talking about Austin and Roky Erickson's name came up and the whole tone of the conversation changed. All these people started coming in around 1980.

Joe King started playing gigs at Raul's where Roky was the elder statesman. [Erickson's future backing band] the Explosives had the haircut and skinny ties but were ringers. Freddie Krc, Cam King, and the rest all came out of the Jerry Jeff Walker orbit. They didn't belong at Raul's. They could play their instruments, but the way they get in there and belong is getting Roky Erickson to perform with them. There's a punk scene up in

Dallas with the new hot band the Nervebreakers. They had a single and a manager. I got to meet [the Nervebreakers' manager] Tom Ordon up in Dallas in 1980. Tom's a fellow traveler, and we could relate. Tom hears about Roky and gets him to come up and play with the Nervebreakers in Dallas. Roky's living with Tom, watching horror movies, and all these people were coming along to do things with him. He would do anything with anyone if they feed him, give him a bed, take care of him. He loves minders. He loves people coming in to do the dirty things for him.[5]

Central Texas–based writer Joe Nick Patoski has authored several major books including Willie Nelson: An Epic Life, Stevie Ray Vaughan: Caught in the Crossfire, Selena: Como la Flor, *and* The Dallas Cowboys: The Outrageous History of the Biggest, Loudest, Most Hated, Best Loved Football Team in America. *He wrote extensive liner notes for the vinyl reissues of Roky Erickson's* Don't Slander Me and Gremlins Have Pictures *on Light in the Attic Records.*

STU COOK

I discovered Roky Erickson when the Elevators played at the Avalon Ballroom in San Francisco in the sixties. Chet Helms had relocated to San Francisco from Texas and had the Elevators play there frequently, but I didn't know they were from Texas at the time. I was hanging out several years later with the guy who was Roky's manager around 1979 when he asked if I would be interested in working some music production for an upcoming album. "Well, I'm not doing anything else," I said, "and I've always been a fan. Let's give it a try." We were cosmically drawn together by his voice. He could howl.

Roky was very present when we worked together but was much more cautious with acquaintances and strangers who weren't in his circle. He was always testing people. Roky had ideas in the studio, but I had to make sense of them as his producer. The Aliens were great. They performed around the San Francisco Bay Area quite a bit when we were working with each other. They were tight and had well-defined arrangements for the tunes I worked with him on, but a song would change every time Roky would sing. I had to lock in the version I felt was strongest. Working with analog equipment took a while before you had a result you really felt worked. The songs were there, so I would mainly reorder and configure them in a way that made sense with first verse, chorus, the whole arrangement. I spent time with and without him working on that.

Roky had a small window when he would stay really focused. My task in the studio was to keep him focused and get the best work and singing out of him. There was conversation along the way which was hilarious and crazy. There are hours and hours of tapes because we always kept the tape machine running and captured every single thing Roky ever said. He was brilliant. I assume that tape is still around. His former manager Craig Luckin would have custody. Craig was instrumental in getting him the two album deals that I worked on. He was Roky's guide for the time we were together. Roky relied on him almost completely in terms of not only his career but personal life as well.

We were working one time at the Hound Sound Studio owned by Willis [Alan] Ramsey, who wrote "Muskrat Love" for Captain and Tennille. He had built a little studio off South Congress in Austin with his earnings. I had to get Roky out of Rusk to do vocals, so I put on a coat and tie to make the doctors take me seriously. I got past the receptionist and was headed toward the ward where Roky was. I was literally accosted by other patients who thought I was a doctor. They wanted to see if I could get them out. I wasn't twenty feet inside the place and was having my mind blown, but I got Roky out and we did vocals until Roky started to drift. "Okay, Roky, you and Craig decide what we do next," I would say. "We're done recording." We did that for three or four days. Roky was right on it as long as we kept it short and sweet. When things start to slow down in the studio after three, four hours we'd say, "Okay. I think we've done our best work for the day. Let's start fresh tomorrow."

Rolling Stone gave *The Evil One* a three-and-a-half out of four stars review in 1980. We recorded fifteen songs total. Ten were on that album and then there was a second release called *TEO*, which are the first letters of *The Evil One*. *TEO* was on 415 Records out of San Francisco. We took five tracks from the first album and five that didn't make that album, so all fifteen tracks were used over those two records. I played bass on "Bloody Hammer." My work with Roky was the most successful in the artist and producer's mind and definitely my most successful as a producer. We were both really satisfied with the result, a long labor of love which was worth every minute. Sometimes you get to the end of a long journey and you go, "I took too many detours." There were a lot with Roky, but in the end we were both extremely happy. That's a win.

Bill Bentley did a great job with the tribute album *Where the Pyramid Meets the Eye*. Bill has been Roky's biggest fan and supporter from the very beginning. Everybody in my band Southern Pacific was a Roky fan. We picked "Cold Night for Alligators" to play for the tribute album because it has that bayou attitude and feel. We thought we could put a little Creedence Clearwater Revival feel into the song while keeping it in the Southern Pacific country rock realm. Bill Miller's autoharp on the original is this incredible, eerie swamp sound, which reminded me of when we were down on the bayou in Creedence's early days. Creedence stayed with our opening band called Smoke because they wouldn't let us check in to our hotel in Baton Rouge. We spent a couple nights out at the house where the whole band lived in the swamps. "Cold Night for Alligators" took me right back there.

I lived in Austin for seven years during the time when Roky had his ice cream socials at Threadgill's during South by Southwest. I saw Roky at one, which was a bit surreal. Billy Gibbons had a tour bus there. I went on the bus, and Roky and I visited for half an hour or so. Roky had a light and dark side as most of us do. I found it hard to find a continual thread through his gift and his challenges. I thought we were really on the same page when we were talking, but then I would find out that he was pulling my leg. Sometimes we couldn't even connect. I'm not sure he even put together that it was him and me that did those songs together the last time I saw him. He told me that he really liked the album that Stu Cook produced.[6]

Stu Cook was a founding member of the singular rock band Creedence Clearwater Revival, whose hits such as "Proud Mary," "Who'll Stop the Rain," "Fortunate Son," Lookin' out My Back Door," and dozens more defined a generation. Cook produced fifteen tracks for Roky Erickson and the Aliens in 1979, which were released in 1980.

CHRIS "COSMO TOPPER" KNAB

Doug Sahm used to come to San Francisco and play around town. He loved San Francisco. He came into the store one day and gave me a forty-five. "This is Roky Erickson," he said. "I just produced a single on him." The single had "Two-Headed Dog" and "Starry Eyes." He said I had to hear it, and he would try to get Roky to come out here. That was the first connection I had to someone who knew Roky. I was a Doug Sahm fan anyway. Roky was known here and could sell out a punk venue like Mabuhay Gardens, but that's about it in San Francisco. He couldn't be a big headliner. He was too esoteric. Everybody thought the Elevators were esoteric already. Only real rock fans who were into that lifestyle knew the Elevators let alone Roky's solo stuff.

Roky was pretty spacey. I had a radio show around that time with Howie Klein called the *Outcast Hour* once a week on KSAN [107.7 FM] radio from one to three in the morning. We played punk rock and other weird stuff. Howie was booking punk rock at the time, and we had bands like Romeo Void and Translator on our label 415 Records. Howie set up a concert at the Warfield Theater in downtown San Francisco to showcase Romeo Void and Translator as the headliners. We invited Roky to open the show. Getting him to open was a big deal. He played very well with Stu Cook from Creedence Clearwater Revival on bass, but Roky didn't really have a draw.

I had gotten to the Warfield early before the show and went into the basement where all the dressing rooms were. I was walking through and saw Roky over in the corner by himself. "Hey, Roky," I said. "How are you doing?" "Oh," he said. "It's the son of Muddy Waters. How are you?" He was really, really out there during that period and not a person you could have a normal conversation with. His situation was sad looking back now. That little interlude with him was short and fast, but the radio show was different. Norman Davis was the guy who anchored our radio show. He was our DJ five nights a week. The show was going out into outer space with the words we got out of Roky. Norman made it sound as normal as possible.

I realized about five or ten years ago that we were making fun of Roky. He was so otherworldly and in his own world at the same time. "Roky, we're on the air," I would say. "How are you doing today?" "I would like to bring my friend," he would say. "I'll buy him a cup of coffee." How do you interview somebody like that? People were trying to get him to say crazy things, which he did. There was a guy who would call up and ask questions because he knew Roky would give crazy answers. It really kind of pissed me off even at the time. He was exploiting Roky and his craziness. Let's face it. Roky was mentally ill. He was a very kind person at the same time. I was in this universe talking like you and I are, and he was responding from his entirely different universe. I regret making fun of him.

Roky's show was our most memorable besides the Sex Pistols. Roky said to one caller, "Don't let them shoot me through the phone line." "Don't worry, Roky," Norman said. "Nobody will shoot you through the phone line." One caller said, "Who is this guy? Are you making this up?" "No," I said. "Have you ever heard of the 13th Floor Elevators?" There were many people calling in angry that we were broadcasting this insanity live over the radio. Someone asked what "Starry Eyes" was about. Roky said, "That was about a monster who bombed us and was falling down the staircase." Roky would lightly berate the caller to make them think what he was saying was serious and real, and they were the ones out of it.

Craig Luckin showed up at our 415 Records office a few years later. He told me that he was Roky's manager. Roky had recorded an album for Columbia Records in England, who had refused to release it in the United States. Craig came to us thinking we might be interested. I was already a big Roky fan and was floored. I ran over to Howie's office. "Howie," I said. "We have a huge opportunity here to put out a Roky Erickson album." "Who's Roky Erickson?" he asked. I used to have a record store called Aquarius Records in San Francisco, and we had to carry the 13th Floor Elevators records. Craig said this would be a one-off deal. I was very honored to put *The Evil One* out.

We would sell copies by playing *The Evil One* on our show. I sold my record store to devote more time to our bands at 415 Records in 1980. I was drawn to Roky's music because it was totally insane. It dawned on me when I listened to Bill Bentley's tribute that Roky was a brilliant songwriter. His song structures were just so different than the typical verse, chorus, verse shit. He would go off and come back to a structure that was totally Roky. Nobody wrote like he did. He was a brilliant songwriter who came from a place where no one ever has. Impossible to duplicate. Listen to the song structures on *The Evil One*—not necessarily the lyrics. Put yourself into the songwriter mindset. Those songs would shatter what a songwriting teacher would teach. Roky should be in the Rock and Roll Hall of Fame. Look at all the bands who have been influenced by him.[7]

Former San Francisco radio host Chris "Cosmo Topper" Knab is currently a music business consultant, author, and lecturer. He serves on faculty for the Audio and Music Business program at the Art Institute of Seattle, where he teaches music marketing and promotion.

HOWARD THOMPSON

There were some real psychedelic rock aficionados in England, but the Elevators didn't tour overseas so nobody knew them there in 1975. Their records weren't even released there until much later. Nobody played them on the radio, but a complete music nut friend gave me the *Nuggets* record, which was the first place I heard the Elevators and which was the case for many people in England. *Nuggets* came in one day when I was in the cutting room at Strident Studios working in A&R. What an array of fantastic singles. My taste was influenced by things my friend Andrew Lauder at United Artists Records was releasing. He got a call from Bruce Young and Craig Luckin of Orb Productions one day.

They wanted to know if Andrew was interested in releasing Roky Erickson's solo album *The Evil One*. Andrew told them they should talk to me since I was at Island Records. The manager of the first group I had signed had sent me a cassette with "Two-Headed Dog" and "Starry Eyes." I absolutely loved that single. Then I did a little research into Roky. There might have been a bootleg seven-inch single from the 13th Floor Elevators that came out on Bizarre Records. The 13th Floor Elevators records suddenly became quite collectible and hip in the independent record stores in London and around the country. I was curious. You read odd stories about Roky. I was completely attracted to him rather than being scared off.

Roky sounded like nobody I knew. He was completely distinct as a writer, singer, and personality. Nobody could touch him. That quality attracted me as an A&R person. I always went where the crowd wasn't going. Doing something second didn't interest me. So, Bruce and Craig phoned and asked for a meeting. I was at CBS at the time around 1979. They played me some tracks, and I fell in love with "Bloody Hammer," the new version of "Two-Headed Dog," and everything they played me. The cassette had maybe five songs. There was still mixing to be done on the record then. I expressed interest and took the record to my boss Muff Winwood.

I was lucky because I had signed Adam and the Ants in the UK. The label let you [work with artists you want] when you have a hit group. I thought, Okay, I'm gonna do Roky Erickson because nobody else will. His reputation had been laid out in the music press by then. The record wasn't likely to sell even in the tens of thousands and didn't have hits galore, but they let me license the album all across the world except America. I don't think the rest of the world was interested. I wasn't able to get "Bloody Hammer" on the record in England, but it was a B side on a single we put out. The record didn't sell. Roky may not have been the household name one always tries to work with professionally, but he was an important guy as somebody who influenced the culture.

I was backstage when Roky played the Ritz in New York City a few years ago. He was fascinating. He would say things that had nothing to do with what other people were talking about, but he was always worth hearing. Sometimes he could be quite interesting and funny. I can see why people might have been frightened to interact with him, but he was incredibly gentle despite his professed love for gore and horror. He just seemed like a really lovely person. I don't think there was anything creepy, malignant, nasty, or scary underneath it. He was just different. Most people can't deal, but I think the different ones are worth listening to for an alternative point of view.

I went to San Francisco to see Roky play another time. Bruce Young invited my wife and I to a room in the St. Francis Hotel where we were to meet Roky and watch *The Creature with the Atom Brain*. Bruce had laid out carrots, dip, and drinks. Roky and [his second wife] Holly [Patton] were on the bed. They had gotten a video machine and the largest television you could get in 1980. Roky was quiet and not very forthcoming, but he seemed happy to be with Holly. We watched *Creature with the Atom Brain*. Roky recited the dialogue two seconds before it was spoken onscreen for the entire movie into my ear. You gotta think, Wow. This guy loves this movie.

That was my first afternoon with Roky, a totally brilliant thrill. We were off to the races and put the record out. We were CBS Records and had to do some promotion and press. I took him into the studio and asked him some questions for my own interview with him. The idea was to send an interview with Roky around to radio stations with the album so they could get an idea of what he was and what the album was about. I wasn't an interviewer and hadn't done this before. I was pretty nervous and my questions were pretty terrible and embarrassing. Roky's answers bore no relation to the questions. I don't think it was ever used except in the sleeve notes to *The Evil One*. I think John Platt, who wrote the notes, claimed the interview was his.

We brought Roky to the label later and journalists from *Melody Maker*, *NME*, and *Sounds* [magazines] lined up all day. I remember the first guy who came in. His name was Tim. He was with the music paper *Zig Zag*. Tim gave Roky a rather ornate, silver, slightly curved dagger in a sheath that fascinated him. They did their interview, and it was time for the next guy, who was called Sandy Robertson from the *Sounds* newspaper. The British music scene stayed very exciting and vibrant for a long time through these papers. *Sounds* was crucial. Sandy came in to do the interview. Roky couldn't stop thinking about the dagger he had just been given in a white plastic shopping bag. He put it on the floor next to his chair.

I was outside and saw Sandy run from the room completely freaked out ten minutes later. Apparently, Roky kept picking up the knife. He would lift the knife, then he unsheathed it and put it on one side, then changed his mind and put it on the other side. That was enough to freak out Sandy. People were bemused, worried, and couldn't deal with Roky's inconsistencies. Nick Kent came by and did a piece for *NME* that wasn't very complimentary. That bothered me immensely. Nick was a highly influential writer at the time. I was disappointed. Nick's a fantastic writer but it was a shame that he didn't have as good an experience as you would hope. He could have sold some records for us, but that's not his job. Roky wasn't in a great place when he came to England.[8]

Howard Thompson, a former A&R representative for CBS Records, worked with bands such as Public Image Ltd., Suicide, the Psychedelic Furs, Adam and the Ants, and Motorhead. Thompson was responsible for bringing Roky Erickson and the Aliens' The Evil One to CBS Records in 1980.

JOE NICK PATOSKI

Roky began recording *Don't Slander Me* in 1983. Instrumental tracks and overdubs were done at Site Studios in west Marin [County, California]. Having Jack Casady from Jefferson Airplane and Hot Tuna play on all tracks except "Starry Eyes" was a big plus. Billy Miller returned to play electric autoharp, although his sound stayed low in the mix except on "Can't Be Brought Down" and "Bermuda." Duane Aslaksen as producer made certain that Duane Aslaksen the guitarist was front and center. The result is the most earthbound, accessible recording Roky ever made. "Crazy Crazy Mama" is straight ahead rockabilly, not punk. "Nothing in Return," "Hasn't Anyone Told You?," and "Realize You're Mine" are unvarnished, sentimental love songs, while "You Drive Me Crazy" conveys the same sentiment in a twangy West Texas rock context with Buddy Holly vocals and Jerry Allison's thunder drums. "Burn the Flames" is a pure power ballad sung with the dramatic flair of a British poet with a demonic laugh thrown in at the end like Vincent Price.

Roky Erickson recordings were becoming as ubiquitous as patchouli oil and paisley patterns. Albums were being made from lost tracks, live tapes, solo acoustic sessions. Roky was being taped playing in a Holiday Inn, any way a record hustler could document him. Roky accommodated them as often as not. *Don't Slander Me* got lost in the avalanche of releases, although "Burn the Flames" found its way onto the soundtrack to the horror film *Return of the Living Dead* alongside the Cramps, the Damned, and the Flesheaters. *Don't Slander Me* was so accessible the album should have rocketed to the top of the charts. This one best showcased the best of Roky Erickson's voice, guitar playing, and songs with a state-of-the-art sound. Never again would Roky Erickson's music be so tight, so together, and so blazing and rocking.

Three Roky albums orchestrated by Craig Luckin's San Francisco music company Orb Productions stand out as his finest recorded works [*The Evil One, Don't Slander Me,* and *Gremlins Have Pictures*]. *The Evil One* broke out of the indie underground and reached a worldwide audience. *Don't Slander Me* showcased his rock and roll sensibilities. *Gremlins Have Pictures* is an anthology of Erickson's solo work beginning with his first live performance all the way to *Don't Slander Me*. Numerous outtakes from *The Evil One* and *Don't Slander Me* were already album ready. The various tracks deftly summarized Roky Erickson's recording career. *The Ritz Theatre* [album] tracks from Austin in 1975 don't just represent Roky and the Bleib Alien's first recordings, they document the band's very first gig with Billy Miller. The Ritz performance was captured on a two-track reel-to-reel tape recorder by Patrick McGarrigle, the man responsible for introducing Miller to Erickson and encouraging Roky to play again after he was released from Rusk.[9]

BILLY MILLER

Roky didn't really talk about Rusk after he got out other than saying he liked when they served cornbread and rice. He also liked [German American novelist and horror film screenwriter] Curt Siodmak's writing. Siodmak was pretty obsessed with revenge. Roky felt like society owed him something. I saw the potential in getting revenge on society, but there were plenty of people around trying to steer Roky away from that. They thought he should settle down and go into country music now that he was through with psychedelic rock, but I thought whatever direction he went in would surpass how heavy the Elevators were. Roky seemed gung ho with the idea.

I ended up going over to his place a few times after that so I could help work on his songs. I would play bass or guitar so it looked like I was doing something [instead of producing him]. Otherwise, it would have been hard to get him to knuckle down to get the arrangements really solid. I couldn't conduct him because he didn't relate to someone snapping their fingers at him. He was coming up with all these inspired musical things, but it wouldn't go anywhere if someone didn't collect his little riffs and write them into arrangements. He was a giant resource so I worked with him to get him accustomed to the idea.

One day he said, "Why don't you bring the zither?" He always called my autoharp a zither. He occasionally would ask me to play the instrument, but I can't imagine any happening producer saying, "Man if this guy only knew autoharp . . ." Autoharp is used in folk and country a lot, but it would seem like an off-the-wall idea [on Roky's songs]. Somehow it worked. Roky encouraged me to get into noise and feedback and talked about horror quite a bit. I really liked [iconic British singer and frequent parliamentary candidate] Screaming Lord Sutch. Roky was more like him than Alice Cooper. I was thinking that probably wasn't the way to go, but then Roky came up with this song "Stand for the Fire Demon." He was talking in that song about [iconic French filmmaker] Jacques Tourneur, who directed [the classic 1942 film] *Cat People*. I took him seriously then. Roky started writing one song after another strictly dedicated to Jacques Tourneur, especially "Curse of the Demon," which was also known as "Night of the Demon." Then Roky wrote "I Walked with a Zombie" [named after Tourneur's 1942 film with the same name].

Roky was very influenced by Siodmak, who wrote the screenplay for Tourneur's *I Walked with a Zombie*. The dialogue in his song "Creature with the Atom Brain" is really brilliant. You wouldn't normally look for such inspired dialogue in a B movie like that, but it had these Shakespearean like themes like revenge and irony, like everything Siodmak did. Roky was really into Siodmak's [1942 classic science fiction novel] *Donovan's Brain* even more than I was. I later could see a strong similarity between those guys and [*Eraserhead* and *Blue Velvet* writer and director] David Lynch, who seemed like the only guy carrying on that type of thing. People didn't notice Roky's influences.

Roky's band the Aliens became more specialized than the Elevators. CCR's Stu Cook came up with the idea to go with only the horror angle, and I thought Roky could take up where Screaming Lord Sutch left off. Plus, Roky was a better writer and way better singer. He was like Screaming Lord Erickson even back in the Elevators days. He actually did more screaming than was needed. Sometimes I wondered where that came from. Roky was really into Buddy Holly at one point when I was into Del Shannon, Telstar, and [British musician and producer] Joe Meek. "I Walked with a Zombie" is filled with these Telstar sounds like a horn or some bass. Stu had me do all the instrumentation on that one, which seemed to work. I really think Stu knew what he was doing looking back.

Roky would say weird things in interviews like Bob Dylan and Lou Reed had done. He was just doing what he thought you were supposed to do. He wasn't that interested in talking about where he got song ideas with interviewers, but with the Aliens he talked about it all the time. We were pretty close. Roky would dwell and communicate on artistic levels. He would talk about his life as much as anyone, but when it came to describing concepts he described them more in terms of films and paintings and certain artist names. The sessions with the Aliens and the

Bleib Aliens before that consisted of him speaking to us in a way a film director would to get people into a certain mood in hopes that they'd do a certain thing. He'd say, "Imagine you're in a long dark hall." He wouldn't say, "This is in G7," though he could be picky about people being in the wrong key. He had an unorthodox way of conducting things, and we took him seriously.

I thought it was perfect when it was just him playing his guitar. Couldn't possibly be any better. Things will only get worse if you alter something perfect, but you can't be a rock star without a band. So, it's preordained to get worse. People talked about "Bloody Hammer" being about shock treatment, but it's not. The song is a folk tale from Central Texas about a frat party that ends in murder. There are other elements that are more mysterious, but it's not about shock treatment for sure. I saw this one documentary called *Acid Casualties*, and the guy talks about Roky getting shock therapy. He's so convincing that it seems true and plausible, and shock treatment could have an unpredictable effect so I don't know. Roky said he never actually had shock treatment, but he talked constantly about the police using some sort of remote control to torture him from a distance.

He would say when he was in a bad mood, "The police just popped my head again right now. Did you hear it?" Someone once asked Alfred Hitchcock, "Is there anything here you don't like?" "Well," Hitchcock said, "I rather dislike policemen." I definitely think that was true for Roky. Someone told me that he might have gotten a hold of a psychiatric textbook. People believing they're being controlled by remote control isn't that uncommon. I don't think Roky would have come up with something like that on his own. Being crazy was something he had studied. Roky was studying himself quite a bit. People who study Edgar Allan Poe [like Roky] are definitely studying things involving mental health.

Roky wrote the Aliens songs. They're all about him. You might have noticed Roky's not a bass player so his music has no actual true bass identity. The music wasn't strict in that way even though we went to great lengths to be very good. [Bassist Stephen] Morgan created things based on signature riffs that Duane [Aslaksen] had already created. I think that's what the Elevators did all the time. Ronnie Leatherman was following Stacy. I think the Elevators were dependent on bass more. The songs wouldn't sound good without Leatherman. They sounded really good when they were working with Danny Galindo on *Easter Every-where*, but they weren't as good as Leatherman and John Ike on the earlier songs. They did sound dedicated to trying.

We recorded shows and rehearsals and would carpool to both. The first thing Roky would want to do on the ride—like, minutes after we had finished—was listen to what we just played. I did, too. We wanted to go from one song into the next with no time for applause or anything. The first note of the next song started when the last note from the song was fading down. Sometimes the drums wouldn't even be fading out. I'd be standing in Duane's face yelling, "Okay, let's go. Let's go. Where's the fire?" I was trying to psych him up and say that we've gotta be obsessed with this. I don't know if that made it any better, but it was definitely different. It was hard getting Roky used to that. "What's this thing of not having dead space between the songs?" he would ask. Sometimes Roky would talk between songs and that was even better than the songs. [Roky's son] Jegar's band and other bands Roky had later followed suit. They don't spend any time fiddling around between the songs.

Stu Cook had a checklist of every little thing that needed to be done. We went down the list, but one terrible thing we all forgot was in the song "The Wind and More." Roky usually would yell "It's the doctor with a knife," which would make the whole song way more dramatic and scary. The idea was everyone on earth is potentially facing a doctor or morti-cian with a knife. Thinking like that's almost hitting below the belt, but that was a major part of the song. Every other tiny detail was on Stu's list. Forgetting it was a big deal, like if we had forgotten the words "two-headed dog" [from "Red Temple Prayer" / "Two-Headed Dog"]. People were always quoting that one saying, *"I've* been working in the Kremlin with a two-headed dog." He never once said those words. He says, *"I'd* be working in the Kremlin with a two-headed dog." He said he would be. Not that he had been.

Roky was a better writer than someone who would write the line the other way. His phrase could be an allegory for an alternate reality. He wasn't there, but he would have been. "Red Temple Prayer" was Roky's Vietnam song. He saw a picture in a tabloid of a little girl who Americans had crucified, which inspired him to write "Red Temple Prayer." The words "children nailed to a cross" weren't in the original version, but that's what it's all about. He finally knuckled down and got serious about writing a final draft that wouldn't change ever again. He experimented with it for a while. The final draft was similar to the previous one, but it did have that line, which inspired the whole song.

"Red Temple Prayer" also was partly inspired by something Roky and I would do late at night. We would tune in to shortwave radio. Sometimes we would turn it up real loud and marvel at these sounds. We would listen to propaganda radio like Radio Moscow. This broadcaster sounded like he spoke perfect English but sounded vaguely European. It would be hours and hours of this guy saying over and over stuff like, "The widest river in the United States is two thousand and sixteen feet. The widest river in the Soviet Union is twenty thousand and eighteen feet. The tallest mountain in the United States is eight thousand feet. The tallest mountain in the Soviet Union is ten thousand feet." He just had all these weird, meaningless statistics with all this static crackling in the background.

Sometimes we would tune in to these rabid mad dog preachers. "You're in your car," they would say. "You better pull over now because you're going to hell if you have a wreck." Some voices on that radio sounded like Wolfman Jack creeping through the static. We wanted the feel of that rabid, maniacal, fanatic voice bleeding through the noise for "Stand for the Fire Demon." The later versions that you've heard are more like rock opera, but in the early ones we really, really were trying to make something really avant-garde. "Red Temple Prayer" still retains a strong, conscious effort to make it seem derived from those Soviet brainwashing broadcasts. The version Doug Sahm produced sounds even more like that brainwashing over the shortwave radio.

People had an image of Roky as this rabid creature. Roky could do a good job if he wanted to act insane. He had this southern cracker preacher sound happening with his voice. People didn't know he was from Texas when those albums came out. We had certain doors slammed in our faces because of the Elevators. I found out later that they had a bad reputation because the albums and shows weren't well produced, but listen to those songs now. That seems like a myth, a symptom of the times. Things really don't have that much meaning in this day and age when you can do anything.

I saw Roky at his last shows in San Francisco. He was really good, but people seemed to have the impression that it might be his last shows ever.

He did nothing but his own songs on Halloween night. He did nothing but Elevators songs the next night including the entire album *Easter Everywhere* in the same sequence as the record. Roky has become an institution since then, but he did pay quite the price. I was always at war with some people who weren't trying to guard against him paying that price. Why did Roky have to be the one to pay? How come Roky has to sit at the back of the bus? I was being his ultimate shill. The mental health angle has been so overdone, but someone has to be the king of that. It would be a cheat for Roky not to be the one, but I hate when people compare him to [legendary Pink Floyd founder and acid burnout] Syd Barrett. Roky was just years ahead of his time like Gene Vincent. He already sounded like something from today.[10]

DAN COOK

We went to a huge Mexican restaurant with a sprawling patio packed with a late lunch crowd and early happy hour celebrants that afternoon. "Hey, Roky," echoed everywhere as we slowly snaked our way through the tables and got seated. Everyone knew him. Roky smiled at his fans but didn't say anything. He ordered a huge burrito platter and tucked it away with food clinging to his beard and mustache. He seemed unaware. Our efforts to interview him went nowhere. He was groggy and responded to questions with an affable smile. His eyes actually twinkled. It occurred to me that perhaps he was from another world where gods walked freely.

His mother, Evelyn, said it was time to take Roky home and asked if we would like to tag along. You bet. Cindy and I followed Evelyn and Roky, but their car turned into a Walmart parking lot before long. We followed. "We need a few things for Roky's place," Evelyn said. We trooped inside. Cindy and Evelyn headed in one direction. Roky drifted about with me in tow. He stopped by a rack of home goods. Perched on the top of the shelves were several lawn chairs. Roky examined the lawn chairs. "Do you think I need a lawn chair?" he asked. "Hey, Roky, I wouldn't know. Do you think you need one?" "I don't know," he said, still eyeing the chairs. "What do you think?" "Like I said, I have no idea if you need one. Do you want one?" "I'm not sure. Do you think I should get one?" He was smiling. He was fucking with me.

"Okay, we're done," Evelyn interrupted. "Let's go, Roky." Darkness was falling by the time we pulled into Roky's driveway. His little cottage sat at the rear of a larger home. The cottage emitted a weird humming sound that grew louder as we approached the door shrouded by trees and kind of spooky in the dark. Cindy, Evelyn, Roky, and I now entered the strangest living quarters I have ever seen. Wires were strung everywhere throughout the house. Radios and televisions were scattered everywhere, all of them blaring out random programs—or were they? The din was deafening. Roky sat down on a worn sofa and promptly fell sound asleep. "Well, we might as well leave now," Evelyn said. "He won't be up for some time. It's the medication." The house was humming behind us as we left.[11]

Dan Cook is the former editor of the In Pittsburgh *newsweekly in Pennsylvania. He currently is a writer and Wikipedia expert for the Portland, Oregon–based To the Point Collaborative.*

JON DEE GRAHAM

There were carpetbaggers who profited off Roky and maybe didn't have his best interest in mind. They were like, "Hey, you wanna see something weird? Watch this." What a disservice. I think that's at best rude and at worst just fucking unethical. Then there was Mike Alvarez. Mike was Roky's friend. He would make him dinner and always, always have time to sit down and play. He played with Roky a lot for a period. Mike put a lot of effort into making Roky's life better. He brought him good food and ice cream. They would sit by the creek and play music together. I don't think Mike ever profited off Roky. He had Roky's best interest at heart. Mike was one of the few people not driving Roky crazier and who was trying to help him integrate.

Roky really had started making his comeback at Raul's by then. He was embraced by the punk rock community as this almost saint-like figure who came with all the dark trappings, spiders, and a backstory that could not be beaten. They said "Starry Eyes" was written about LSD overdoses. Then there was this superstitious but popular folktale that went around in my circle that Roky had done so much acid and had so much electroshock that he had developed psychic powers and could read your mind. People said you had to be really careful with what you were thinking around him. He would respond to what you were thinking even if you didn't say it. I saw it happen more than once. Think about the pathology involved in both sides of that situation. I went to see him play at Raul's with the Explosives before I was even in the Skunks. Somebody said, "Dude, just stand in the audience and think, Hey, Roky, look at me. Watch his eyes. He will seek you out in the crowd."

Then True Believers backed him up at the Austin Music Awards in 1986. Look it up on YouTube. The footage is wild. We were this ideologically sophisticated group of guys trying to put punk rock and American music into one thing that included songs in Spanish and covering the New York Dolls and Hank Williams in the same set. We were thrilled that we were getting to play with Roky. Rehearsal was at Mike Stewart's house, who was our tour manager at that point. Roky came over with a handler. He was pretty out there. I asked Roky, "Man, are you writing? That Doug Sahm recording of 'Starry Eyes' is in my top ten perfect recordings of a perfect performance of a perfect song." I would put that up against anything. He goes, "Yeah. I wrote one just today." "What's the title?" He struck his right fist into his left palm. "Wait, that's the title?" He smiles and hits his right fist into his left palm again.

Roky wanted to do "Two-Headed Dog" and "You're Gonna Miss Me" with us at the awards show. "You're Gonna Miss Me" is actually a pretty complicated and sophisticated song. There are weird and unnatural chord changes, so we had to work it out. Roky would play with us for about forty-five seconds to a minute, then go, "No. Y'all aren't getting it. It's E, D, A, G." We're like, "Okay." We would play the song that way, but then he would stop again. "No, you're not playing it right. I said it's B, F, G, B." We're all looking at each other. "Oh, okay." We did it that way and he threw his arms up and said, "Man, I don't know if this is gonna work. Y'all aren't playing it right. I said it's A, B, F, G." Every time he would pick four different chords. We decided that he would play on "Two-Headed Dog" and just sing on "You're Gonna Miss Me." That worked. We got past it.

So, Roky shows up at the awards show. You never know with him. We go out onstage and put the guitar on him and made sure it's in tune. We go into "Two-Headed Dog" and do one verse and a chorus. He does another verse and chorus. Everyone is freaking out about how good it is. Then Roky starts playing a solo after the second chorus. He was a really good guitar player when you got him focused. There's nothing like jamming on a rock and roll song. He's playing his solo, but he won't stop. He keeps going round after round after round. We had to stop when our slot was over. We didn't get a chance to play "You're Gonna Miss Me" because Roky couldn't stop playing his solo.

The last times I saw Roky were a little before he died. He had gotten his teeth fixed and had shaved off his beard. He was looking good and had his meds right. He wasn't with someone who was pounding him down with antipsychotics. There was less Roky the zombie and more the guy who was pretty charismatic and engaging. He was still crazy but more in the way that he blows your mind. Roky got a third act in which he got to be Roky again. Did him being manipulative make him be less crazy? No. He had that survival instinct because he had no cultural or social skills whatsoever. It's a pretty good trick to make people put your guitar on you and make sure it's in tune. He figured out he could pretty much do what he wanted.[12]

Jon Dee Graham was a founding member of the pioneering Texas punk band the Skunks as well as the literate rock and roll band True Believers with Alejandro Escovedo. The longtime Austin resident is a critically acclaimed solo artist today.

MIKE ALVAREZ

Roky and I were together like brothers for four years starting in 1984. Roky's brothers brought him to my doorstep on Clyde Barrow Avenue. "Hey," they said. "Roky can't live with Evelyn anymore." I only had a bag of carrots and some corn tortillas in the refrigerator, but I said, "Yeah, come in." That's the way South Austin is. Musicians always take care of each other. [Texas Tornados bassist] Speedy Sparks was always there for Roky. Roky was always living with one of us during these years. Roky was highly intelligent. I could relate to him very well. He communicated fine. His brain was a little fried around the sides, but otherwise he was fine. I found him normal, but he'd put up a little show if we were around people. He didn't want to talk to anybody or shake hands ever. We started working on music. "Hungry for Your Love" came out of us jamming. He never recorded it. Nobody knows about it or cares, but he played amazing lead guitar when I cut the song.

No one cared about Roky at all during those years. He was just hanging out at my house. We lived together in a few different places and became close. I was in Max and the Makeups and was producing and recording everyone in Austin including the Reivers, True Believers, and Daniel Johnston before anyone knew him. Roky was hanging around because I always had weed. We were a bunch of potheads in South Austin. Roky looked like Howard Hughes sitting on my couch. I had all these bands coming in and nobody recognized him except one guy. It was probably [Alejandro Escovedo from True Believers]. He said, "Is that Roky Erickson?" "Yeah." I didn't know anything about the Elevators then. "Oh my god," he said. "I'm not worthy. I'm not worthy."

I was always gigging at the clubs. Roky would go with me to the Continental Club and restaurants around town, and I started noticing that seas would part for him. "What the hell is going on here?" I had only heard the Spades' "You're Gonna Miss Me." Mike Jensen introduced me to that music. Mike was a young kid like nineteen years old, but he was the biggest Elevators fan you could imagine. He was in the documentary I produced called *Demon Angel: A Day and Night with Roky Erickson, Halloween 1984.* Mike brought Roky over to my house one time when I was kitchen manager at Raw Deal on Sixth Street. All the musicians worked there. Mike put on the Spades' version of that song one night in 1983. I was going into my psychedelic phase without the Elevators. What is that?" I asked. I dropped everything. Jensen was a big musicologist and steered me toward Syd Barrett and [Pink Floyd's] "See Emily Play" and the Chocolate Watchband. Then he turned me on to the Spades.

I was rehearsing for Max and the Makeups' last show on October 31, 1984, when Roky comes in wearing a cape and a crown. He always looked trippy and especially on Halloween. "Hey, Mike," he said. "You wanna be in my video?" "Yeah, sure." We were always recording or shooting something. I didn't know what he was doing, but I figured maybe his mother was shooting something. Evelyn had shot something at a gig down the street from the Continental Club last time I had watched him do a video. I went with him. I was a surfer, so I put on a hang ten shirt for

Halloween. He drove us to this place that had a whole television crew there. The stage was in a hole in the ground by Forty-Fifth Street. You would have to get down there by a ladder.

Roky and I had only been jamming blues up to that point. I figured Roky would play his songs and I would play guitar solos and dance around it for the video shoot. Didn't happen. He grabbed the electric guitar, and I got the acoustic. "Oh shit," I said. "I don't know any of these songs." I faked it pretty good. Then we swapped, and I had electric guitar. Roky knew what he was doing. Everyone thought he was just a jelly brain all those years sitting on my couch. I knew differently. We were playing guitar one day just sitting there. "Hey, Mike," he goes. "Let me see that guitar." What are you gonna do with that? My jaw dropped when he started playing. There's an A League, B League, D League with guitar players. Roky was A League. He blew my mind. Then I had [bassist] Karl [Remstam] from Max and the Makeups and Jensen come over to jam. We played "Cold Night for Alligators" and "You're Gonna Miss Me," which was so psychedelic and wicked. We decided to put a band together.

We went with a couple German guys in suits from CBS Records to a little motel where Roky was living around that time. Jensen told me that the Germans told him he was too young, but I don't believe that. He was nineteen. Roky had this little mafia around him, which really prevented us from doing much. The True Believers' bass player and drummer backing us, and me and Roky. Nothing really materialized, but we did get *Demon Angel* and some singles out. They were too psychedelic and wicked for 1987. Roky was in fine form.

Then I got an offer to move here to Los Angeles to produce at Paramount Recording Studios. I had a big house and remember talking to Roky from that house. "Roky," I said, "we've got plenty of room for you here." I felt like I left him. "Nah, I'll be okay, Mike," he said. "I'll be fine." That was probably 1988. "Mike, I'm gonna hide away," he said. "You'll probably never find me again, but you have the right to represent *Demon Angel*." I have my own version that has Mrs. Erickson and Bill Bentley in it. Bill Bentley is a historian. I interviewed him and one of the musicians in the Aliens who had a snake crawling all over him during the interview. I got the rights to do the Elevators movie called *Reverberation*, and Jack Ortman knew I was with Sony and said, "Mike, you ought to take that version of *Demon Angel* and cut it. Redo it." I did. It's really sweet.

We later put a band together and toured *Demon Angel*. A big Roky fan and publicist named Dan Cook put me together with a couple gigs in Cleveland and Pittsburgh. I went to Pittsburgh to promote *Demon Angel* in 1992. There was still nobody paying attention. Sumner [lived there and] had a band, and we opened up. They were terrible. I did "Slip inside This House." I'm a horrible singer to begin with, but then I showed up in Pittsburgh with laryngitis. I met Roky's dad there. It was winter and I'm sliding everywhere and I'm sick. "Oh my god," I said. "I went cross-country for this. Nobody's gonna be at this show." We rehearsed in a storage unit with no heat. We did what we could and got through some songs. Then the gig happened the next night. We show up and the place is packed to the rim. I guess they don't let snow bother them. Then the next night Sumner was playing in Cleveland, and he asked me to play guitar at the Grog Shop, which was more serious than just a bunch of kids showing up. Lots of known musicians showed up for that gig. Roky knew what he was doing when he nabbed me to play on *Demon Angel*.

I was working as a sound man at CNN during the midnineties and was doing a set visit at the *Donny & Marie [Osmond] Show*. Dick Clark was standing there by himself running the show and doing what producers do. He was up against the wall, and I said, "Hey, Mr. Clark. I'm Mike Alvarez. Do you remember the 13th Floor Elevators?" "Oh my god," he said. "Yes. Whatever happened to them?" "It's a long story," I said. "I'm working on a screenplay about them. Can I pick your brain?" I called him first to get the footage from *American Bandstand* for our documentary. "Oh, no," he said. "We have to charge ten thousand dollars a minute," but he was a great guy. I would call his office, and he would pick up the phone and say, "Mike, I'm right in the middle of a meeting, but call me back in ten minutes." Amazing. I called him back to talk about the movie. "Mike," he said. "I think you're beating a dead horse. Let me give you an example. My daughter has rights to the Otis Redding film, and she's having a hell of a time getting any interest in an Otis Redding movie." I was thinking to myself, god, and this is Dick Clark's daughter with an Otis Redding movie.[13]

Mike Alvarez produced Daniel Johnston, Roky Erickson, and several other icons in Austin during the eighties. Alvarez produced and played guitar in the hour-long documentary Demon Angel: A Day and Night with Roky Erickson, Halloween 1984. *He currently lives and works in Los Angeles.*

MIKE JENSEN

I grew up in the projects in New York City until I was eleven, but I was very much a part of the South Austin music scene and culture. Our small band of people still stick together and always will have each other's backs. One thing I have never appreciated about other people calling to get Roky information—and I assure you that you are not the first one—is that they all want dirt and trash. "How crazy was he? Did Lucifer have satanic rituals?" I can't tell you how many people I've hung up on over the years. The legend and persona promoted by the record company of Roky as America's Syd Barrett isn't how Roky was as a person. There's another side many people didn't get to see. He gave me advice that I follow to this day.

I'll give you an example. Roky invited me to join his band for the 1984 tour, but I wasn't making any money with him. I needed to make money another way. I got a restaurant job and felt like it was important to keep it for minimal money. I was getting ready to leave this recording session with Roky one day. "Hey, Mike," he said. "Where are you going?" I told him I felt obligated to go to this party the restaurant was having. "I don't really want to go, but I have to," I said. "I have to keep this money coming in." "You know," he said. "You don't owe those people anything. You're with us." He asked me if he and the band mattered more to me than the job. "You do," I said. "You do." "You gotta think about this, Mike," he said. "What matters more in your life: a restaurant job that will come and go or hanging with the people you really want to be with? Where do you really want to invest your time?" That stuck with me. I was nineteen years old. I was twenty and he was thirty-six. Roky most certainly had [a good head on his shoulders]. The craziness you see in video interviews was something that he promoted because it's what people expected.

Here's another example. We were at a midnight movie in 1983. Roky wanted to see this movie and was gonna pay. Hey, this is great, I thought. I'll go. Sure. We were standing in line for this movie when I noticed this guy in the distance looking at us. I thought, Oh no, here comes a Roky fan. We'll see how this goes. This guy finally worked up the courage to come over. "Excuse me, sir," he said. "Are you Roky Erickson?" Roky changed immediately. He takes a drag of his cigarette. "Yes, I am Roky Erickson," he says. "I'd like you to meet my friend Mike Jensen. Mike played with me on my first record in the Spades. He was the drummer." "Roky," I said. "I wasn't there." "Oh, come on, Mike. You are being so bashful. This man wants to meet you. Tell him about when we played in Dallas and we played on the Spades record." This guy was convinced I was being modest by the time Roky was finished. Roky had this guy completely bamboozled.

Roky was funny, but very few people really knew him. I think most musicians who reached the status Roky did are like that. He would go from band to band to band and has this great catalog of music both with the Elevators and his solo career, but very few people actually talk about who was Roky Erickson really? What was it like to be with him and just talk? I'm very privileged in that Mike Alvarez and I were his friends first. Roky was a guy from the neighborhood who invited us into his incredible world of music. I wouldn't trade it for anything. Roky absolutely was hilarious when he was in the mood. I only saw him really, truly angry a couple times, but his sense of humor was really great, dry, understated.

He also was an incredible musician. I went over to Mike Alvarez's house for a recording session one time when he was pouring all his resources into recording Roky. Everyone was doing drugs, which is what people talk about, but something else was happening. "You know what, Mike," Roky said. "I've had this syncopated rhythm going through my head for a while. I wanna see if you can do it." "Yeah, okay," I said. "That's fine." I was dubious. Roky couldn't play the drums, but he sat down behind mine. "It's okay if I play your drums, right?" he said. "Yeah. No problem." He belted out this syncopated rhythm that I cannot reproduce. It was correct musically and had a beat that invited someone who didn't understand music to dance and feel the music. Incredible. Blew me away. "Mike," he said when he was done. "Do you think you can do that?" "I don't know," I said. "I can try." I did. Couldn't come close. No way. I finished and he said, "That's pretty good. I like it. We're not gonna use it for anything, but I wanted to see if you could do it."

Mike and I were waiting for Roky to show up another time. Here's his sense of humor. Mike started playing "You're Gonna Miss Me" on guitar. I was singing, but I'm a terrible singer. I'm belting it out and having a good time but didn't realize in the meantime Roky had come in and was sitting down next to me to my right. I had an "oh shit" moment. I'm singing a song this guy wrote, and he's sitting there smoking a cigarette and smiling. I stopped. He said, "Why did you stop?" "Because it's your song," I said, "and I'm terrible." "No, you're not," he said. "I loved it. I thought the whole thing was great. Keep going. Keep going." I was overwhelmed. He knew I was terrible. I must have been. Roky was funny.

We started playing music together on and off starting in March 1983. Roky and I hung out at his house a lot. We sat on the back of my car and would talk for hours or sit by the swimming pool that his father designed and built behind the house. He talked to me about this Elevators reunion that was coming up. "First of all," he said. "I don't want to do it." "Okay, Roky. Don't do it if you don't want to do it." "I'm being forced into this. This guy and his band Cornerstone somehow cornered me into doing this music. They've got me on the hook for the Elevators reunion at the same time. Mike, they're not gonna let me play. I'm angry. I don't want anything to do with Tommy Hall or the Elevators music." "Okay," I said. "You've spoken to me about that, Roky. I empathize, but it's an opportunity to make some money." "It's not about money," he said. "I don't want to hear about money."

I went to the studio way out on Menchaca Road [in Austin], and the first thing I noticed was that they didn't let Roky play a note. They were doing his solo stuff and this band was dressed like Devo. They had this new wave persona that didn't fit Roky at all. His singing was flaccid. He wasn't into it. Didn't scream. He walked out shaking his head. His arms at his sides. The drummer's yelling, "Play, play." He drowned the whole thing. Didn't do anything these people expected. It wasn't because he was an incorrigible mental case. It was because Roky chose to do it that way. Period. He was in control every second. He was very adamant. He was mad at these people. He was mad at the Elevators. He was mad at Tommy Hall. He was angry at being micromanaged and doing things he didn't want to do. They weren't letting him play.

The band that Mike and I had with him was very different. Roky played everything. We didn't keep him from playing his music. He played a lead or a solo if he wanted. He could extend a song if he wanted. We all followed each other as musicians and professionals, but the band and music was Roky's. He didn't tell us what to play. Never, ever. We played what Roky wanted as far as songs. We had a big brother and little brother relationship. He protected me from some things.

Like the time Roky was booked for a solo show at the Continental Club. The club manager told me, "I paid Roky six hundred dollars up front. Can you help see that he gets there and gets onstage?" "Sure," I said. "I'm giving him a ride over there anyway." I got him to the show and was taking his guitar and amp inside. I talked to the manager while Roky's talking to this woman I'd never seen. "Hey, Mike," Roky says. "I'm just gonna take off for a little while with this girl. She has some pot. Let the manager know I'll be back." Not a problem. I see him take off across the street to the Austin Motel, which was a dump back then. This woman was a fan who wanted to have her own good time with Roky. I didn't see Roky again for two days.

The manager started to argue with me over the six hundred dollars. "Hey, listen," I said. "First of all, I'm not in control of an adult. Second, you paid him up front. Third, are you going to go to Roky Erickson and ask for the six hundred dollars back? I'm not." That's his qualm with Roky, not mine. All I did was give him a ride here. Turned out that he went and spent the money on this woman he had just met and had himself a good old time carousing around. Never gave the six hundred bucks back. I don't know if he planned that, but he didn't tell me that he was gonna have a festival of sex and drugs. He just said, "I'm just taking off for a while. See you later, Mike." He knew if he told me I would have stopped him from taking off like a little brother would.

Roky was planning to tour Europe with our band, but we had never played a live show because of contract problems. He wanted us to go there and record his next EP. I never had a hard time working with him musically, but at the same time I didn't try to enforce any control over him. Other musicians have said he was difficult. You would have to speak to them. The Explosives in particular might say that. I've heard stories about Roky literally exploding and going off on them over simple things. The only time I saw him go off the tracks was when they tried to impose the Elevators tour on him.

Roky felt like he was losing more and more intellectual control over his music. He was being told what to do until the point it got with CBS where he didn't play one note on *The Evil One*. We sat down and said, "How would Roky like for this to go?" We tried to give him the creative process and atmosphere that he had early on but was taken away. We decided that the practices would be recorded just like they had been in the sixties and we'd play them back for Roky to hear. He'd give feedback on what he liked and didn't like and proceed from there. We auditioned for CBS to go on tour and laid down the tracks for the EP we wanted to do. We got into the thinking behind "Bermuda" at one point.

We were out having a talk and walk in the neighborhood because we didn't want to smoke pot at his mom's place. "You know," he said. "I wrote 'Bermuda' when I was at Rusk. I was gonna follow a certain path, but I ended up with 'The Interpreter.' 'The Interpreter,' where is he now? Does he burn with the devil? Did he leave Moscow? 'The Interpreter' is about this guard at Rusk who I would speak with. He and I worked out a relationship. We were able to talk to one another. He wasn't like the other guards. He had these piercing eyes. You seem to have the same eyes as the guard in Rusk. It makes me wonder about you when I look at your eyes. I decided this: he's not the interpreter. You are, Mike."

Then he dropped it just as quick as he brought it up. He brought it up one or two more times. "Mike, you're the interpreter." He would just say it in passing. Then it faded. A Rokyism. He was an intelligent man. He was also grasped by his devils. He was mentally ill. I don't know what his diagnosis was. Depressed? Sometimes. Just like all of us. I think doctors used medications on him that were probably unnecessary in the sixties and seventies. I know that he suffered at Rusk. The conversation with him about those two songs was a window into Rusk, a window into how he thought about his songs and the people around him. Roky took me back to his room one time where he wanted to talk. We were bullshitting and he said, "Mike, I have something I want you to look at." He handed me an old notebook. I opened it and said, "Roky, what is this?" "It's the journal that I kept at Rusk." "Why are you showing this to me?" "I want you to take your time and see this." It's hard to describe what was in this book. It left an impression. He was writing on one page to Dana. The writing was on the left-hand side.

"Dana," the words said, "I'm so glad to have the opportunity to write to you, but I have to tell you that everything is turning into demons as I write." The letters and words he was laying out in the book were becoming the demons he was describing. It was very surreal. The word "demon" melted on the page as he wrote it into this horrific demon depiction. The whole journal was filled with these images of Dana, demons, the devil, god. He was giving me something that was extremely personal and absolutely overwhelming for me. I have no idea what happened to that book. I saw it once and handed it back. He asked me what I thought. How am I gonna answer? What do I think? "Roky, this is very personal and a window into your experience at Rusk. Do you really want me to see this?"

"Yeah," he said. "That's why I handed it to you. I want to know what you think." "Roky," I said, almost out of breath from what I had seen in this journal. "I think this was a really hard time for you, but I like this artwork." "You do?" "Yeah, I like the way you made the words melt into pictures." "That's what I wanted you to understand." Then he dropped the whole conversation. I'm a nurse so I can superimpose my experience as a nurse over what I experienced with Roky. I think he reached out to many people trying to say, "Hey, this is really what happened. This is what's going through my mind." I don't believe that he shared that with lots of people.

He despised the Elevators and their music then. "Tommy Hall this, Tommy Hall that," he would say. "It's all his fault." I was flipping through some records. "Mike, pick out a record. Let's go smoke some pot out back while mom's not here. I wanna go out but get high before we go." I'm flipping through the records and there's a copy of Roky's first album. Holy crap. He has such disdain for it. I pulled it out to see if it was mono or stereo. I took the LP out and in Roky's handwriting it said, "To Sumner with love on Roky's fortieth birthday." I put it back in its sleeve and put it back. I think Roky tried to have someone understand what had happened and what was happening in his head. I very well may have been one of those people.

I was with Roky a few times when he experienced audio and visual hallucinations. I believe that he believed what he saw was going on. I was sitting with Roky by the empty swimming pool one evening. There were frogs in there, but it was one place he liked to sit down. We went there after a session with Mike Alvarez and Roky started talking about Dana. She was the love of his life. He said, "You know, Dana watches me." "She does?" "Yeah, in fact, I know she's watching me right now." "Watching us from where, Roky?" "She's right over there across the pool." He stood up. It was one of the few times I ever heard him use profanity. "Dana, you bitch," he yelled. "I know you're watching us. You wanna listen to what we say? You're not invited." He started throwing rocks in that direction.

I let him go through it and didn't say anything. He finally calmed down, and I said, "Roky, is she gone?" "She's never gone, Mike," he said. "She's back again." He got up and started throwing rocks again. "You bitch. Stay out of my life. This is none of your business." Then he sat back down. This continued all evening, but the outbursts became shorter lived and took a longer time to manifest. I didn't even smoke cigarettes then, much less pot. I was totally sober. Didn't drink. Smoking marijuana was the heaviest thing Roky did that evening. Marijuana was everywhere in South Austin. Seeing Dana was something organic that was either brought on by bad care, lack of care, or lack of understanding at Rusk. I truly believe that Roky Erickson was one of the most intelligent people I've ever met and that his intellect was his greatest asset and one of his greatest problems.

Roky's intellect could get away from him. His intellect outstripped what he was able to process in real time. I don't believe he was nearly as psychologically incapacitated as these stories that you see. That's all BS. The Roky I knew had a grasp of reality for the most part. He was able to string sentences together. He was fun to be with. He was able to produce music that made sense. It wasn't a chore to be with him. I have a lot of psychiatric experience because lots of my nursing experience has been in corrections facilities. I think overall the electroshock treatment that Roky received at Rusk is criminal. Rusk wasn't the right atmosphere for a person suffering from his maladies.

I don't believe he was a paranoid schizophrenic. I think that at the very worst he was depressed. I have dealt with people who really are mentally ill—murderers and murderesses who have hacked their children to death and buried them—and Roky's issues were nowhere near the level people have given them either because of some legend that people have made up and stuck onto his persona or rumors. Roky was depressed at times, but all of us have reasons to be depressed. Life can be depressing. He would talk about the Elevators and his solo career and I think what depressed him wasn't that he didn't have a number one hit. I know that he wasn't interested in being a millionaire. He was depressed over the fact that he had lost control of his creative process.

The Ericksons blame me for the money that was lost on the 1984 tour. They see me as the problem, but I didn't scuttle that tour. Roky did. CBS had three bands in mind even though Roky's contract with them stated that he had the right to pick his musicians. It was black and white in his contract. "Mike, I have to tell you something you're not gonna like," Roky said. "CBS made up their mind about the band. They chose the band I chose, you guys." "Fantastic, Roky." We had talked about the dates, getting work permits. This wasn't just a ghost or music BS. There's a paper trail with the hotels we were gonna stay in, the food we were gonna eat. Details were mapped out. "They like the band," Roky said. "The one problem is they don't like you." "Is it my playing?" "No, it has nothing to do with how you play. CBS believes you're too young to go, that you're a liability not an asset." "Roky," I said. "You need to get another drummer and go." "No, I'm not gonna do that. My contract says I get to pick my band and I picked you. They're telling me no and I'm not gonna have it. I'm not going if they don't let me have the musicians I want."

"Roky," I said. "This is potentially millions of dollars. This could jump-start your career. You could get another album out of this." This is where he got mad. "Mike," he said. "You have to listen to me. You need to mind your own. Back off. Listen to me. Let me handle this. Mind your own, Mike. Stop." The conversation stopped there. Of course, he scuttled that tour, and they blame me. I'm very sad as I say this to you. I'm almost in tears sharing this even after all these years. The whole thing is very upsetting. It hurts me to this day and ruined my relationship with Roky. That destroyed all the years of friendship we had. Destroyed it. I didn't have a hand in that. I was twenty years old. I wasn't a kid. I don't know what their rationale was.

Maybe because Roky was "The Evil One." Why would The Evil One have this really clean-looking guy playing the drums? I think losing control over his creative process, losing control of the music, now he's losing control over the musicians. I think he was pretty mad, but I still believe to this day that he should have gone. I tried to approach it a couple days later with him and was shut way down. I tried to talk to Mike Alvarez, who was about twenty-nine then. I told him to get another drummer in my place. Maybe I could play with those guys again when they came back, but they couldn't pass up this opportunity. "It's done," Mike said. "There's nothing I can do. I can't change his mind. No one can." So, yeah, I'm upset. Roky was loyal to people.[14]

Mike Jensen was a drummer in Roky Erickson's Austin band during the mideighties. He works as a registered nurse today.

MIKE HASKINS

The Nervebreakers were shooting the shit one night after rehearsal in the midseventies when our keyboard player Walter Brock said, "Wouldn't it be cool to get Roky Erickson out of retirement?" Roky was retired as far as anybody knew. Our fantasy was we could be his band and record an album. I had seen an Elevators reunion gig on March 25, 1973, when Roky still had his institutional burr hair, and he had released the "Two-Headed Dog" single around then, which is why he was fresh on our minds. Time went along. Then the Nervebreakers were playing regularly at this concert club called the Palladium in Dallas in 1979. Touring new wave and punk bands would play there, and the Nervebreakers were the first-choice opening act. The club owner had contacted our manager saying Graham Parker canceled, and he had an open date next month and did we have any ideas for a show?

Nervebreakers' manager Tom Ordon had connections from spending the late sixties in the Bay Area. He was friends with Roky's manager Craig Luckin. Tom said, "Hey, what's Roky doing?" "Well," he said, "he lives with his mother in Austin. He's not doing much of anything. He's not playing." "Would he be interested in playing a date in Dallas?" He told Tom to give him a call. Tom called Roky's mom's and asked him. "Sure," Roky said. He said he would pay $300 and a bus ticket. "Sure." The Nervebreakers would be the opening act and his backup band. He had never heard of us, but he was agreeable. We asked him to send a demo tape of his new songs so we could learn them. Craig sent a cassette, which is the same stuff that became the *Roky and the Aliens* album.

We were blown away. The whole demo album was great. We practiced around the clock for two weeks. Tom was a good singer and stood in for Roky on vocals when we rehearsed. We learned the songs without ever having met Roky. Then Roky came in from the bus stop on show day. His communication skills were not one hundred percent. We asked how he was doing, if everything was cool, whether he wanted to run through some tunes. I told him our roadie was gonna run to the store for Cokes

and asked if he wanted one. Then I said even better he would get peach
Nehi soda. His answer to everything I said, over and over, was "Yeah."
Then one guy said, "It's hard to tell what key 'White Faces' is in on the
tape. What is it?" Silence. "Roky," I said. "A minor, right?" "Yeah."

I thought, Oh man. This is rough. So, we plug in, start playing, and
Roky's one hundred percent and nailing it as soon as the music starts. We
ran through about three songs and were thinking everything would be
fine. "Roky," we said, "this sounds great." "Yeah," he said. "Sounds good.
Well, I'll see you at the show." "Wait, Roky. We need more than three
songs." "Nah, it'll be fine. See you later." It turned out to be okay, and that
first show with almost no rehearsal ended up being the record *Roky Erickson Live in Dallas 1979*. We had a really good turnout. People came up
from Austin because he so rarely played a show at that time. I don't know
the official count, but capacity at the Palladium was about a thousand.
The venue was reasonably full. I had friends that had the "Two-Headed
Dog" / "Starry Eyes" single, but almost all the material we played was
unfamiliar to us and the crowd. The response was surprisingly positive.

The Nervebreakers played a few more shows with Roky in the Dallas
area over a three-month period. Everything was okay, but playing with
Roky was like babysitting. He was very generous and spirited toward his
fans, which included taking any and every drug he was offered. He was
offered drugs all the time. He was generally a sharp guy, but the results
were unpredictable. We felt like we were ready to go on with our music
after those few shows, but Roky thought it was fun and good and wanted
to go on the road. We didn't feel that way. "Hey, Roky, let me hook you
up with a band," Tom said. "The Explosives would be perfect for you, and
they want to go on the road." I loved Roky's music, and he was a sweet
guy, but I don't regret not going on the road with him. Having a chance
to play his music with him was fantastic and a dream come true, but a
few months was my limit.[15]

*Mike Haskins was a founding member of the Dallas-based Nervebreak-
ers in the midseventies. The group earned recognition as opening act for
pioneering punk rock bands the Ramones and the Sex Pistols. Additionally,
they served as backing band for Roky Erickson for several shows in the late
seventies.*

GREGG TURNER

Roky Erickson was in tow when Doug Sahm was playing the Palomino Club in North Hollywood one night right after they had recorded "Starry Eyes" and "Two-Headed Dog." My friends and I couldn't resist showing up, and I was wearing my Elevators T-shirt like a dizzy groupie. The Palomino mostly had watered-down country and western music for slobs who came in to chew steaks and swill beer, but Doug was more rock and roll. I think they figured it would work because he also was a good old boy. We were sitting there and saw Doug wandering around. "Hey, Doug," I said. "Is Roky here?" He goes, "You know Roky?" "Well, sort of." Sahm brings me backstage.

Roky was sitting at a large wood table. He was explaining how he knew he was a Martian to a hippie woman next to him. "My mother was the first one to tell me about it," he said. "What do you call your mother?" She said, "Mom?" "What else?" he goes. "Ma, right?" He writes "MA" on the table with a big felt pen. "What's the first letter of my first name?" he says. "R," she says. So, he adds that to make "MAR." "And what comes after 'R' in the alphabet?" She goes, "S." He adds the "S" to make "MARS" and underlines it about twenty times. "I couldn't believe it either," he says. "It scared the hell out of me the first time I found out." I thought, Okay. I had heard all the stories about Roky and Rusk. There was allegory and lore behind him that made him interesting, but this upped the ante.

Anyway, we weren't sure if he was gonna play that night. Sahm played three sets, and the last started at midnight. There was no Roky playing until about halfway through the [last] set. "I want to bring along a good friend," Sahm said. "He's been through some hard times, but he's back. I think he'd really like to play a few songs. Would Roky Erickson please stand up and come to the stage?" Roky tromps down the aisle from the backstage area looking hapless and shuffling to the stage. I thought, Oh, this is gonna be bad. Then the minute he hits the stage he comes to life like a live wire. He goes around to everybody's amp and turns them to thirteen so they're feeding back and blasting. He starts playing the first four chords of "You're Gonna Miss Me." My jaw dropped.

Roky was so much better and crazier than I imagined. You should have seen the faces of these beer-swilling cowboys in the audience. Their mouths were so open it was like their tongues were gonna jump out. Then he went into "Don't Shake Me Lucifer," "Starry Eyes," and "Two-Headed Dog." The show was a remarkable game changer for me. The only other game-changing rock show I'd seen was Iggy Pop and the Stooges at the Whisky a Go Go in Los Angeles, but that was for different reasons. I was so hooked on Roky so quickly. I had never seen anything come to life and manifest with such energy, craziness, and power. I couldn't believe it. I started constantly flying up from Los Angeles to the Bay Area to follow Roky around wherever he was.

I started writing for *Creem* magazine in 1976, and it became a mission for me to spread the word. I was evangelical about it. The autoharp player Billy Miller was just as crazy as Roky every time I saw them play but incredibly talented. I play with Billy on my solo albums today. He does these beautiful harmonies and dissonant back melodies that sound like Lou Reed and Jimi Hendrix. Roky also had Duane Aslaksen, who is one of the best lead guitar players I've ever seen. They had this understated all-star lineup that got better and better with Roky on top. Then things would get crazier and crazier as Roky would tell these stories onstage that made no sense, like seeing crawling hands strangling a guy in jail. Then he would say, "This song's called 'You're Gonna Miss Me.'"

I was a different person before and after that Palomino show. The show made me want to do crazy, weird stuff. I was very conventional in terms of the kinds of things I liked, like hard rock and punk rock. Roky sprayed out visceral angst and energy like a fire hose. I wanted to be in a band just like everyone else who'd seen something that influenced them. I wanted to write for magazines in a way that was out of control. I wanted to write songs that were evocative in the same way without emulating or imitating but dialing into something that was just as out there.

Our very first Angry Samoans show was opening a crazy and out-of-control show for Roky at a theater in Richmond, California. In fact, Roky was absent that night. Billy and Duane had to sing the songs in his voice because something came up. There were always things coming up. Roky was a huge variable in terms of dependability. I had a psych garage band out here in Santa Fe called the Blood Drained Cows, and we opened for Roky at a place called Ruta Maya on Roky's birthday one year, which was his first real coming out playing with the Explosives. Everybody had to do Roky covers that night. We did half a dozen and our secret weapon was Billy because he had played as one of the Aliens.

Then there was the time Roky was playing the Whisky a Go Go when I reintroduced him to Leland Rogers. I had been working for the resurrected International Artists label for two years, and they hadn't seen each other in a while. Roky goes over to Leland. "Leland," Roky says. "How come you're not dead yet?" Leland's eyes opened. "What?" Roky was always out there and had to be tethered to you to make sure he went from Point A to Point B, like the time we took him to see the Swarm at the Whisky. He had a breakdown at his motel room, thinking killer bees had come through his ventilation system. He said he had what he called a "brain hernia." Fortunately, he said, as the hernia happened and his brain fell on the ground, the woman behind him happened to be a brain surgeon and threw it back in his head. She sewed it back up. Unfortunately, he told the manager and all of us in the room, he couldn't sing anymore. There was still one more Whisky show and an interview left to do on the tour.

Roky was a bigger-than-life gory cartoon who kept morphing. He took shape right in front of you. Each incarnation would be even more compelling than the last. Then I lost touch with him around 1981, and that's when he started disappearing into the psychiatric abyss again. Roky could have been putting us on a little with the crazy, but I do think the base was anchored in the schizophrenia. Schizophrenia comes to life if you take acid five hundred times a day and then go to a hospital that feeds you Thorazine and electroshock. Roky was very cognizant about how people reacted to him even then. There were times when I would come over to his apartment in San Francisco in the seventies and he would say, "Who's there?" "Roky, it's Gregg." "Did you bring me a horror toy?" I bought him a little toy gun that he loved. Then he said, "I have a new song you'll like." He'd play "There's Nothing Better That I Love Than a Severed Head Bouncing Down the Stairs."

We took him down to this twenty-four-hour delicatessen in the Fairfax area in Los Angeles called Cantor's Deli after one show when he was playing the Whisky. We sat at the table, and the waitress gave us all a water. Roky looks at his water and is really troubled. He hadn't even ordered yet. "What's wrong, Roky?" "Well, probably nothing," he said, "I don't know." He's holding up the water looking through it. "What's wrong?" "Well, Gregg, there's a seed in my water." Oh shit. Here we go. "Roky," I said. "It's probably a grapefruit seed. I'm sure the glass is clean." "It could be a dirty seed. It could be contaminated." "No, no," I said. "It's probably been in the dishwasher and is sterile. It's probably a good seed." "A good seed?" he says. "I don't know." Now, people at adjacent tables are looking up. He gets up and starts tromping down through the restaurant holding the cup up. "Oh, my god," he goes. "It's the goddamn demon seed." He throws the glass up in the air. That was it. We left a hundred-dollar tip for the manager just like we did other times.

We were at the Old World Cafe on the Sunset Strip another time. There were about ten of us for dinner. Roky's manager Craig Luckin was there. "You know," Roky goes, "I'm pretty hungry tonight. I'm thinking I want one of everything on the menu." The waitress goes, "What?" "Yeah, every single thing on the menu. I want one." It's clear Craig is in charge, so the waitress looks at him. "Do it," he says. She fills ten tables with food. "This is gonna be so good," he says. "This is gonna be a feast. I'm so hungry." Chefs and managers are looking around the corner. They can't believe it. He looks at the waiter at some point and goes, "Can I have some takeout boxes?" He was hilarious and very witty. There were some times when you wouldn't think there were any psychiatric issues besides his humor being a little eccentric. He was a very clever, bright, humble, sweet guy.[16]

Former Creem *magazine writer Gregg Turner helped found the Los Angeles punk band Angry Samoans in 1978. He has served as associate professor of mathematics at New Mexico Highlands University in Santa Fe for more than two decades.*

FREDDIE "STEADY" KRC

We formed the Explosives in 1978. I had been a drummer for B. W. Stevenson and Jerry Jeff Walker but wanted to do something on my own. I knew Cam King and Waller Collie were rock guys like me. The Explosives would woodshed, do a few gigs, and start writing and demoing our songs. We all wrote and sang, and the wonderful Stu Cook produced our album [1982's *Restless Natives*]. Stu was good at overseeing everything and knew how to get good sounds no matter who engineered. We had started playing in June 1979. Coincidentally, Roky moved back from San Francisco about a month later. Roky's manager knew my friend Tom Ordon and said, "Roky's coming to Austin. Do you know a good band for him to work with?" "Yeah," Tom said. "The Explosives." Stu had already produced that *Roky and the Aliens* album before Roky moved to Austin and started playing with us.

Of course, I knew about Roky and the Elevators before working with him. I grew up in a little town called La Porte, Texas, between Galveston and Houston, and started playing in bands when I was ten in 1965. Kenny Rogers's brother Leland produced the Elevators, and he had moved from California to La Porte to work with International Artists Records. Leland had a son named Danny, who was a year older than me, and we both played drums in the school band and in rock bands. Danny came to school one day when I was in the seventh grade with his arms full of records. He started passing them out and said, "My dad just produced this record, *The Psychedelic Sounds of the 13th Floor Elevators*." Tommy Hall's esoteric songs appealed to me more than the more straightforward "You're Gonna Miss Me." I loved the electric jug. There was nothing like it then.

Roky and the Explosives played together for two and a half years through the end of 1981 and did approximately ninety shows mostly around Texas, but we also did quite a bit in California. Roky was in a great state of mind. He had been taking medication for his schizophrenia, which I knew absolutely nothing about at the time. We knew that he had taken a lot of drugs and was different. We knew the songs he was writing and rehearsed at my house. Roky would come over, grab the guitar, and play great rhythm. He still had all his high-range voice then and was great to work with. I'm also a rhythm guitar player in addition to being a drummer, and I'm telling you nobody was better than Roky in that aggressive way to play rock. He was on top of his game during those years.

Roky had a great sense of humor and so did the Explosives. We treated him like one of the band members. He knew we loved him, but he got no special this or that from us. We were like, "Get the guitar, get onstage, and let's go play. Then hop in the van and we're going to Dallas." He responded that way. We had a wonderful time. Roky's manager started getting us gigs like the Whisky a Go Go in Los Angeles and opening for the Psychedelic Furs at the Warfield in San Francisco as a result of the Roky and the Explosives Halloween show we released, which is a great testimony to how we played back then. We tore it up. We played Sacramento, San Diego, all over the Bay Area like Berkeley, Oakland, San Jose, and Santa Clara. We were always very well received. I remember seeing [*The Basketball Diaries* author and poet] Jim Carroll at the Berkeley show. People came to see us. Roky still had that mystique. We were starting to build up and get to the next level and that's when Roky started getting dark and reluctant to practice. He went off his meds.

The Explosives coming back with Roky was a big deal in February 2005. Cam King had just come back to Austin from living in Los Angeles and Nashville. Tracy Kluck was Roky's friend who organized the gig for the album *Live! Live at the Ritz 1987*. Tracy told me that he was driving around with Roky in 2005 and said, "Listen to what Freddie did." I had been in England in the eighties starting my solo career. Tracy played him one of my CDs to try to get Roky interested in playing again. "Do you think those guys would play with me again?" Roky asked. Tracy said, "Let's call and see." Cam and I met them at Threadgill's and said, "Yeah, we would love to play with you."

Honestly, we didn't expect it would turn into much. The only plan was to play two or three songs at Roky's Ice Cream Social [during South by Southwest in Austin], but the show was so well received we started getting offers to play Noise Fest in Chicago, Austin City Limits Music Festival, and other festivals. The Chicago gig was the first time Roky had been out of town to do a gig in years. We played huge festivals in Norway, Scandinavia, Finland, Sweden, Royal Festival Hall in London, northern Spain, Lollapalooza, Bumbershoot, Coachella, all the big American festivals. We had a blast overseas. We always had a good time together. We played for three years through 2008 until Roky went off his meds again and wasn't quite the same. Then we left for the same reasons as the first time. The shows weren't as good as they could have been.

We saw other bands play with him over the years, but they were more sycophants. "Oh my, what a lovely cape you're wearing, Mr. Erickson." "You're the best, Roky." He loved that rock star treatment, but he'd go do it if you treated him like we did. "Come on, dude, it's time to go kick butt." I do think he understood he was unique, but not in an egotistical way. He understood that he brought something different than other people did. We never really talked about [fame], but I liked the air about him. "I do what I do, and it's great if people like it. I can't do anything about it if they don't." I never saw him get desperate and say, "Man, we gotta break outta here." It just didn't matter to him if he was playing Royal Festival Hall or the Boom Boom Room [in Los Angeles]. He just wanted to play his music. I mean, there was a buzz and people knew he was special when we started playing together in the eighties and got to California, but we were still playing the bars.

I noticed his behavior. Roky would be crazy for you if you were apprehensive and think he's crazy, but he'd respond normally if you talk to him like we are talking now. I think guys who have been institutionalized have learned to behave however they needed to behave to get along in whatever circumstance they were in. Roky talked to me at length about Rusk, and the stories were heartbreaking. He was a tough guy to get through that. He talked about the fact that Rusk was a mental institution for the criminally insane. "I was in there with people who chopped up their family," he said, "and they treated me worse because I had long hair. There was one nurse who would hold my hand when I had shock treatment." That story made me very sad. So, I did go through some dark and weird times with Roky, but I prefer to dwell on the [positive]. I'll always remember the second day we rehearsed over at my house. He brought the first *Openers* book. "Fred," he said, "I know you're a Christian. I was writing about that when I wrote this. I want you to have it."[17]

Freddie "Steady" Krc has been a session drummer for Sir Douglas Quintet's Augie Meyers, Carole King, Pink Floyd's Roger Waters, and the Faces' Ronnie Lane. The Texas Academy of Music's Lifetime Achievement Award winner served as drummer in Roky Erickson's Explosives.

HAROLD F. EGGERS JR.

I visited Roky one day with Townes Van Zandt and Kay Sexton. Everything felt intense and uncomfortable with all the televisions and radios on. The vibe was like going into a danger zone where the dark got darker with fear and unknown. We went in, but I could see Townes looked uncomfortable. "Roky, Roky," Kay said. "Roky, Roky." No answer. She walked into his bedroom. We followed. Roky was sitting on the side of the bed staring off. "Roky," she said. "Roky." "Oh, Kay," Roky said. "I didn't know you were here." The volume was on high on everything. "Hey, Townes, man," Roky said. "How are you doing?" Roky had asked Townes to be the bass player in his band [years earlier]. Townes told him he didn't play bass. Roky said, "It doesn't matter."

Townes always said he felt like a square peg trying to fit into a round world. I would imagine Roky felt the same. We stepped into another dimension when Roky and Townes were in the same room. I've never felt that with anyone besides them. They both had their own strange brew going on. They both had electroshock therapy. Townes told me that Roky had become the mascot for the Banditos [Motorcycle Club in the sixties]. They were constantly feeding him handfuls of acid. "Roky would go off for a long time," Townes said, "and not come back." Townes heard voices like Roky did, and they both did things to the extreme. They say most people have one cup full of life. I always thought Townes had dozens. Same with Roky. You know, John Lennon went through primal scream therapy. Roky and Townes lived primal scream.[18]

Harold F. Eggers Jr. road managed legendary Texas singer-songwriter Townes Van Zandt for nearly twenty years through the end of his career. Additionally, he worked for iconic Nashville music publishing company Acuff-Rose.

WILL SEXTON

Roky would come to our house when I was a kid. My brother and I woke up one morning and thought the house was on fire because Roky had been up all night smoking cigarettes. I went over to Evelyn's house many years later with my daughter. The dynamics were strange. My daughter had youthful eyes for Evelyn to share some strange anecdotes. The odd thing in the house was a painting above the piano in the main room. Someone from the state hospital had done a small, peculiar painting of a torso that was replicated on the ceiling. Evelyn was singing and doing her operatic thing. My brother and I were from more traditional music. Loud and dangerous music like Roky's wasn't around us, but Roky was respected and revered by more traditional musicians that I loved. He was a beautiful powerhouse of singing and playing.

Speedy Sparks lived in a house with Roky. Roky had one room with a mattress. They asked me if I would see if he could get comfortable playing a show, which was never gonna happen. Roky had his mattress, a black-and-white television, and horror movies. That was it. I remember playing him a song he had written, and he acted like he didn't know the song. I was concerned. It was weird. The song was something everybody knew like "Bloody Hammer." He was watching movies and just wasn't engaged and paying attention at that point. Then someone told me that he had convinced someone to raise the money to get security for the house. The story was that he was attempting to get a security system on his room because he was concerned about people getting to him rather than taking from him. He didn't really have anything in his space besides himself.

We ended up helping him get ready for shows [in the eighties and nineties]. He felt safe because he had known us since we were little kids. Roky was different early on. He was intense in the early seventies but very disconnected in the period we worked with him. The first time I performed with him was [opening for] the Butthole Surfers at the Ritz in 1987, which was three days getting him to get ready to do the show. The venue was crazy and packed because the Butthole Surfers were playing. Roky wanted to leave immediately. Then he starts talking about the guitar amp like it's a cold heater. The show seemed disconnected from the very beginning.

I did two shows with Roky at the Austin Music Awards where I would go over to his other house across the street from the airport on Highway 71 behind the smut video rental place. Very jarring. He had every noise going on in the house. He asked me if the noise was bothering me at some point, and I said it was distracting. He went over and turned one television down. There were still thirteen other noises going on then. The television was the least of the worries. He shouldn't have been by himself at that place. He was falling apart. The last show that I did with him was a performance with Lou Ann Barton, Derek O'Brien, Mike Buck, John Reid, and Speedy Sparks. I wasn't interested in talking him into getting into the car to go do the show. He didn't seem like he was enjoying it. My job was to sing the songs with him and give him cues to start. You could tell that he was uncomfortable. I asked him flat out after. "You want to do this?" "Eh."

My brother played guitar on [*All That May Do My Rhyme*]. They decided to do some more unreleased songs before I was brought in to work
with Roky on the record, which was impossible. They couldn't piece
together anything. They kept trying different tempos, so they wouldn't
comp anything. They were thinking I would be the person to help him
get through some songs that no one really knew. He could tell that I was
getting incredibly frustrated. "Are you okay?" Roky asked me. "I think
your hat is too small for your head." "Yeah," I said. "I think you're right.
Something's wrong here." It was getting to a point where I was too frustrated with that attempt. There were too many people trying to structure
a song and complicating it more with coproduction ideas.

People always say Roky's was a drug thing, but I thought it was from
childhood trauma and mental illness. I'm not saying it helps to do psychedelic drugs, but I don't see anything that would hurt him like having
the life he did. Townes Van Zandt was always talking about his connection to Roky and Billy Gibbons and others in that area who were drug
in from the mental places. It was a strange time with reefer madness,
which is a story in and of itself. You grow up around people who were
drawn to Roky like they were to Daniel Johnston. They think, Isn't this
interesting? They want to be involved with something that has created
madness all around them. It's not very healthy. That's the tough thing
about iconology. We have that here in Memphis from drug addicts and
nut bags to people who are just drawn to weird energy. They want to wire
themselves into the story and art. It's unbelievable how connected people
are with these crazy rock and roll threads and random loose stories.

Roky was just a human who happened to make great art sometimes.
The people who blow my mind are ones like Terry Allen. Terry is someone I want to be close to because he's healthy. He's not only a great artist,
he's a great human being. It's a whole different thing. It's great that there
are all these interviews now that are giving him fame now in a certain
area. People are talking about how he's been so overlooked, but Terry has
kicked ass forever. He has art in all the biggest museums. He's been very
successful in his work. I think that's the fascinating thing. I know you and
I are a couple of the biggest Townes fans of all time. He was so influential
to me as a human being because he was one of the most decent people I've
ever known, but I would never trade writing one tad bit of his songs for
his pain. I wouldn't want to be him. I'm in it for the long race now. That's

what I'm counting on. I want to be more comfortable and healthier than ever. I own a house for the first time now.[19]

Will Sexton and his brother Charlie both learned guitar from the "Godfather of Austin Blues" W. C. Clark while still in their teens. They began opening for Stevie Ray Vaughan around the same time. Will Sexton has collaborated with marquee names such as Joe Ely, Waylon Jennings, and Stephen Stills.

JOE NICK PATOSKI

Fast-forward to the nineties when Roky's really torn down out in Del Valle [outside Austin]. He's living crazy times behind the corner bookstore in public housing. He'd gotten in trouble with the law several times. It's crazy time out there. He hasn't taken his meds or been discovered by Henry Rollins. Casey Monahan was a regular out there taking care of Roky. King Coffey of the Butthole Surfers starts coming around. You basically go over to Roky's and take him to Luby's to eat or over to Evelyn's house. This is a period when Roky's not playing anymore and is certifiably crazy. This was leading up to his brother Sumner intervening and getting him back on his meds and reviving his career, but Roky's in the middle even at his most torn down in that house with three television sets all on static with white noise and visual chaos with the verticals flipping and making strobe light effects. "Hey, Joe," he says when we walk in. "How you doing?" We go over to Evelyn's house and Roky plays three, four songs for us on guitar. I keep thinking, This guy is not as crazy as people make him out to be. Maybe this is what it takes to get a free meal.

Craziness is something Roky doesn't deny or chase away, but it gets him things. He doesn't have to do shit. He has people coming over, bringing him shit, taking care of him. Why bother getting out of that comfort zone? The deterioration was from 1975 to '80 and certainly through the nineties when Sumner comes in and famously rescues him—before Sumner too is pushed aside when things went awry again. It's concurrent with all these people coming out of the woodwork with love. "Aw, man, I dug the 13th Floor Elevators. They changed my life." "This guy's the greatest." "'You're Gonna Miss Me' turned my head around." So, all these people are paying homage and Roky's letting them during a period when he's clearly suffering mentally.

Roky was doing a shitload of recording for anyone who would come around and pay him money. He liked doing it, but it was also when he played the Austin Music Awards with the True Believers, which was pretty cool. I remember about three years after that Doug Sahm was coming back with his band. Roky was showing up and performing all the time with his arms crossed, which is a defensive measure. You're really going inward when your arms are crossed like that. He wouldn't uncross his arms. You'd ask him how he's doing, and he would say, "I'm relaxing." He really was kind of relaxed, but he clearly wasn't comfortable in the live realm. Then it got to the point he wasn't performing at all, but then there was the Will Sheff and Okkervil River comeback.

Roky lived a pretty fucking good life. Everybody wanted to be his best friend because he had a great talent and was the leader of the first psychedelic rock band. Roky died for our sins. He took too much acid, went to Rusk, and had electroshock therapy for our sins. None of that should have happened. His should be a really happy story, but instead all this dark stuff happened. Roky liked people to take care of him. You get used to people doing things for you if you're a rock star. People who knew his work were willing to do whatever they could to help him. People thought they were doing him a favor by bringing him acid and even heroin in the seventies. Roky was not one to say no. They were really hurting him. All that left him very bruised and battered all the way through to where he wasn't a very cogent human being. Is it worth it that he could still sing like James Brown? I don't know.[20]

BRIDGE

Starry Eyes

HENRY ROLLINS

I was aware of the 13th Floor Elevators from college radio, but then the artist Raymond Pettibon played *The Evil One* for me in 1984. I was hooked immediately and have been a Roky Erickson fan ever since. You realize that there's no one like him as soon as you listen. It's all there the more you drill down on what he's saying, his phrasing, subject matter, tone, and musical excellence. People don't even know they're Roky fans. Hopefully, they'll hear him and get clued in. I play him a lot on my radio show [on KCRW 89.9 FM Santa Monica, California, public radio] so he's always getting out there as best as I can do it. He's an artist that you will never outgrow. Roky's records get better with time if anything.

You hear Buddy Holly in Roky's music with songs like "Starry Eyes." His sympathetic chord structures come from Texas blues and early rock and roll. His phrasing has always grabbed me the most. Where he puts words, and how he works with syllables and beats is fantastic. "I Have Always Been Here Before" or "Click Your Fingers Applauding the Play" are as good as music gets. Also, Roky was able to articulate all the hardships he went through with great lyrical intellect. "If You Have Ghosts" and "I Think of Demons" are perfect examples. You have to have gone through something intense to come up with those songs. "I Walked with a Zombie" is completely scorching live. The guitars are so great. You don't know what it is those guys know, but you know they know it. "Red

Temple Prayer" is fantastic insanity. "The Interpreter" is amazing. "The Interpreter, where is he now? / Invisibly transparency disguise." "I Have Always Been Here Before" is a masterpiece. "In the night," he says in "If You Have Ghosts," "I am real." One of the best lines I have ever heard. Roky's music is full of moments like this. He had talent beyond talent and had the thing.

I saw Roky play at least twice. There was never a time when I could have seen him and didn't, but touring often keeps you from seeing shows. I was at his birthday party in 1995. The band was playing, and people were trying to get him up on the stage. He got up there and stood nervously for a while and then finally started singing. I think the song was "Red Temple Prayer" or "Starry Eyes." You could see that it was a struggle for him to be up there, but it was great when he got going. I saw him in New Orleans in 2011, and he was really good, much more relaxed. The place was packed and the audience was with him all the way, a great thing to experience.[1]

Henry Rollins entered public consciousness as lead singer for the ground-breaking hard-core punk outfit Black Flag for six years starting in 1981. The singer-songwriter, actor, and activist currently hosts a weekly radio show for KCRW in Los Angeles and is a regular columnist for Rolling Stone *magazine.*

CASEY MONAHAN

I was hired to the Texas Music Office in the governor's office in 1990. Roky had a real rebirth in his life. He got sober and was doing drug treatment in prisons. I went and had a meal with Roky and saw how he was living in government-subsidized housing. I counted nineteen different sound sources constantly playing, from weather-band radio to police-band radio and AM and FM and several TVs. I couldn't believe someone could live like that. I started taking him out to eat once or twice a week. We really liked going to Arkey's together on Cesar Chavez.

I started recruiting people to come with me to see him or take him out. Roky had limited human contact when I met him. He had spent a couple months in that prison for mail transfer before he got sprung. Houston White was cofounder of the Vulcan Gas Company. What a mind he has. Tary Owens and Houston got together when Roky got out of prison and created a trust so that people could give money to Roky. Evelyn had power of attorney over his affairs. I was thinking, Okay, how can I get some income streams going for Roky? He had signed away the rights to lots of his publishing to his first manager, Craig Luckin. I spent 1990 through 1995 with Roky. He never received any publishing money, which I thought was wrong. Craig will tell you he was trying to recoup his expenses for taking care of Roky in the seventies.

Roky was in such a bad way. I started getting what recordings together I could. Evelyn gave me a VHS tape. She was an early adopter of using the public access ACTV to video herself and Roky singing. He gave me this tape with a bunch of songs that had never been copyrighted. I was so excited about it. Roky playing guitar for his mother in his childhood living room was an amazing document. I could copyright these songs since they had never been released. I was driving around with Roky one day and said, "Your mom gave me this tape and these are songs that you own. What would you think about recording again?" He hadn't recorded in nine years then. "Sure, Casey," he said. "As long as it's fun." Roky didn't wanna do anything that wasn't fun.

I went over to Speedy Sparks's house and told him that Roky wanted to record. He said, "No way." "It's what he told me," I said. I gave Speedy a copy of that VHS tape, and he worked it up. I booked a time at Arlyn Studio with Stuart Sullivan. Stuart was Roky's only engineer in the nineties and two thousands. He did the Okkervil record and *All That May Do My Rhyme*, which I coproduced with Speedy. We recorded six tracks and I brought in Paul Leery of the Butthole Surfers to play guitar on it. That record was really difficult. Roky was unpredictable, but he liked the vibe Stuart created in the studio. He did really well, and we had a record to make some money for Roky. I started compiling lyrics for his songs in the process of getting it together.

A local writer named Rob Patterson said, "You know, Henry Rollins would publish these as a book." "Really?" "Yeah, Henry's a huge Roky fan." We had never met, but I contacted Henry Rollins, and he was really excited about working with Roky. I'll never forget when I got to introduce Henry to Roky. Roky had an amazing capacity of disarming people. He could read people's minds. He was very in tune with the world. Henry came down for the contract signing. I went to a couple labels. Peter Buck from R.E.M. was really into it. He said, "If you don't have enough money to finish the album, talk to this person and I'll help you out." I'd never even met the guy. You mention Roky's name to musicians who are knowledgeable, and there's total respect. He was such a groundbreaking figure in rock and roll.

My whole thing was to do fun things with Roky that would help his health. I took him to the dentist twice, and he wouldn't open his mouth. A dentist really can't work when you don't open your mouth. That's the one rule. He had abscesses, and you're dead if those things explode. I was really worried. I really wanted somebody to look over my shoulder as I did the book and help me edit. I didn't wanna get any words wrong. Craig Luckin was no help. Billy Miller, who played autoharp with Roky's band the Aliens, was a big help in finding songs I hadn't transcribed. I sent him a draft of the book, and he made all these helpful marks. I called Sumner Erickson out of nowhere, and he really wanted to be involved. I brought him in and even let him play his tuba on *All That May Do My Rhyme*.

I kept having to go through Evelyn if I wanted to do anything of substance. Sometimes she would agree and sometimes she would balk. I told her, "I took him to the dentist, and he wouldn't open his mouth. I need your help." I'm not complaining, but Evelyn really wasn't there for me. I didn't push it. Sumner helped a little editing the book. I had a cassette deck that had a pitch control so I could really slow it down and make sure I was getting the words right. Rollins came down. The way Roky was living blew his mind. Then Roky was reunited with Sumner, who he didn't really know. There was twenty years between them. I kept asking Evelyn to have my back on some of the medical stuff. "Well, Casey, we will just have to agree to disagree," she said. It just broke my heart.

Sumner took it upon himself to right the Roky ship around 2002. He convinced Roky to get on a plane to go with him to Pittsburgh. He realized that the teeth were the most important thing. He got Roky his first therapist and got him to open his mouth in the dentist chair. The dentist said, "I can't save any of these. They all need to come out." Dentures aren't cheap. Roky didn't have insurance so I suggested Sumner contact Henry Rollins. I said, "I'll bet you he'll pay for dentures." He did. Henry paid for Roky's first set of dentures. I think Roky had a fear of not having self-control. You're very vulnerable as a patient regardless of the type of doctor. The more you try to force someone with mental illness to do something the more they push back. They've only got a slight hold on reality.

Sumner got him to Pittsburgh for almost a year. He got his teeth fixed and made sure he ate better food. Troy Campbell is a true hero in the Roky world. Troy introduced him to Darren Hill. Darren is a musician and a manager. He's managed Paul Westerberg and knew about Roky. Darren and Roky got along. Roky had his first real manager of his life thanks to Troy. Troy suggested to Jegar that he go on tour with Roky because Darren got him on the road where he could make some real money. Concurrent with Darren's arrival, Troy tells this amazing story where Sumner was basically trying to be Roky's manager even though he knew nothing about management or the rock and roll industry. It came to a head one day. Troy was there. Roky, Sumner, and Troy were talking. Sumner asks his eldest brother, "Well, you do love me, don't you, Roky?" "No," Roky said, "I don't." They never spoke again. Roky did not enjoy working with his youngest brother.

I'm always in awe of Troy because he took advantage of the opportunities that were presented and made the best of them. Bringing Jegar into the fold was just so important. Troy's an honest person. Do you know how rare that is in the music business? I would bring Roky into KUT [90.5 FM in Austin] to play. That's when I really broke with Sumner. Larry Monroe called me up and said, "Why don't we do some Roky?" Sumner was in town for Roky's birthday. I asked him to come with me. Sumner hates his mother, which is never good. You know what the most important thing is? Compassion. Everything comes back to treating people the way you want to be treated and putting yourself in their shoes. Sumner was so angry. He will tell you he's cured. Whatever. Sumner's objective that session was to have Larry play Roky's song "Crazy Crazy Mama." You could easily say it's Roky talking about his mom, but it could be about anything. Roky never said definitively that it was about her.

Larry asked me to come in. It was my show. I told Sumner, "We're not gonna play that song." He got so pissed off at me. Roky's playing on the turntable there at KUT, and Sumner started to get into an argument with me. "Motherfucker," I said, "I'll stop the show right now. We're not gonna fucking play that song, Sumner. Get over it. Go get some help. The way you think isn't healthy." Don't forget, Roky always wanted to be having fun. He didn't wanna be around people who were negative or working an agenda. He hated that shit. He wanted to explore the mind. That's why his mind is such a trip. He wasn't elliptical. He put stuff in his songs that could be interpreted one way, but I don't want to hear about it unless it came out of his fucking mouth.

There were stories like Sumner abandoning him in an airport. They didn't communicate for the last thirteen years. Then Sumner organized Roky's memorial without any involvement from Jegar and Roky's closest brother, Mikel. I was like, "Wait. This ain't for Roky. This is for Sumner." Three lawyers got up there and talked. It was basically a tribute to Sumner for stuff he had done for Roky twenty years before. Jegar didn't go. I couldn't believe it when Sumner didn't include Roky's son in the planning. Roky reunited with Dana when he came back from Pittsburgh. Sumner had given Roky posters that he had framed and he came and took them back. Then he sued Dana and Roky. I had stepped away, but I'm basing this on what Jegar told me. Ugly. Sumner sued over possession of property that in his mind he loaned to Roky but didn't give him.

Jegar invited everyone over to his backyard before the memorial. That was the true Roky wake. Mikel and Dana were there. Mikel walked into the memorial and stayed five minutes and went to the parking lot. "I can't believe this is happening." PBS had this reality series called the *Loud Family* in the nineties before reality shows existed, the saga of a fucked-up American family. Well, let me tell you, nobody holds a candle to the Ericksons. Nobody. I don't have animosity toward Sumner. I feel sorry for the cat. Sumner really saved Roky's life. Being hardheaded can be good. He got Roky away from his mother and up to Pittsburgh. Roky would have never gotten well as long as his mother was part of the picture. Sumner hated his mother so much he made that happen. Troy, Darren, Jegar, and me just roll our eyes. How can you take such a positive act of saving your brother and fuck it up? Tragic.[2]

Former Austin American-Statesman *music writer Casey Monahan served as director for the Texas Music Office for more than two decades.*

STUART SULLIVAN

I came to admire Roky a great deal. He was otherworldly. Many musicians experience unspoken communication, but Roky really lived there.

He was always in "the zone." I don't mean that as a sad thing. I say it like, "Holy fuck. This is the first person I've ever met who lives there." I tapped into that and want to be in that state as much as possible, but I simply don't have what Roky had to live there. Maybe because I'm too connected to the normal world and have too many responsibilities and obligations. Roky was basically free of that. Roky was extremely perceptive and extremely disconnected at the same time. He truly was King Baby. Everybody did everything for Roky. He didn't have to do squat. He became very manipulatively dependent as a result.

I recorded most Roky songs since about 1991. Working with him in the studio was interesting. I feel weird even saying this, but he would speak to me without talking. I didn't always understand him, but I could tell something was there. He seemed like a child, but I knew he was intelligent. He had an ability beyond me to exist in almost another dimension that's very real but unavailable to most. I started off by making real subtle jokes you had to think about to get. Roky got them over and over. So, I was able to work with him, but that doesn't mean everything was smooth. He would be weird. He would fuck with you. I would say, "Roky, do you want to stand or sit [when you sing]?" I would set up the mike, and he would stand. "So, you want to stand?" "Yeah." I would adjust the mike. Then he would sit. This would go around and around three or four times before he would do something. He was saying, "I don't wanna do this."

Roky had times of relative verbal lucidity that were wonderful. I have worked with Daniel Johnston and Junior Brown, so it wasn't that offputting to have a guy like Roky who was out there like that. We struggled a huge amount with vocals to get him to sing the songs in time and with the right lyrics. [All That May Do My Rhyme] sounds unfinished. We didn't have the freedom to move things around with Pro Tools then so it's a little discombobulated. The same core people I spoke about were getting behind him and giving him energy in the meantime. Then his brother Sumner decided he was ready to leave the Pittsburgh Symphony and wanted to help his brother. He was able to generate interest by getting an attorney to get the rights back to his songs. Roky was getting nothing from his songs.

His teeth were a great sense of humiliation. You see this disheveled guy who was embarrassed and wouldn't smile because he had no teeth. Roky was in detritus splendor in his apartment, but you could tell he was self-conscious. He was highly sensitive and insecure about himself. Roky got teeth when Henry Rollins ponied up ten grand. Then people started getting him real clothes, not Dollar Store ones. These steps were huge. They didn't just make him more presentable. They made him be more willing to be presentable and be presented. He was more engaged. Sumner took him up to Pittsburgh for a year and got him therapy. He did some really great things for him. Roky was more of a guy when he came back. He was still out there, but he was a dude.

Roky started getting requests to do vocals with bands like Mogwai. He would come in the studio and sing. He always sang in this shaky high voice, which wasn't the Roky Erickson voice that I knew, but it was Roky. I thought, If that's what he wants to do, that's what he wants to do. I'll help him. He got familiar with me. Familiarity and knowing that person cares can really make him a different person for you. He was always very nice to me and really enjoyed the little jokes. I started doing them at first, but then he started doing them. We were seeing facets of a coherent person mixed in with the chaos in his mind. It was fascinating and a little scary. I liked knowing I'm not the only mix of crazy and healthy.

Roky did not want to drive the bus. We dragged him in the studio early on. We would have to promise him stuff like if he would come in and sing a song we would get him a smoothie. I had the same experience with Daniel Johnston. We would have to promise Daniel another Mountain Dew or two more comic books or that we could go to this restaurant if we could just do another vocal. Roky's health got better over time and he started singing more. There was chaos in the family, to put it mildly. Who was in good or bad graces shifted. Everyone had strong minds and their own desires. His mom was one way and Sumner was another. They were totally on the outs, and then they became close. There was drama in the family growing up. I believe Roky was mentally ill, but it was exacerbated by his home life.

Roky was doing pretty well somewhere in this picture. He moved out of the Del Valle place, moved into an apartment, and started playing with a band. The attorney who had worked on getting his rights got those scumbags Charly Records to agree to something like a fifty-fifty split. Roky at least got some. I told Shawn Sahm, "There's this issue we have. Three classic songs—'Starry Eyes,' 'Don't Slander Me,' and ['Two Headed Dog']—ended up in Doug's collection." Shawn very quickly gave Roky the master tapes and copyrights back. So, Roky started building up his catalog and was able to get a decent income as a result from his old records as well as from touring.

Things were going well enough that they booked him on [episode number 3312 of the long-running PBS music series] *Austin City Limits* [in 2008]. I remember going to that show. I had only heard the high, shaky voice to this point, but now he had Freddie Krc's Explosives as his band jumping around and going all crazy. John Sanchez looked like an angel with the backlighting and played all the classic guitar melodies. Billy Gibbons played with them. The band commanded the stage. I was thinking, This is terrible. These guys are gonna swallow up Roky. Then Roky shuffles up to the mike with his head down, the whole stage goes black, and there's one brilliant light shining on Roky. He blew my mind. How could this homeless-looking guy come on that stage and completely dwarf all those guys including Billy Gibbons by doing nothing? That was his intangible power.

Then he started to sing. I get chills even now. He had the voice, the scream, and everything I had been enamored with. I was bawling. I couldn't believe what was happening. I had known the guy for ten years and hadn't seen it. That night was so beautiful and powerful. I asked Roky after, "Why did you use another voice before?" "Well, that was my voice." I guess the high, scared, shaky voice represented where his head was. Then he got more confidence and was socialized now. He was confident enough to use that voice that drives you out of your mind. That was the voice that got him whatever girl he wanted and captured imaginations all around the world. So beautiful.

Roky made *True Love Cast out All Evil* with Will Sheff and Okkervil River two years later. Will went through all these songs and tried different tempos and pitches to make sure they worked. Will really went through and put together amazing tracks. We would record a song or two during the day. Then around six or seven Jegar would bring Roky around, and we would listen to soul and rock music from Roky's sixties and seventies heyday. We were just hanging out and got him to do vocals when he was comfortable. Will took him to Brian Beatty's after and got more beautiful vocals. There was a need to shift around to get him in the right spot to sing, but it worked when he did. That's one of his best records and certainly his best post-Rusk. The album was artfully done. I have to tip my hat to Will. He did a brilliant job and really let Roky shine in a way that didn't cause him stress. Will's a smart dude.

There were memorable moments. Jegar brought him over one evening and immediately said, "Can I talk to you outside?" "Sure." He was obviously upset. This sounds like a simple story, but you know the impact if you know Roky. "I went over to get Roky this evening," he said. "I went over and knocked. No one answered, so I walked in. Roky barked at me." "I'm really sorry," Jegar said. "I knocked three times and nobody came to the door." Then they were getting ready to leave. "Jegar," Roky said. "I'm really sorry I got mad at you. You don't deserve that. You've done a whole lot for me. I really, really appreciate it." I used the term King Baby earlier. King Baby never apologizes or recognizes anything anybody does for him because it's expected. Well, King Baby Roky apologized and told Jegar he appreciated him. That was as powerful a moment as I can remember.

Roky also became comfortable around this group of people when Will would be around. That was huge. Roky usually only would be comfortable one on one and he was limited even then. These were baby steps, but with Roky it was one small step for man and one giant leap for mankind. Roky was having a second renaissance with the Okkervil record. He even got a driver's license. That doesn't mean I want to be on the road when he was driving, but he got one. Then he remarried his wife, Dana, they bought a house, and lived off his royalties and touring income, which was nothing short of a miracle if you knew him twenty years before. Roky and I connected well because I never asked or wanted for anything. I was like, "How can I help?" Same with Casey, Craig, and King. They just wanted to help. I can't speak highly enough about those guys. They established a ring of protection. They were trying to keep all the users at bay. I felt so honored to be involved.

I produced Roky's ten-CD box set of the 13th Floor Elevators. [Elevators biographer] Paul Drummond in England put the thing together. He came in the studio with Walt Andreas, who recorded most of the original records. I was supposed to be in charge, but I was in awe of Walt. I was the boss in that I would say, "What do you want to do, Walt?" We had every known recording of the 13th Floor Elevators at the time. Lots was garbage from bootlegs or bad radio things, but there was so much material in there. Oh my god, the voice. It was a wide array of stuff. We spent a week just going over and over it trying to clean stuff up and decided to remix some. Walt did a crazy echoed-out version of "Will the Circle Be Unbroken." He insisted that I mix "Starry Eyes" and "Don't Slander Me." Talk about a highlight in your life. I was mixing the original tracks. That was mind boggling and exciting.[3]

Stuart Sullivan is an Austin-based engineer and record producer who owns Wire Recording. Sullivan worked extensively with Roky Erickson and bands like Butthole Surfers, Meat Puppets, and Sublime.

SHAWN SAHM

I met Roky when they were doing the "Two-Headed Dog" / "Starry Eyes" sessions at my dad's infamous Soap Creek house in Austin in 1975. I was ten years old and admired him. Roky seemed like the wheels were always turning and knew more than he let on about what was going on around him. My dad, Doug, produced that session, but I don't think people know he also played that weird, fuzzed-out guitar with the phaser that's on [Doug Sahm's 1979 album] *Texas Rock for Country Rollers.* They did several other songs like "Don't Shake Me Lucifer" and "Goodbye Sweet Dreams." I don't know how small that studio was, but I would imagine it was pretty tightly crammed because three thousand people have claimed to have been there.

We were at the Tropicana hotel in Los Angeles with my dad and Roky later that year. They played "Starry Eyes" and "Two-Headed Dog." The single was on the Mars record label. Look at that record. There's a weird little symbol on it. I remember Roky saying, "This symbol needs to be on the cover of the single. I saw this on a UFO in a book." He drew it. There are squiggly lines on the top and bottom and one that went right down. Doug owned the publishing to "Starry Eyes" and "Two-Headed Dog," but I gave Roky the masters and publishing after Doug died. Roky was on the mend and trying to get better then. Everyone was talking about helping him, and I thought it would be the soulful thing to do. They were staple songs for him, and that was the point. I hope he made some coin.[4]

Shawn Sahm performs with the iconic Texas country rock band Texas Tornados, which was founded by his late, legendary father, Doug Sahm, and equally celebrated players Flaco Jiménez and Augie Meyers.

DYLAN CARLSON

[Screaming Trees lead singer] Mark Lanegan and Roky would have these marathon phone calls [about horror movies] all the time. They were obviously vastly knowledgeable. I knew and admired Roky because my roommate had a collection of psychedelic garage rock from the sixties with all the International Artists records like Bubble Puppy and the 13th Floor Elevators. My favorite Elevators record was *Easter Everywhere*. The Elevators' music had a rock and roll sense of transformation that anything was possible through music. Their music transcends when it was made and the time when you're listening to it. They obliterated any preconceived notions or worldviews and were light striving to move beyond possibilities. I also loved Roky and the Aliens. "The Wind and More" is so amazing. I was with Lanegan once when he handed me the phone. Roky wanted to talk about a horror movie he was watching.

Roky had a big impact on the [Northwest music scene] in bands like Girl Trouble in Tacoma. I feel like every band starting out in the late eighties probably did a cover of "You're Gonna Miss Me." Roky and the Stooges were the big thing in the nascent [grunge] scene. Maybe that's because I was listening to him and so were the people I hung out with. I think it was the lyrical themes and attitude [that drew us to the music]. Anything that has some drone like the 13th Floor Elevators was something I was into. They had the jug and the pseudomodal playing. I've certainly used those techniques over the years and wouldn't have a career without that stuff. Maybe it's an atavistic thing about bagpipes because of my Scotch heritage, but I like the trance-inducing sound that grabs your attention and transports. The universe is all vibrations and banding waves, so it taps into the whole being.

I was drawn to Roky's songs because the lyrics weren't about the norm. The lyrics I have written are not about conventional situations. They're not a love song or a woe-is-me song. Roky obviously was obsessed with the demonic, and I have used angels and demons in my songs a number of times. I like the idea of writing about transcendent beings, space, and the supernatural. I guess you make that a serious idea by being subtle so it's not the cartoonish way like a black metal band. I can sense the difference between Roky and a more cartoonish metal band. He has an intent and brings up these subjects in a familiar way that's real to him.

He's saying, "This is my perception." People worship Satan in the cartoon version. They want to be evil. Roky wasn't like that. He was just saying he sees demons as an everyday thing. "What, you don't see them too?" I think he was saying he saw demons so you don't have to see them. He's giving a gesture. "You can chill out. I'm taking care of this." That gives the songs a reality that's removed from the cartoon.[5]

Dylan Carlson, born March 12, 1968, in Seattle, Washington, is the lead singer and guitarist of the drone rock group Earth as well as his solo project Drcarlsonalbion. Carlson was friends and roommates with legendary Nirvana front man Kurt Cobain.

MARK LANEGAN

I think [Screaming Trees bassist] Van Connor turned me on to Roky Erickson. Van had the Elevators' *Psychedelic Sounds* and *Easter Everywhere*. "You're Gonna Miss Me" and "Fire Engine" were the first songs I heard. "You're Gonna Miss Me" was one of the first songs we started playing as a band. I got heavily into the Elevators albums *Easter Everywhere* and *Bull of the Woods*. I listened to nothing else besides those two records for a long time. Roky's intensity in the singing drew me to the songs. The tunes were great. I was twenty-two and came from a really small town and had never heard anything like "Slip inside This House" before. Getting any music wasn't easy, but there was a small comic book shop there that had a bunch of punk rock singles. We had to look for it. Music was something we had to travel to get.

I heard a couple people sing and thought, Wow, I would like to do that. Roky was definitely one. [Love's] Arthur Lee and [The Gun Club's] Jeffrey Lee Pierce were the others. "I wanna do that for sure." It hadn't occurred to me to sing myself, but the music spoke to me in all three cases. There was something about the way they hit me. Roky's solo stuff appealed to my weird, perverse, horror movie–loving sides as a young man. He could have sung anything and been compelling to me because he was so balls out. Even his sweet love songs were amazing. His cover of the Velvet Underground's "Heroin" is the definitive version to me. I loved *The Evil One* and the later records like *Bermuda*. He looked badass.

I'm in my studio right now where we have a framed photo of Roky
backstage somewhere wearing a cape before the show in a classic shithole
someplace with graffiti. He looks like a dark lord. I met Brian Curley
[who was a member of Erickson's band the Resurrectionists in the nine-
ties] in the mideighties. Brian found out I was a Roky fanatic. He said,
"Look, I can give you Roky's mom's number, but I can't really give you
his. Everything has to go through his mom. You should give her a call
and say you wanna meet Roky when you come through Austin. I'm sure
she'll okay it if she likes your vibe." I gave her a call. She seemed like a
sweet old lady. She realized that my intentions were [good]. This is the
only time I ever sought out a hero. I just wanted to have a relationship
with the guy. I have never done that before or since. I'm not exactly an
outgoing person. I'm definitely not a stalker fan. I would never ask someone for an autograph.

Something made me want to get to know him. His mother gave me his
number. I would call once a week for months. He picked up the phone
eventually. He was really outgoing and wasn't guarded. Roky would only
talk about horror films with me. He completely ignored any attempt I
made at steering the conversation toward music, but he found out that I
had worked at a video store. That's how I got into my first band. I worked
for the parents of the guys in the Screaming Trees in their video store.
They rehearsed out back, found out that I like the same kind of music,
and wanted me in the band. Roky asked me what the horror movie section was like. We only talked four or five times over the course of a couple
years. Then he was arrested for taking his neighbor's mail.

I never did meet him in person. His mom had said to take him out for
barbecue when I came to Austin. I planned on it, but I wasn't in Texas
at all during that time and didn't have the opportunity. I remember him
questioning what I was into movie-wise. He went deep. I had never heard
of some of the obscure stuff he brought up. He was a real aficionado. I do
remember that there was a strong white noise going on in the background
like I had a bad connection, but I was told later it was because he had all
his [televisions and radios] on at once. I could definitely hear something
weird in the background that was quite loud. I couldn't always hear what
he was saying because of the background noise.

I had an opportunity to see him live once in Los Angeles maybe fifteen
years ago, but a family emergency came up. I missed it. I was out of town

every other time. I planned on traveling to go see him, but that always fell through. My wife got to see him one time when I was out of town, and she was blown away. The greatest thing for me was that he was able to get past what was ailing him so long and get out and play fucking music again. It seemed like that would never happen for so long. I haven't seen the documentary, but I heard the gist of his turnaround. I couldn't have been happier. He was one of the all-time great singers, songwriters, and performers. It was such a fucking crime to be derailed so long, but I thought it was beautiful that he had a chance to come back.[6]

Mark Lanegan was a founding member of the highly influential psychedelic grunge band Screaming Trees in 1984. Additionally, he performed with Mad Seasons, which included Alice in Chains singer Layne Staley and Pearl Jam's Mike McCready. He recorded a cover of Roky Erickson's "Burn the Flames" on his 2012 solo album Dark Mark Does Christmas.

BILL BENTLEY

I think being in possession of drugs made the Elevators paranoid and standoffish in the sixties. I did hang out with Roky a lot in the seventies, though. The seventies weren't great for him. I don't know if he was schizophrenic then, but he was definitely challenged mentally. He wasn't a street person, but he was out on the streets. He really wasn't doing much when he got out of Rusk. He had the book *Openers*, and I was around Roky a lot when he did that single ["Two-Headed Dog" b/w "Starry Eyes"] on Mars Records with Doug Sahm because I was really close to him. Roky hooked up with Craig Luckin later in the seventies and made a record in Berkeley and got going pretty good. I didn't see him as much because he was actually touring then. I moved to Los Angeles in 1980. He probably played there at the Whisky a Go Go five times.

My old friend Tary Owens told me during the first South by Southwest in 1987 that Roky had been having some problems and was institutionalized again for stealing mail. We wanted to raise money for his living expenses once he got out of the federal institution in Springfield, Missouri, with [1990's *Where the Pyramid Meets the Eye*]. So, Tary and I decided to make the tribute and hopefully the publishing money would be filtered to Roky and Tommy for his cut to help them live. It didn't sell that well and might not have even broken even, but Primal Scream put their Roky and Tommy song ["Slip inside This House"] on their own album *Screamadelica* [released in 1991], which sold about five hundred thousand copies. I have a feeling the publishing on that made money. However, Charly Records in England owned the publishing, and I have a feeling they never gave them any money. I asked Roky's manager a few times, and he said, "Nothing from the Elevators ever comes to Roky— not album sales, song publishing, any of it." I have heard that Charly isn't very honest in their royalty payments to American artists.

I'm in love with every song on the tribute record. They're all very different. Every time I would get a new track I would go, "Wow. That's my favorite." I listen to it all the way through and every song excites me so much that I couldn't really tell you that one is my favorite. Some days it's the John Wesley Harding track "If You Have Ghosts," which is completely amazing. Then it might be the ZZ Top or Poi Dog track. The only regret I have is that when Lou Ann Barton was doing her track I had heard secondhand that Stevie [Ray] Vaughan wanted to do the guitar part because they had been in a band together. We couldn't pull it off logistically, but that probably would have been one of Stevie's last recordings.[7]

BRUCE HUGHES

Roky getting busted with two sheets of acid, eating it all, and going to Rusk was the myth going around when I was in junior high and high school in North Austin. Then nobody heard about him ever again. There was music and discoveries going on in Central Texas in the seventies. We had all the guitar-driven rock and blues from the redneck hippies and cosmic cowboys, the Armadillo World Headquarters, and Willie Nelson coming back from Nashville. There was always a market here for anything that was youth driven. I started at University of Texas in 1979, which had punk rock and the do-it-yourself ethos and new wave scenes. Some guys from the Delinquents ended up joining Cam King and the Explosives. They ended up becoming Roky's backing band.

Roky suddenly was playing live again, a pretty amazing era. "Wow," I said. "This guy's being reborn. He may be damaged, but he's risen from the fire like a phoenix." The Explosives were so supportive and so badass with Roky in retrospect. They were giving him a vehicle for "I Walked with a Zombie" and "Two-Headed Dog" during the Bleib Alien era. I loved it and was in tight with the Club Foot scene and Raul's. Club Foot was an alternative venue that would support everyone from Roky Erickson and the Explosives to U2's first world tour. I was friends with Troy Campbell and Mike Alvarez, who was active in the music scene and lived next door to Roky.

I ended up becoming a part of the Austin-era Poi Dog Pondering in 1987. We were a real folk-driven busking operation, and then we developed and added more members. We always had six to nine members and got some buzz and a following. I met [Poi Dog's lead singer] Frank Orell on their first go-round rolling through the country. I was friends with his girlfriend, who later became his wife. I loved what they did. I was playing in a group called Seventh Samurai at the time with Alejandro Escovedo and [Austin disc jockey] Jody Denberg. We put that group together to back up [former Small Faces leader] Ronnie Lang. Poi Dog ended up opening up for us on our tour of the country. I was fascinated with Poi Dog and saw them at our co-op in town and suddenly got involved with their thing. Frank reached out and asked me to put together songs for an EP.

We started picking up steam after steady touring around the country for a year and a half. College disc jockeys were driving music and there was hunger in great music towns like Austin, Tucson, and Columbia, Missouri. They were all over the country and you just had to drive to get there. We built up a good following and labels were interested. Half the people in Poi Dog weren't from Austin. They had connections but not in a deep way. Nobody was from here but me. Bill Bentley was with Sire Records at the time, and he was reaching out to Austin folks like us because we were signed to Columbia/Sony in 1989. "Hey," he said. "I'm involved with this idea." The tribute record idea had only been done a couple times at that time.

I asked Frank if he wanted to be involved with this Roky tribute record and told him there were other people like R.E.M., John Wesley Harding, and the Judybats involved. Frank and Susan were like, "I don't know who that guy is." "We have to do this," I said. "It's Roky Erickson. You don't understand just how powerful that is to the Austin myth." "Oh, okay," they said. "Then you run with it." I thought, We have to do the Elevators' "Levitation." Of course, that was taken. Well, we're not gonna do "Fire

Engine." I started looking and luckily I had all the vinyl. I pulled out records, and the hidden track on side B of *Easter Everywhere* is "I Had to Tell You," a song was written by [Roky and] Clementine Hall. I had forgotten about what a poignant and potent song it is. I thought it could work in a quietly powerful way and fit instrumentally with the Poi Dog ethos.

We were in between a US tour at one point and flying to New York to go to London to do a European tour for Columbia. We booked half a day at Arlyn Studios here in Austin. I played guitar and Frank played a water jug, but he didn't play it like the electric jug in the Elevators. He turned it upside down and played it like a percussion instrument. Ted played mandocello, and we did very basic tracking, sang it, and overdubbed the bass with a broke-down crew at Arlyn that day. We worked on it for about five hours, and then our time was up. I was hoping that was enough. We had to pack up and go to the airport the next day. That was all I heard about. It was mixed and sent off as far as I knew.

I had seen Bill Bentley around Austin. He reached out and said that was one of the very first tribute records, but even though all these people had signed on with interest nobody had turned anything in six months later. He was about to shelve the project. Our song was the first he received. He heard that and was like, "I have to finish this tribute record." He suddenly got fired up and reenergized. "Holy shit, this thing could be phenomenal." He reached out to everybody again and in pretty quick order they started submitting songs. The album is so lovely and it was great to honor Roky and have things come full circle as an Austin musician who deeply respects the creative spirit of Roky Erickson. It was really delightful for me personally to give back to Roky in some small way.

Austin was a classic hippie town back in the day. There was a lot of what we would consider the underground Haight-Ashbury culture with underground comics and music. Janis Joplin, [artist and cartoonist] Gilbert Shelton, and [concert poster artist] Jim Franklin came from here. Commander Cody left here and went to the West Coast around 1967. Then they went, "I don't know. It's kind of expensive and unruly out here." People clamoring out in California, and they thought they could hide out better back here in Austin. The counterculture idea and ideal existed everywhere here. I would catch the UT shuttle bus when I was growing up and go to the Drag and You Scream, I Scream, which was an ice cream shop entirely lit with black lights. There were all of these crazy bootleg record shops.

I think Roky found comfort in the counterculture. Also, there were many places to play music as opposed to places like Dallas and Houston. There were quarter beers at the Armadillo. I grew up with all this and thought every town was like that in the seventies. It wasn't until I started touring the country in my midtwenties that I realized the rest of the country is not nearly as comfortable as Austin was. They were all uptight other places. There was a free spirit and really strong do-it-yourself attitude encouraged in film, photography, sculpture, writing, any art. We had a very interesting crossover between higher education and graduate education whether chemistry or tech, and the political schism about being extremely democratic in an extremely conservative state. Artists and writers found a home here. So, it's not too surprising that Roky found a home here.

I was really drawn to the psychedelic soul movement in the seventies. I saw Roky play with the Explosives and his Bleib Alien–era stuff with "Two-Headed Dog" around 1982, and I was like, "Holy shit. I wanna do that. Roky and these guys are great." Then my friends gave me records to get into. Roky presented such an inescapable spiritual force onstage. His voice was such a cool instrument. Mike Patton from Mister Bungle [as well as popular nineties rock band Faith No More] and Arthur Brown from the Crazy World of Arthur Brown are like that. There are a handful of singers who get up and do a thing and you go, "Holy fuck. That's a hundred percent more than most people even pretend to give." Roky showed up. Energy comes out and shoots out of his mouth. Roky was wild and had a connection to some source that was stronger and deeper than most people. He was desirable and wired, and it felt electric and dangerous. Also, his subject matter is hilarious and campy.[8]

Austin, Texas, native Bruce Hughes was a founding member of Poi Dog Pondering, Ugly Americans, and the Scabs. The widely diverse bassist has toured with acts from Southern California rockers Cracker to pop star Jason Mraz across the United States.

JOHN WESLEY HARDING

We weren't really exposed to Roky Erickson in England, but I had heard "You're Gonna Miss Me" at university. I was on Sire Records, and almost as soon as I got to the label, they said, "Oh, we're doing a Roky Erickson tribute album called *Where the Pyramid Meets the Eye*. Would you like to be on that?" "Yeah," I said. "I don't actually know a lot of Roky Erickson songs, but that sounds cool." I had an amazing band at the time which was two of [Elvis Costello's] the Attractions, a guitarist called Steve Donnelley, and a keyboard player called Kenny Craddock. I asked what song I should do. Howie had been head of 415 Records and said, "Well, you should do one of the songs off the 415 record [*The Evil One*] I put out." He was trying to get those records in front of people.

Primal Scream, Julian Cope, T Bone Burnett were amazing on the tribute album. I chose "If You Have Ghosts," which is very prominent at track two on that record. We went to the studio in London to record with the producer who did my first and second albums with the same band on those albums. My songs had little bits in them and were folksy and Kinksy. The Roky song came to us and we listened to it to get it right. I'm obviously biased, but I'm so proud about being on that record. It just came out on vinyl for Record Store Day, and that brought how great that record was all back to me. People like Bill Bentley at Warner Bros. really understood Roky's music and what a great recording that was. That song had such a great pop-rock structure with the call-and-response vocal. My band was relieved to play that after doing my herky-jerky folk-rock stuff. They liked tearing into that. We did that song in a day. I remember heading back to Hastings in England with Kenny Craddock, and we were listening to it on the train. He went, "This is fucking great." I think that whole album was excellent.

I became associated with that track and I started doing Roky's Ice Cream Social at South by Southwest. [Dinosaur Jr.'s] J Mascis did it one year. I really like Sumner. He would bring Roky out if I was playing in Austin somewhere. I remember hanging out with him one night when we went out to see Ian McLagan at the Saxon Pub. Roky was aware who I was because I had that song on the tribute album. He was always very friendly and nice. I did the in-store for *Where the Pyramid Meets the Eye* at Waterloo Records. That was the first I had ever heard of Daniel Johnston.

Roky was there. I remember a woman asking Roky to sign an autograph on her arm. "I'm sorry," he said. "I don't sign flesh."

I don't know the ins and outs of Roky's life other than what everybody knows, but it seems to me I had seen him not at his best once in real life. The next time I saw him was when he was on his comeback tour at Bumbershoot in Seattle about ten years ago. I couldn't believe how powerful his performance was. He was really rocking, and the band was great. He sounded fantastic. I was like, "Wow. That's a great story." He kept on touring, and then he was dead. Amazing. I was surprised. He seemed frail to me the last time I saw him, but the power of his voice at Bumbershoot was amazing. I didn't think he'd be up to it. I was blown away when I saw him. He did all the great songs and his voice was blood-curdling. He was on fire.

I have a book of Roky's lyrics. I don't like to overintellectualize these things, but he was one of the greats. His lyrics are very mysterious. They're profoundly confessional but mixed in with his cultural touchstones in science fiction, aliens, and horror movies. He wrote confessional lyrics the same way Leonard Cohen wrote them, but the touchstones and imagery were Judaism, the Catholic church, Rilke, Lorca for him. Roky chose imagery from a different set of cultural touchstones, which I thought was really cool. Unfortunately, I think I sang completely the wrong lyrics on "If You Have Ghosts." That was before the internet, and you couldn't figure out lyrics without listening to the record. I think what I sing on the record is like a phonetic version of his lyrics. I only found out later when I bought his lyric book. I looked at "If You Have Ghosts" and said, "Fuck me. That's nothing like what I sang."[9]

John Wesley Harding (née Wesley Stace) has released more than two dozen albums, from the live It Happened One Night *(1988) through the covers album* Greatest Other People's Hits *(2018).*

JEFF HEISKELL

Someone was talking about this compilation album when we were in the studio, but I knew nothing about Roky Erickson. Most songs were taken, but I was drawn to how simple and straightforward "She Lives (in a Time of Her Own)" was. I thought, Whoever wrote this song is probably someone who does lots of acid or mushrooms. The lyrics were disjointed and unhinged, but we learned the song in one day and recorded the next. That vocal track is the third take. Sometimes I hear bands that everyone's all goo-goo and ga-ga about, and I'm like, "Shit. They're just taking the same chords and melodies and sound like this band." I thought R.E.M. listened to a bunch of Roky Erickson albums and then started making music. They patterned everything they did after him. I never listened to their music the same way again. I went through a period where I sent Roky's mother Christmas cards and talked to her. She said he spent most of the time in his room during the day.

The band thought putting "She Lives (in a Time of Her Own)" on [the Judybats' 1991 debut, *Native Son,*] would sound great on the record. I don't remember being resistant. They said they liked it so much they wanted to do a video. You're not gonna say no when somebody says they want to shoot a video with a budget. Things have changed so much. No one had shot a music video in Knoxville, Tennessee, back in 1991. The video was a huge, big deal in town. That was back when MTV was reigning. There was so much horrible resentment within the little music community for signing us to a major label [Sire Records]. Then doing the music video was hilarious. We were in the newspaper and everything.

I didn't think much about the song back then, but the last two, three years I've heard [our version] on the college radio station in Knoxville. The song sounds so good, so fresh and fun, a good recording. People don't know it's not an original. We played "She Lives (in a Time of Her Own)" live on our first and second years touring. The song isn't complicated or hard to play. The singing range wasn't like doing aerobics. I always wanted to do a cover of Madonna's "Live to Tell." She's not a great singer and somebody else wrote that song, but the vocals were so hard to sing and wore me out. You would have never thought that. I could listen to "She Lives (in a Time of Her Own)" three times and go out and do it right now because of the range. Plus, the crowd just loved the song live.

I probably thought [having a hit with a cover song] was bad as a younger person, but I don't really feel that way now. Sometimes you have songs where you've always wanted to do your own version. Recording "She Lives (in a Time of Her Own)" actually started a pattern. There was a cover on every Judybats record because people liked the Roky cover so much. Our cover of the Kinks' "Animal Farm" was popular. I'm up for any challenge. I don't care what it is. I had never heard that song, but [vocalist and multi-instrumentalist] Peggy [Hambright] played it, and I was like, "Let's do a cover of that." They threw around a couple others, but I said, "No, that's a kooky and a nice pop song." We used to play that live and people enjoyed it.

People were calling themselves indie rock back then because they were independent and thought you were selling out if you signed to a major label. The people acting that way would sell their mothers to a whorehouse for five dollars to be on television for ten minutes. There were ugly things written about us on bathroom walls in bars we hung out in. I started doing music through depression problems. Playing live completely weirded me out, but I still make music now. Those people making music back then were only playing to get attention and become famous. None are making music now. They're all fat, old, and divorced. I never even hear about them even getting drunk and playing the guitar on the front porch. They wanted to be famous. Our video for the Roky song was more than they could bear.[10]

Jeff Heiskell fronted the Judybats for about a decade from the late eighties through the midnineties. The Knoxville, Tennessee–based alternative rock band's first major label release for Sire Records was a popular cover of the 13th Floor Elevators' "She Lives (in a Time of Her Own)."

CRIS KIRKWOOD

Roky was the *Austin Chronicle*'s musician of the year during South by Southwest [in 2011]. They had asked us to play the Austin Music Awards, but I don't think my brother Curt was really into performing because we didn't win anything that year. They came back and asked if we wanted to back Roky for his live set after being named the best musician, which was very appealing. "Yes," we said. "We will happily do that." Curt lives in Austin and had hung out with Roky, but that's when I met him for the first time, which was a novel experience. I thought it was nice to see someone who has had to struggle with his day-to-day existence being embraced and celebrated while he was still alive. I felt a kindred spirit and could relate to him. Roky had helped my development as a psyche-delic warrior. He was primal with a great voice and an interesting artist with surprisingly far-out lyrics.

We did a photo shoot for the cover of the *Chronicle*. What a fucking trip. We met at the photographer's apartment and were standing out on the street waiting for Roky. He was an odd duck to say the least. They pulled up, and he told his wife, "Wait in the car." Jesus. He walked over to his son Jegar. "Look, Roky," Jegar said. "Gibson sent a new guitar as a congratulatory gift." Roky said, "I don't want it." Classic. Then he said, "I'll look at it. Thank you." My drummer at the time was Doug Sahm's kid Shandon Sahm. We had a big slice of Texas rock and roll right there. Doug and Roky were serious contributors to making Austin a musical place. We all gathered around Roky for the shoot. He's sitting on a little stool with his arms crossed over his chest. "What do you think, Roky?" the photographer asked. "Maybe you want to put your hands on your knees?" "I would rather not."

Then we had arranged a plan to go back to my brother's house and run through "Starry Eyes" and "You're Gonna Miss Me" a few times with Roky so we felt comfortable together. "Roky," someone said. "Do you want to head over to Curt's house?" "I would rather not." So, we ended up not doing it. Instead, we set it up to play the next day at his rehearsal space after he had finished practicing with his band. We got there, and Roky wasn't really chatty. I said, "Sure is a nice day out, isn't it?" He said, "We're supposed to like that." "Aren't the trees in nice bloom?" He said, "They do a good job with that." Fuckin' A. I was touched and moved. I got to catch the side of Roky as a head, a conceptualist. The practice session was seriously far the fuck out. He obviously was living in his head in a pretty significant way. We started to run through the numbers. He was starting to feel it choogle and lift off, and I was getting a big kick. I started smiling and was having a cool moment. He looked into me and broke into a big grin. Far out. That moment was so cosmic and touching.

So, we went to the show and were sitting backstage. Billy Gibbons was presenting. ZZ Top is seminal in my DNA. Getting to run into people I really dig while they're still around is pretty sparkly. The Texas greats just go on and on: George Jones, Janis Joplin, Roy Orbison, Buddy Holly. Roky absolutely was one of them. Getting into the stuff that he did was very interesting, but you pay the price for whatever you do. What they did to him [at Rusk] and how they did it was fucking gross, but he did leave behind some great tunes. Anyway, Roky and his wife were backstage. This guy Dennis came back and said, "Roky, I got you cupcakes." "For me?" he said. The funny thing that happened is that we arranged the songs so we would do "Starry Eyes" and then "You're Gonna Miss Me." We had practiced and had it all arranged for Jegar to come out and play harmonica. So, we walk onstage, and he starts into the songs in reverse order. He threw us all.[11]

Brothers Cris and Curt Kirkwood formed the Meat Puppets in Phoenix, Arizona, in 1980. The band's psychedelic rock and country style earned them a loyal cult following and caught the eye of Nirvana front man Kurt Cobain, who asked the band to accompany them on their iconic MTV Unplugged *appearance in 1993. They performed the Meat Puppets' "Oh Me" and "Lake of Fire" together.*

JEFFREY "KING" COFFEY

I discovered the 13th Floor Elevators when I got into punk rock. They were a revelation, so out there and from Texas. I felt like I could relate to them as a kid from Fort Worth more than what was happening on the West Coast or London. The Elevators were homegrown Texas psychedelia and even invented the term. That played heavily on me. I was lucky enough to have hippie parents who had hippie friends, and they had all the Elevators' records. I would borrow them and be blown away. Of course, as the years rolled on I got into Roky's solo stuff. Here was one of the premiere voices of sixties music transitioning into what was happening after punk. He created his own version of punk that was so scary and real. He had always been a legend.

I moved to Austin in 1983 and would hear rumors that he was here and there. You might spot him at the [Texas grocery store chain] H-E-B. He would play local shows pretty regularly around that time in town. Seemed like he played a weekly gig for a while at the Continental Club. You would almost take it for granted. "Oh yeah, it's just Roky Erickson's weekly gig." He was only drawing so many people. The Butthole Surfers had a song we wanted Roky to sing on. We had set up our own recording studio and were recording [the band's 1987 album] *Locust Abortion*

Technician. We played the song, but he didn't feel it at all. I think it was taking him too far out of his element to expect him to sing on a song he didn't write. He wasn't interested in that, but he did like our song "Cunts," which is just a tape loop of Thai music sped up and slowed down and makes no sense.

I was beginning to drop acid more and more by my sophomore year in high school. Hard-core music got so boring. You couldn't play that much faster or angrier. You couldn't be more macho. My friends and I started discovering all kinds of great music like psychedelia and world music. We realized that the Elevators were creating their own thing in Texas and making a template in their own way. They were a huge inspiration. Roky's songs are timeless and work great with just an acoustic guitar. They're so amazing and beautiful yet the lyrics are so out there when you analyze them. They're gorgeous and cryptic with beautiful melodies. The lyrics are like complex Beat poetry.

I think his songs will reign supreme. Listen to his voice. He might be the greatest singer to come out of Texas. He's certainly in the conversation with Janis Joplin and Gary Floyd from the Dicks. He had such an incredible, intense voice. He channeled his demons into his music. Roky and the Elevators showed us to not be afraid to let our freak flags fly. The Buttholes took cues from Roky in embracing our Texas roots and then frying them at the same time. The Elevators could not exist without Texas. Their approach was laid back like Texas and the music is ours. I think every Texas punk took inspiration from them.

My real introduction to Roky himself was when I was doing our record label Trance Syndicate. Casey Monahan was working at the Texas Music Office. He called me and asked if I would be interested in doing a new Roky Erickson LP. I freaked out. Of course, I would love to do it. I felt like I had won the lottery, but it was a scary thought because all the bands I had been working with at that point were young and unknown. It was no big deal if we failed miserably with them, but this was Roky Erickson. This was presented to me as a chance to finally make Roky some money. He never got a solid royalty check. I felt it was all upon me to make the world right for Roky, being the overly dramatic person I am.

I way overreacted, but he did need someone like that. The guy was struggling. So, Casey invited me to go out to dinner with Roky. I quickly gauged how unchecked his schizophrenia was. We assumed he was a little kooky and an acid casualty. No. He was a hard-core schizophrenic. He was yelling at imagined voices and had that nightmare scene of twenty radios and televisions at his house twenty-four seven. His teeth were rotting out and giving him grievous pain, but he was afraid to see a doctor. He refused to take pills for any of his ills whether they were psychological or physical pains. The only person he semitrusted was his mother, who really just wants to pray everything away. "If we just pray a bit more, things will get better for Roky."

You can't reason with someone who has an intense dogma like Evelyn, or Roky, who has intense schizophrenia. The situation was really tragic, but here was this guy in need who recorded this amazing record. I told Casey and Roky that we would give him a solid paycheck. We gave him an eighty/twenty cut while our usual cut was sixty for the artist and forty for the label. Of course, he had all the publishing. We promoted the hell out of it and did a good job. Part of having him on our label was some friends and I taking him out to eat every Tuesday. We basically wanted to check on him, so we would go eat, go grocery shopping, or take him to go see Evelyn. Sometimes he had a crazy mission like going to cash a thirteen-dollar check at a convenience store.

We did these small things to make his life easier, but you wonder if you're doing more bad than good dealing with an unchecked schizophrenic after a few years. We wondered if we were enabling him. I didn't make a conscious decision to drop out [of his life], but after a few years you get so beaten down by it. It was fun at first. "Cool, let's go out to eat with Roky." Then a few years later we were tired of another three or four hours of dealing with schizophrenia. "Oh god, we have to see Roky again." It was a shame. I didn't think he had much time left on this earth at that point because he was declining so much. People who wanted to help couldn't. It was horrible and tragic. Then Sumner comes in out of the blue and saves his life. He's a true hero.

I really don't know if we ever made a human connection, but I was the only person he called by my name. He had nicknames for everyone else. I guess because I already had the crazy nickname King he just went with that. He would call me King and definitely knew who I was, but as far as actually talking, we could never. I only saw him once after Sumner came into the picture and Roky was being treated for schizophrenia. We were at a restaurant and Roky came up and said, "Well, hey, King. How have you been doing?" He was clearly in a better place. He had Sumner and more family helping than just Evelyn. He talked for a few minutes and I was like, "Oh, my god. I would have loved to have been able to do this all the years we were together."

I was around him instead when he was screaming at random things. Every now and again he would pick up an acoustic guitar, belt out twenty seconds of a Buddy Holly song, and leave your jaw dropped, but you couldn't have a conversation. Schizophrenia is very one sided. He was very cryptic. You couldn't tell the meaning behind it. He would give you an answer if you asked him something that may or may not have anything to do with what you just asked. You would try to decipher what it would mean, but it was very frustrating and hard. That was my first time being around someone with intense schizophrenia and hopefully it will be my last. It's absolutely devastating.

I saw his solo shows in 1986, and you could tell that even though he still had the voice his schizophrenia was getting more intense. The Buttholes played with him at the Ritz and his schizophrenia was really problematic at that point. He played, but there was a lot of doubt whether he would even show up because he was late. Apparently, his handlers were doing their best getting Roky into the car and to the show, which I could relate to because I did the variations on that just going to the store or to Eveyln's. You can't corral Roky. He's a man of his own intentions. He was literally a different Roky when Sumner stepped in and got him medicated. He was clean shaven and playing songs and engaged. He still had that voice. He really had a rebirth once he got treatment and his teeth fixed and not giving him constant pain. He could focus on the music again.[12]

Jeffrey "King" Coffey serves as drummer for the iconic psychedelic rock band Butthole Surfers and founded the independent record label Trance Syndicate. The Butthole Surfers contributed the 13th Floor Elevators' "Earthquake" to Where the Pyramid Meets the Eye: A Tribute to Roky Erickson.

JEFF SMITH

Roky Erickson was the alpha and omega of psychedelic rock. Others might have produced what you may consider trippier and more intricate recordings, but you find something infinitely more primal in Roky's music. His songs are not only songs of a man's brain but also his heart being thrust through time and space while encountering demons and monsters along the way and trying to make sense of the seen and unseen world around him. His voice was the haunting sound of a man being thrown down a well, singing arcane lullabies to himself in the knowledge that his fears—real and imagined—could not harm him if he confronted them. Many folks may have considered Roky a burnout. Institutionalization, highly questionable treatments, and drugs no doubt took their toll, but he was an intelligent and canny lyrical genius with an ethereal voice that is rarely rivaled in recorded rock and roll.

I moved to Austin in 1982 and had seen Roky's name around, but I didn't hear his music until around 1985. I was pretty deeply immersed in punk music then. This was after his Raul's revival era so the album *Don't Slander Me* probably was the first I heard. We were listening to it at a friend's house in Austin one night. Then Roky was my friend Mike Alvarez's roommate in the summer of 1986. They lived in Mike's little house together in north Hyde Park in Austin. He was helping out Roky at the time. I knew that Roky was somebody famous, but he wasn't playing at the time. I probably saw him every day that summer for five or ten minutes at a time. I never saw him pick up a guitar. Pretty much all he did was watch black-and-white monster movies on a little bitty television on Betamax. Mike did some recording with Roky.

I am not a famous musician, but I run into people who know so much about me it's almost creepy—flattering but creepy at the same time. I don't lean into people like that. I give them their space. Our friendship will go forward if they take a liking to me. Roky was always in his own headspace so I didn't push those boundaries. I didn't really have any conversations that I remember. "Hey, Rok," I would say. "How are you doing today?" We were smoking a joint. "Want a hit?" "No," he would say, "but you can roll me one." He had that awkward OCD thing going on. Most of the conversation was more like a non sequitur, but that voice is what initially drew me to the songs. He had a very ethereal and unusual voice in rock music, but not in a hyper pretty way. He sounded like he was singing to something else.

I really loved the demo version of "I Have Always Been Here Before." Our guitarist Davy Jones, who was my musical partner off and on for thirty-plus years, had just been diagnosed with stage four lung cancer. We had a month-long tour of Europe scheduled, and Davy found out he was ill about two weeks before we were scheduled to go, so we got somebody else to play guitar while he began his treatment. We started working on some recording when we got back to raise his spirits. He had declined really quickly so we decided to cut cover songs by some Texas artists. Of course, Roky was one, but I didn't want to resort to the go-to songs in his catalog. "I Have Always Been Here Before" is one of the more obscure. I felt like we could do something cool with it and get back to the Buddy Holly vibe Roky had on that demo. I don't think we ever played it live.

If there is an upside to the many injustices suffered by Roky, it is that the stripping away of the ego allowed Roky a pure conduit that stemmed from his soul and poured from his body even on the campier B-movie-inspired tunes. I only saw Roky [perform] five or six times. He always seemed a tragic figure in spite of all the joy and inspiration he provided to others. I know well-meaning folks tried to help him out, but, as is always the case with a troubled icon, an equal if not bigger number of wannabes and users who were trying to hitch their aspirations to his star were on the scene. It seemed in the last decade he was relentlessly trotted out and he appeared confused and truly joyless onstage in spite of the great adoration paid to him.

Thankfully, his final San Antonio appearance at Paper Tiger a couple years ago left me with a good memory. He was seated but smiling broadly and playing electric guitar and singing well even if he did not match up the correct lyrics to the assigned melody on a couple songs. The bottom line was that he was enjoying himself and looked genuinely happy playing music, which was gratifying. Maybe that wasn't sufficient payback for his significant suffering, but it was comforting to me in some way. Roky played more after that, but that night was the perfect last time for me to see him. I'll always consider that show a great memory. I'm not an expert on Roky's music, but I definitely have lots of admiration for him. He was one of the three or four most talented people ever to come out of Texas.[13]

Jeff Smith is the lead singer and guitarist for the Hickoids. The Austin-based band played their first show opening for Henry Rollins' Black Flag

and the Meat Puppets in San Antonio in March 1984. They shared stages
with the True Believers, Poison 13, and the Butthole Surfers over the years.

CAROLYN WONDERLAND

I bought my first records from Grateful Greg in Houston, and we ended
up hanging out quite a bit. Greg had worked in a record store for years
and had a bunch of videos. He turned me on to Roky Erickson. I think
the 13th Floor Elevators' *Easter Everywhere* was the first one I heard. Then
I moved to Austin, and Roky was everywhere. I got into his solo career
with *The Evil One* cassette. I was drawn to both the lyrics and music, and
mostly because they scared the shit out of me. What he did with his voice
was the best and nothing like anything I'd ever think to do. I had never
considered screaming when I was angry in a lyric. He was so fucking
honest. The way he ripped your head off like that was quite something.
Then he would be as soft as "Starry Eyes."

I have listened to "Don't Slander Me" and "Cold Night for Alligators"
the most at home. Folks have been inspired by Roky and try to write like
that, but I have never heard anything like it lyrically. Maybe Sun Ra does
that musically. I love how "Cold Night for Alligators" is scary, freaky, and
sets a good mood, but then [the album] *True Love Cast out All Evil* is the
other side of that coin. Roky's so gentle but yet still so screaming and
perfect. He taught me that you can sing what you want, write plainly, and
use a certain economy with words. You don't have to be all floral with
them. You can get down to the point and just say what you're seeing. It's
cool to hear people argue about meanings to songs. They're fairly open.
His half was writing, and the other half was up to the audience interpre-
tation. They mean different things to people. The meaning is tied into
where they heard it for the first time a lot. He got away with "I Walked
with a Zombie" because he sang it differently every time.

We set up [the Instruments of Freedom benefit in Austin in 2006],
which was after we did Roky's Ice Cream Social at Threadgill's. Roky
and I were in a song pull with others. How scary to perform in front of
him. You're sitting in front of your hero and go, "All right. This is a little
song of mine that's not exactly 'Two-Headed Dog,' but I wrote it about
a broken heart." That seems so insignificant compared to his songs. The

biggest gig I saw him play was at the Rock and Roll Hall of Fame in Cleveland for the Janis Joplin tribute in 2009. The way he maintained himself at that show was fucking awesome. He was just "plug in and go." His voice is unmistakable and so beautiful. I remember seeing him and Guy Clark and a bunch of others side stage beforehand just waiting and going, "What's gonna happen?" His cable had fallen out of his guitar, but he just plugged it back in and slayed. He was better than I had seen him the past three times. It was really cool.

Roky was really sweet if he liked you and was in his space. Everyone has to get their space and time together. He would have that beautiful look in his eyes. We did a Threadgill's show one time where I saw him in the crowd at the beginning. I thought, Cool. Then he left during the last minute, and I thought, Oh, I get it. Well, it turned out that he had gone to Waterloo Records, but he came back later. "I didn't know if you were selling your CDs at the show," he said. "So, I went and bought a couple. Then I bought a couple of mine." He signed his albums and gave them to me. I was like, "What? You came to my gig and did what?" Roky would do that to people. He was very sweet. The fact that everything he went through didn't dull that part of him is an amazing testament. True love really conquers all. So does true music.[14]

Singular singer Carolyn Wonderland wails like Roky Erickson and plays guitar with Stevie Ray Vaughan's passion and precision. The longtime Austin resident has made significant marks with several studio albums from Peace Meal *through the defining* Miss Understood.

SHELLEY KING

Roky Erickson was already a legend when I moved to Austin in 1992. I looked up to his whole musical generation, which represented the city to me. Roky's part of the rock of Austin. I found a lot of great stuff the year I came here. Roky was reemerging. He and Lou Ann Barton sang "Starry Eyes" with Charlie Sexton at the Austin Music Awards around then. That was my first time seeing Roky live in person. I started digging a little deeper. Then we were out in Kerrville a few years later and we ended up going to his old drummer [John Ike Walton]'s house with the band late night after the show. He played on the old 13th Floor Elevators drums, and we got the full lesson with all the Elevators memorabilia and albums.

We really got into it and loved the originality and musical vibe and how it really started the psychedelic movement. I relate to psychedelic rock and have respect for that whole genre as a songwriter myself. I don't write those types of songs, but I dig them. I love a good song and a good vibe. Roky had great songs. My friend Jason Richard played bass with Roky in Hounds of Baskerville. Now my son is a teenager and is discovering music of his own. He recently played a band called the Murlocs for me, who I thought were reminiscent of the 13th Floor Elevators. So, hopefully it's getting passed on to the next generation. They're very cool, an offshoot of King Gizzard and the Lizard Wizard from Australia.[15]

Shelley King was named Texas Musician of the Year *by the state legislature in 2008. Her most recent album,* Kick up Your Heels *(2019), deftly mixes the gospel, roots-rock, and soul influences that have been a common thread throughout her music.*

TROY CAMPBELL

Roky was very quiet when I first went along on his trips to Amy's Ice Cream in Austin. He mostly wouldn't even reply to me. Then I brought my future wife, Michelle, one time. She's a psychologist and started having a full-on conversation with Roky. I got pissed. I thought, Well, yeah, you'll talk to the cool blonde girl, but you won't talk to me? I would ask him a question, and he would go "yes" or "no" to anything. Then he went to the bathroom. I said to Michelle, "Great, you're really getting him to open up." "You never say his name," she said. "He's on medication that makes everything sound the same." Michelle had worked in the Santa Barbara Mental Institute when she was getting her master's degree and said, "You call him 'man' or 'hey, dude.' Never 'Roky.'" I watched her after that. She would always lead by saying his name loud, then asking a question. Roky could pinpoint who you were and focus on what you said. The machinery, cars, everything blended together to help suppress the voices when someone is on the medication he was on.

We started having an interesting relationship once I addressed him by name. We were having ice cream at Threadgill's one day around 2005, and he decided to play two songs, which was extremely rare then. He had given up and was burned out by the idea of performing, but he got up on that stage. It was fucking awesome. He sat down to eat after. "Roky," I said. "That was amazing, man. What do you want to see happen next in your life?" He goes, "I want to be on TV." "Well, man, *American Bandstand* isn't on television anymore." That's what I knew him from. "No," he said. "*Austin City Limits*." "Well," I said, "you should be on that. You definitely should be on that." He goes, "Can you make that happen?" "I don't know if I can," I said, "but they own a festival called Austin City Limits. I bet if you played that festival and kicked the crowd's ass they would have to put you on the TV show."

I knew the festival cofounder Charles Attall and called to pitch him. "What if I told you I could give you Roky Erickson?" I made up some figure that sounded like a shitload of money because Roky was living on nothing. I was thinking there was gonna be a debate, but Charles goes, "Troy, are you kidding me? Do you know what a massive Roky fan I am? I grew up with Will Sexton, and he used to play with Roky. Man, I would do anything to have him play our festival." This was the first time in however many years he would perform. Charles goes, "Look, we're gonna announce who's playing the festival in a few days. I'm gonna have to move some people around. Do you think this will happen? Do you think Roky is . . ." I knew what he meant: "Is he well enough?" "Yeah," I said. "In fact, he said he would kick your ass." Charles told me to call him back.

I called Roky and Sumner. "Guys, this looks like this is gonna happen. Also, we're gonna get money." Roky goes, "How soon is this?" I told him six months away. He just needed to get the band back together. Roky goes, "I don't know if my voice will be ready by then." He was dead serious. I knew to say, "Well, that's fine, Roky. Let me know when your voice is good and ready." I never wanted him to do anything ever that he didn't want to because he was messed with for too long. Sumner said they would call back. I got a call in fifteen minutes. "We've talked about it," Sumner says. "Roky wants you to know that he'll do it. He also wants you to know that he's secretly been rehearsing his scream." "Guys," I said. "You just paid me. That's the coolest thing I've ever heard." He was secretly rehearsing what he was famous for.

We got the Explosives to play with Roky so everything would sync up like the last time he was performing. We spent months with them to rehearse together. Cam and Freddie couldn't have been more wonderful with Roky. They spent years touring with him and totally got him. Everyone was really excited. Roky hadn't played in about twenty-five years, and there were several times I didn't think it would happen. I remember there was a massive crowd when they were getting ready to go onstage. Oasis was onstage across the way, but Roky had this huge crowd who couldn't believe he was gonna play. Roky looked at me on the side like Renfield [the vampire's sidekick in Bram Stoker's 1897 classic *Dracula*]. He looks up at this gorgeous totally full moon and walks onstage. The crowd was so Austin. They were chanting, "Roky. Roky. Roky."

Roky stood there and didn't do anything. I thought, Fuck. Oh no. Then he just powered into "Cold Night for Alligators." The whole place went nuts. I started weeping because I was so excited. Roky played the most professional set. He said "thank you" between every song. I saw something in the crowd that I hadn't seen in a long time. He and I got into the golf cart, and I was so excited. He was all sweaty. "Roky," I go, "that was so awesome. I can't tell you how much that meant to me." I looked at him. He was starting to get upset like he was gonna cry. "Roky, what's the matter?" "I'm sorry," he said. "I'm sorry. I can't remember your name. I should remember your name." He was so worked up from the set he couldn't remember. "Roky," I said. "Do you remember my face?" "Yeah." "That's all you need to know." He said, "Thank you."

I knew I didn't have the capacity to manage him and didn't think Sumner did either. I've been around, but neither of us had the business sense and acumen. I just knew I didn't want him to play in clubs. He should do a comeback—if he was gonna do one—on par with the New York Dolls. I knew the guy who did that comeback and managed Paul Westerberg. The Dolls had a third act that was dignified and well paid. I said, "Darren Hill is the guy." I called him and said, "I want you to manage Roky and do what you did for the Dolls." "I'm a massive fan of his, Troy," he said, "but I'm up here in Rhode Island. I'll only agree to do it if you look after him and go on the road with him. I can get him on course." We both basically wanted to get him to the other level that he deserved. I was all about making sure his third act played out properly. His legacy shouldn't be that drug-addled guy, but the architect of a very important sound in

American music. He was an inspiration to a lot of people. We picked up a good booking agent and were playing Coachella, Lollapalooza, Roky's first real European show in Sweden, which was really amazing.

We were in a trailer side stage at a massive festival called Hultsfred in Sweden. We got a considerable payday—like the biggest payday of his lifetime that was basically ten years of his salary. We said it was a one-time thing. Roky and I were sitting in the trailer talking about cartoons because we both loved them. We could hear people making loud noise, so loud that he goes, "They're really loud here, don't you think?" I said, "I'll go check it out." I went to the stage and there were easily forty or fifty thousand people spread out yelling, "Roky. Roky." This was forty minutes before the show began. I got shook up. "Fuck. This is a lot of people. This is like two or three times bigger than Austin City Limits festival." The people were pumped. I go back to tell Roky. He says, "Oh, really?" He was easily amused.

We walked onstage. Freddie and the guys took their places. Roky was with me. I was holding his guitar and was starting to put it on him. I was really nervous, but I didn't want him to see. "Roky," I said. "What do you think about this?" He said, "I expected it." Then he went out and rocked the shit out of them. I stood to the side thinking about what he said. I think he meant, "I've been waiting on this. I knew this would be here after all that shit I went through." He wasn't saying he deserved it. He was saying he dreamed about this. You know, I realized something right then. I battled with health issues and alcoholism for a long time. I realized I needed to pull my head out of my ass in that moment. Roky didn't want to be schizophrenic. He would have loved to be in reality, while I did anything to avoid it.

We kept working after that and were pitching to the *Austin City Limits* television show. We got the call one day. They agreed to do it if Billy Gibbons performed with Roky. Billy had been helping us with the Ice Cream Social at Threadgill's. Billy has been a really beautiful, wonderful friend to Roky. He agreed to do it. I remember playing that show after three years of touring everywhere—the Meltdown with Jarvis Cocker in England, we met every amazing hero from Patti Smith to Jello Biafra. They all wanted to meet him. Talking to people like the folks from My Bloody Valentine in England was so fun for me. They just wanted to meet Roky. He inspired all these folks.

Cut to *Austin City Limits*. I was doing the sound check because I love singing like Roky and didn't want him to sound check. I didn't want to waste his voice—or he might go, "Okay, that's the show. I'm done." I knew what to dial in his guitar, where his mike should be, what he needed in the monitors. Then he would show up, I would walk him onstage, and he would do it. We were getting ready to do ACL, and I was going to quit. My agreement was to get him on television three years before. "Roky," I said that night. "We're done. I'm very proud of you and proud to know you, but you're doing the show and I've done everything I said I'd do. I'm gonna leave." He looked me right in the eye with that beautiful gaze and said, "Do you really have to?" I thought about it. "No. I'll do whatever you say, dude."

I hung in a little longer to train his son Jegar [how to tour manage] because he would never have gotten to know his dad, and I wanted him to be in Roky's life. I figured this was an interesting opportunity. "You know," I said. "You guys might never develop that dad-son-buddy thing, but at least you get to see who he is." Jegar went on the road with us for a year, and then I split. I would still produce the Ice Cream Socials and chime in on branding, but I needed to start working on my own stuff and developing the House of Songs. We knew we could do the comeback tours for a couple years, but that would just be beating it into the ground and not be rewarding for Roky. We had to figure out how to get the young acts who look up to him to record some of his songs. I think he wrote more than four or five hundred on yellow notepads in Rusk. Those had been worked through and compiled. The demos were shared with not only Billy Gibbons but Okkervil River, who showed a real interest. They were a really smart, up-and-coming band, and Will Sheff loved Roky. I thought that would be a chance for Roky to get a Grammy if they could do something cool.

Then there was the Patrick Swayze situation. Cut to Will working on the songs and making demos in Brooklyn. He was calling and saying, "I need Roky to start practicing the songs before we get there to record." I told Roky that I would come by with a guitar to go over the songs that Will had chosen. Roky said, "Okay." I showed up at three in the afternoon, and he acted like he was totally surprised to see me. He'd ask, "What's going on?" "Well, Roky, we're gonna go through the songs today." "Can you come back tomorrow?" This happened twice, and then

I got pissed about it. I came in on the third day and answered, "No. We really gotta do this." "I'm watching *Powerpuff Girls* on television," he said. I said, "Oh, I love television." I was just trying not to leave. I sat down, which I knew would make him terribly uncomfortable.

I watched a bunch of *Powerpuff Girls* with him. He was like, "Well, it would be great to see you tomorrow." I brought a guitar Gibson gave for him to use. I thought, Okay, he'll play this guitar. I handed it to him, and he said, "Can you put it over there?" "Oh, shit." Another strike. I left and came back the next day with another idea. He had perfect pitch. So, I untuned the guitar, sat next to him, and quietly played his songs incorrectly. I watched him cringe and thought he would take it away from me. He didn't. This went on for a long time. I said, "Look, Roky, Will is coming in a few days. My job is to make sure you're doing what you feel like doing. I need to let him know if you don't want to do this record and move on."

He looked me right in the eye and said, "So, that's your job? That's really your job?" He was staring me down. "Well, let me ask you something then. This isn't gonna become one of those Patrick Swayze situations, is it?" Jegar looked over his shoulder at me and mouthed, "What the fuck?" I said, "Explain, please." "You know, where everybody wants to be together, and they want to be friends. Then they're hanging out at a bar and start fighting." "Are you talking about [Swayze's 1989 film] *Roadhouse*?" "Well, yeah." "No, Roky, we're not gonna do that." He picked up his guitar. Jegar goes, "How the hell did you know that?" "I watch a fuckload of television like he does," I said. "Today it paid off."

I called Will later. He goes, "How's it going?" I said Roky was practicing, but I hadn't called Will in a week because I was panicking. He goes, "Well, great. I'm excited." "So, Will," I said. "This isn't gonna be one of those Patrick Swayze situations, is it?" "What are you talking about? Are you talking about *Roadhouse*? That's been on Showtime all month. Tell Roky, No. It'll be nothing like *Roadhouse*." I said, "Wonderful." Isn't that wonderful? Roky just wanted to make sure it wouldn't be a Patrick Swayze situation. Will was asking me some questions when they were making *True Love Cast out All Evil*. "I'm gonna play Roky some cool records in the studio," he said, "and make Roky feel relaxed." "What records are you gonna play?"

"I was thinking Lou Reed because Roky covered 'Heroin.'" He was naming people. I told him I wouldn't do that. I didn't think Roky wanted·

to hear those guys. We were in the studio, and Will was playing Neil Young. "Hey, Roky," Will says. "What do you think?" "Uh-huh." "It's Neil Young." "Uh-huh. He's all right. He's got that one song." One song? Then Will played Lou Reed. "He's okay," Roky said. "He's got that one song." He was slagging them. Will finally gave up and started playing Muddy Waters. Roky lights up and started talking. He still was that nineteen-year-old rock and roller who had that ego about what he was doing. He didn't want to hear [contemporaries]. He wanted to hear guys who inspired him, not the guys who went on to be great successes while he was languishing in a mental institution.

We worked with the Black Angels another time. I thought they had a 13th Floor Elevators sound. We worked on them doing some demos and then them doing a West Coast tour together. They did cool drone sounds and [Velvet Underground drummer] Moe Tucker rhythms. They played "Red Temple Prayer" and those songs really aggressively like they were on the records. Roky wouldn't do "You're Gonna Miss Me" or any other Elevators songs at that point, but we were working them in with a band that could really emulate that sound. I told Roky, "Why don't we do like James Brown did at the end of the shows and come back out and surprise everybody." Roky loved Little Richard and all those who came before him, so he agreed.

We were backstage at Great American Music Hall in San Francisco one night with the crowd going berserk after he had just finished the set. The Black Angels walked back out on their own [for the encore]. Roky and I were behind the curtain. It was really dark, but there was a little beam of light coming in. I was like, "Hold on, Roky, it's building up." I was really into it. I looked over at him, and he goes, "Do you see an eyeball on the floor?" I went, "Excuse me?" "Do you see an eyeball on the floor?" I looked down. "No, Roky, I see a beam of light on the floor." "You don't see an eyeball with a Band-Aid on it?" "No, Roky." "Well, neither do I." He walked out and rocked the shit out of it. I freaked out. I didn't know if he was messing with me, but I did what I was supposed to do. I gave him reality. I know you see this, but this is not happening.

We were in London another time when I had to spend a shitload of time with him at the airport. I should have murdered whoever did the booking. I had an eight- or nine-hour layover with Roky by myself at Heathrow just hanging around. You run out of shit to say. I had gotten a text that someone had written a little mention of him in *GQ* magazine. "Hey, Roky," I go. "You're in a magazine. Angelina Jolie's on the cover in a bikini." "What?" "Let's go look for it." "What kind of magazine?" he said. "Well, there's a beautiful woman on the front." "I'm in a girlie magazine?" I said, "Yeah." I didn't know what he meant. We were walking to find it, and he kept saying, "Oh, my. I'm in a girlie magazine." He thought he was in *Playboy*. That's what they called those things in the late fifties when he was a kid.

Then we were headed to the airplane. Roky still had obsessive-compulsive issues at that point where he would wash his hands a lot. I was used to it and would help. Also, he would only eat something if there was a fork and a proper plate. He and I really wanted a piece of cake, but you could only get one at Starbucks. They wouldn't give you a plate. So, I got the cake and walked into a restaurant I didn't know, went into the kitchen, took a plate, and put the cake on the plate. We started walking to the gate, but we were out of things to say. "Roky," I said. "Are you working on any songs?" "Yes," he said. "I am." I got really excited. Roky Erickson has written a new song. "What's it called?" "It's called 'Gerald Ford Is a Square Queer.'" I went, "What?" He just kept walking and thinking about it. I thought there must be these hidden meanings.

I was breaking the song down about the Nixon era. I would ask him every few days, and he would say the song was coming along. It went on awhile, and I was excited. So then we went to play a big show in Los Angeles, and I'm doing his sound check. He was supposed to do an interview with a big Los Angeles newspaper. He's upstairs in the dressing room above the stage. I get done with the sound check and want to monitor the interview to make sure nobody's gaslighting him. I go up and hear them talking. I hear Roky saying to the journalist, "You know, people will believe what they want to believe." I enter the room. "Like some people wanna believe that I wrote a song called 'Gerald Ford Is a Square Queer.'" I go, "You didn't write that song?" He said, "No." The journalist is like, "What the fuck is going on?" "I'm gonna get you back for that, Erickson," I said. He started giggling. He was turning red. He kept me going for months.

I would be in charge of money at the end of the night to collect the rest of the guarantee or what was left of the door sales. We went to pick up Sumner one night in this rough part of New York City after the gig and were in the cab. I had the money in my jacket. Roky never talked about money, but this time out of nowhere he said, "How did we do?" "We did really good." "Did we make some money?" "Yeah," I said. The cab driver was this huge, scary guy. "I'll tell you about it later." "No, tell me," he said. "How much?" I opened my jacket. "Oh, my god," he goes. "That's a huge bag of money." "Shhh. Stop it." "I mean, that's a lot," he said. "Like thousands, right?" I was like, "Fuck." I'm trying to get him to stop talking. He just went on and on. I think he was messing around. He thought it was funny. It is, but at the time I'm protecting Roky Erickson. That's not how I wanted the story to go.

The only way he could make money was playing again. Darren was trying to fight to get back what little publishing he had. Sumner was making sure that Roky had a trust, funding, and a way to protect the money he did have so he could retire. That was what I bought into. He gets a salary, an apartment, money is put aside to live off. My hope was to get his branding back up to sell T-shirts and posters I had different artists to do. I wanted to sell that slowly but surely over the years so that Roky could have some dignity. There isn't really a musician's retirement plan, especially with his publishing exploited. We were trying to build up content. That's how he made a living toward the end.

I didn't want him just playing any gig given to him. I watched from a distance, but Roky was able to buy a house. Jegar told me that they bought the house, and they had the cash to do it. Roky had been living in Section Eight housing. He walked through the place, and Roky asked Jegar, "Did we get this from all the flights we took?" He hated flying, but he did it because he knew it was good for us to do. Jegar said, "Yeah. It was." I thought that was really beautiful to hear. I wasn't there, but I heard Roky was amazed that he had this nice house.

His place on West Gate [Boulevard in Austin] was decorated like a Halloween house. There were pictures of ghosts on the walls, which was everything that you would hope for. Then you would go in the kitchen, and his wife would be making chicken. I came over one time to ask about signed posters. His wife was cooking. "Hey, Dana," I said. "How's it going?" "He's in his studio." He turned the middle bedroom into a studio. I could hear a keyboard playing a really good, full-out performance. I said, "Wow." "Yeah," she said. "He's been playing that all day." I thought, Roky Erickson plays keyboard? I'm the first to know that. "Go in and say hi," she said, "but he's working." I pop in and Roky's standing over a keyboard—one of those that you push a button and it plays a song. He's standing over it with his arms crossed. I said, "Hey, Roky. What's going on?" The keyboard is playing *The Lion King* theme, which I didn't put together before. He touches a key and it turns into another song. He'd been doing this all day. "Troy," he said. "This one's got a mind of its own." You know what I got out of Roky Erickson? I learned how to live.[16]

Former Loose Diamonds leader Troy Campbell and Danish star Poul Krebs founded House of Songs, an organization that proves music provides a conduit for connecting diverse cultures together. House of Songs now sponsors collaborations in thirteen countries and operates out of Austin, Texas, and Bentonville, Arkansas.

DARREN HILL

My friend Troy Campbell had seen my [management] work with the New York Dolls and the Replacements and thought I would be the right person to resurrect Roky's career. He arranged for me to meet up with him. Sumner was his guardian then. We hit it off, and Roky asked me to manage him. I was a little apprehensive. Frankly, Roky had this mythological reputation that was a little frightening, but I was completely at ease when we met. He was so sweet and genuine and nothing like what I had read or seen years ago when I went to Baylor [University in Waco, Texas] in the late seventies and we would go to Raul's in Austin on the weekends. I think we saw Roky's first gig with the Explosives at Raul's. I was converted instantly. The man was a true otherworldly genius. Anyone in his circle would agree. He almost single-handedly invented two genres of music: psychedelic rock and punk rock. He completely reinvented himself in that phase. How many artists can do that? *The Evil One* is always a go-to for me. The songs on that record are insanely good. Then there was a third side to him that was more like a folk artist. He wrote beautiful country folk ballads.

My job as Roky's manager was to oversee his career. I was kick-starting a career that had been dormant for a while for obvious reasons. He was doing so much better than he had been when he was in Section Eight housing and not doing well mentally or health-wise. Then Sumner came back into his life and helped turn things around for him. His documentary *You're Gonna Miss Me* was wrapping up. Roky seemed like he was ready to start performing again. I hired a booking agent who I knew was really into it and could do a great job. I had to clean up a lot of his business dealings. They were a complete mess. I oversaw his publishing and merchandising and created public awareness about how important he was. The Elevators record deal was notorious. International Artists signed them to one of those deals you read about in history books. International Artists owned their masters and Roky's publishing in perpetuity. So, that was a lost cost—particularly when International Artists was signed to Charly overseas.

Roky was very tentative when he started playing live again, like he wasn't comfortable onstage. I remember the second time he played Austin City Limits festival. The show was cringeworthy. I don't know what happened. It was outdoors, and he was looking up into the sky almost was like he was somewhere else. They made it through the set fine, but there was definitely a disconnect. There was adjusting required. He had been on a lot of medication and had been taken off. I think he was growing a little uncomfortable with his relationship with the Explosives at the time as well. We made a change not too long after that. We tried out different sets of musicians, which eventually led to the Okkervil thing and finally ended up with [the Hounds of Baskerville] that Jegar was working with. Some shows were great, though. There were absolute flashes of brilliance. He still had that vocal range, scream, and intensity.

I'm so happy and proud about the Okkervil record [*True Love Cast out All Evil*]. I still listen to it once a week. That record is inspiring. I had been talking to a couple people about doing a project where we take the old songs that Roky had written but not recorded and having Roky do them properly. I was talking initially to Britt Daniel from Spoon. He was really, really interested. Then Will Sheff came into the picture. Along with that came assurance from his manager Ben Dickey that they would help fund the project and we could sell it a label, which ended up being perfect with ANTI- Records. I knew right from the start that Will was the man. He was so invested. We needed that. He persevered and did an outstanding job. Will was moving much faster than I could in the studio.

You needed to know what you were getting into with Roky and whether you're cut out for it. Will was. You saw the changes that were made in his family and who was looking out for Roky. His mom was initially. Then Sumner. Then his ex-wife, Dana, reentered the picture. Then Jegar wrestled the reins from her. Here I am stuck in the middle of all this. That goes back to what I do as a manager. I had to get involved in personal things with him that I would never, ever entertain with any other artist. That just became part of the job. I'm considered part of the family even today. I did what was necessary to work with him. It was very rewarding and satisfying for all the work and stress to see how Roky changed and became more full of life.

I think the last fifteen years of his life were the happiest he had ever been. You could see that in his eyes. Turning the world on to this great talent was very rewarding. People had forgotten or didn't know about him at all. Roky had absolutely no ego. He wasn't thinking, I should be this or that. I should be the one getting credit for this. I think he was content just being who he was. He certainly embraced the accolades and attention he was getting on his fourth or fifth chance. I think he really appreciated it particularly when I would bring fans backstage to meet him. He was so friendly and appreciative that they enjoyed his music.

Unfortunately, I wasn't at the show when the Elevators got back together [in Austin at Levitation fest in 2015], but I was the one putting it together. I had the Replacements doing their reunion tour at the same time. There were conflicting dates. I was trying to fly in that morning for the festival but missed my flight. That was a very, very difficult situation. Honestly, I don't think Roky wanted to do it. I don't think he had any interest in looking back or revisiting that time. There were many things that pulled the scab off for him. He wouldn't play any Elevators songs other than "You're Gonna Miss Me" for a long time. We introduced a couple into the set, but he resisted playing anything he didn't write lyrics to. I think that's primarily because he couldn't remember the words.

I decided I wanted to work with artists I really loved when I went into management. Unfortunately, most great artists and geniuses come with baggage and problems. Let's call them challenges. [Longtime *Chicago Sun-Times* music critic] Jim DeRogatis wrote an article on Roky's comeback, and he devoted one paragraph to me and how I only worked with the most difficult artists in the world. That didn't really dawn on me. I was just working with artists that I love. It was such an honor to work with Roky and continue to work with his legacy. I think Roky was quite misunderstood. He was very reserved and quiet. I always called the writer beforehand when I set up interviews with him. I prefaced the interview by explaining how Roky was. "He's gonna give you a lot of one-word answers," I would tell them. "You have to dig a little deeper to get him to elaborate." It could easily be interpreted that he was just a burnout with mental issues. I think Roky was just on a higher level than any of us. You had to understand that to be with him and work with him.[17]

Darren Hill owns Ten Pin Management. Hill has managed the Replacements' Paul Westerberg, Roky Erickson, and the Mighty Mighty Bosstones. He lives in East Greenwich, Rhode Island.

CHORUS

True Love Cast out All Evil

WILL SHEFF

My band Okkervil River had been signed to Jagjaguwar Records, and the most famous act associated with them at the time was [late Magnolia Electric Co. leader] Jason Molina for [his 1997 breakthrough album] *Songs: Ohia*. Jason was on their sister label Secretly Canadian. Those two labels put a festival on in Bloomington, Indiana. This was our first time playing outside Austin, and we wanted to make a good impression. We piled in our van and drove up to Bloomington, which was my closest first experience to being on tour. We got to the Bloomington offices for the label and were very excited. Then we needed a ride somewhere. Jason showed up. We had never met. "I've got my tour van," he said. "You guys can just hop in." He was very outgoing, nice, and playing the elder statesman.

"I've been listening to Roky Erickson lately," he said when we got in the van. "Have you ever checked him out?" I was familiar with who he was mostly because I was a big Daniel Johnston fan. Unfortunately, everybody always mentions Daniel and Roky in the same sentence. Jason was playing the horror rock like "Night of the Vampire" or "Bloody Hammer." He was rocking out in the van, so I'll forever associate Roky with Jason, which is a beautiful thing. I always appreciated Roky through the years and certainly loved the Elevators and horror rock, but it wasn't until we were boning up on material to play a show with him that [longtime

Austin Chronicle writer] Margaret Moser wanted us to do at the Austin Music Awards that I got to appreciate it on a deeper level. Meeting Roky was exciting and intoxicating.

I find Roky's songwriting fascinating because he's not about sophistication. He gets into this really strange headspace that's dreamy and cosmic. I hear Lewis Carroll in his writing. He does weird things with language and puts words out of order like, "Also thought-lost and never-known treasures /coming back to we" [from "God Is Everywhere"]. Listen to "Be and Bring Me Home." He has this combination of incredibly heart-felt lyrics that come from the Bible: "They told me you were dirty / I don't see no dirt / They told me you were strong; funny, I don't feel hurt / They said you were a criminal / no one sees no crime." Then he'll do something like, "No foot moves through you trying for to kick / I won't jump on you though we are all rubber." It sounds nonsensical until you puzzle through. It sounds like he's saying, "We're not gonna hurt you, but in reality you're strong and you can bounce back from being hurt."

That complete and total freedom with syntax and language is something I admire so much. You have to be willing to let nonsense in to get to where Roky gets, which is a really scary thing. We hold on to our egos and sense of order so dearly. They say that if you give someone LSD and give them an MRI, their whole brain lights up because parts of the brain that don't normally talk to each other are talking. You can't get along in the world like that because you don't want to hear a sound and have it smell. You're just trying to drive your car and have to be able to process information in a linear way.

Roky's manager reached out one day. "Do you want to produce a new Roky record?" he said. "Here are sixty songs you can sort through." Really heavy. I heard this side to him when I was listening to that Rusk material that's incredibly spiritual, emotional, and transcendent, which grabbed me more intensely than the other stuff. I wasn't sure I would be the best choice to produce that record, though. I love the Elevators, but they were so removed from contemporary context that I wasn't sure exactly how to work my way into it. I love the more rock stuff, but I'm not the best choice for a hard rock production as much as I love it. The Rusk stuff wasn't hard rock. I felt there was a visionary quality. I'm always looking for transcendence in art and life. Roky caught me with that.

Roky went into a wide-open space where anything goes emotionally, spiritually, and psychically. He went beyond into deeper or higher self-consciousness. Transcendence has religious, spiritual, and sublime sides, but also a negative side with obliteration, annihilation, nothingness, and ego death. Roky was open to both ends of that spectrum. Roky's music is very exciting and scary. The pain and yearning in his music—especially the music he was working on in the time around the Rusk period—excited me. He was beseeching the universe for help and at the same time asking his fellow man for understanding. That brokenness and tenderness is really compelling to me. He was fighting demons in and before the horror rock stuff, but then there's a turn in his experience where he embraces and makes friends with his demons. That's a big part of the horror rock period. Those are the qualities that made me want to work with this guy and the material.

Roky's story is complicated. I think the *You're Gonna Miss Me* documentary isn't entirely accurate in terms of what happened, but it is true that he had a really good period shortly before I started working with him. He was reconnecting with his family and son, which wasn't quite as sunny when I came into the picture. Somebody had decided to not give him his full dosage of meds for whatever reason. The Roky we got was more shut down than the guy at the very end of *You're Gonna Miss Me*, which was a real shame. He wasn't anything like the Del Valle housing project Roky who was completely floridly psychotic, though. He was just undermedicated.

Roky is in touch with his emotions and talked about the difficult stuff in his life, so [revisiting the Rusk songs] didn't seem to be too much of an issue for him. We were very frustrated because we were trying to pull him out of this hole he was in. He was really out of practice with guitar. So, it was like training for an athletic endeavor. "Okay, we've gotta hit the track." We would rent venues and get him onstage to rehearse and rehearse and rehearse again. We were getting him used to playing again, but we were also giving him a support system. He grew up in a band, which is like a gang with your best friends and sometimes worst enemies. He didn't have that. He didn't seem to have social contact besides Dana and Jegar. I wanted to get him back in the gang and into the clubhouse.

We would play and hang out. He would tell us stories about his life, and we would do songs I knew he liked. I have no illusions, though. You can't save someone when they're schizophrenic by jamming, but I do know that it really helped. We didn't talk about this openly, but I got a sense that he was fighting this stuff. He knew the record was important. He respected us, and I could tell for sure he trusted me. He knew that I cared and wanted him to do his best, but he would run up against moments when his brain was betraying him. He wasn't as much fighting painful memories as fighting his own demons. He wanted the record to be great. Roky, Jegar, me, and all the band members were doing our best and fighting to make the best thing we could. I'm really proud of that record. We made a good record slowly, which cost a lot of money, but we made a good record.

Roky didn't play guitar on the album. He started out playing guitar, but I quickly realized that would make his vocals worse. I wanted him to sing with us, so everything on the record was performed as a band with the exception of "Please Judge," which is Roky singing and me playing piano. Roky was always present. Roky would be bored easily, so we would have our instruments set up and settings marked down before he arrived. He wouldn't want to do anything more than once. Twice maybe. Every single day we would rehearse in the studio. Then he would show up, and we would play. Then we would take breaks, listen to music, and get him a cold brew coffee. Then we would go again, but we almost never did the same song twice in a row, which is really tough.

We realized some songs were a little high for Roky's voice and would transpose them into a different key. We were thinking on our feet. We would play these songs so many damn times that we didn't even know what a good performance from us was. The goal was getting the best Roky performance. I took all the vocals he sang with us and went into a different studio. I had him sing everything again. Then we took the best parts from where he was rocking with the band and the best from when it was just him and me in a room intensively talking about the songs. I would be literally standing in front of him dancing half the time. I was like a one-man cheerleader for Roky during those sessions. I would sing along with him and give him encouragement and energy. He talked about [Rusk] freely and sometimes with emotions. He talked sometimes like he was talking about the plot of a movie that he saw a while back. That was more emotional, like therapy.

I wanted to show how Roky unites American music on *True Love Cast out All Evil*. He is a country boy who grew up on Buddy Holly, got into James Brown, joined a band that invented psychedelic rock, did a bunch of psychedelic pastoral folk music, and then went on to do music that was influenced by hard rock and heavy metal. He unites real Texas country, fifties rock and roll, soul, funk, psychedelic rock, and power pop. I wanted to show the breadth of him being a true American original. He was a formative American artist. "Goodbye Sweet Dreams" falls into that because it feels like the Stooges, a bit like proto–punk rock. "You're Gonna Miss Me" is one of the most famous garage rock songs. I wanted to give that song this dark, gnarly garage Stooges feel, like the Stones' "Gimme Shelter."

"Goodbye Sweet Dreams" was one of the first songs we did for the album. Roky was always very engaged with that one. I put some jug on there at the last minute when we were recording. I doubled the jug with tremolo on electric guitar, but I'm not sure how audible it is. Maybe it's a slightly cheeky Tommy Hall reference. I thought about Tommy because he was really important to Roky even though he seemed like a very bad influence on everyone. There's something special about the intellectual and the wild man working together. I wanted to include the good Tommy Hall version of light instead of the Tommy Hall of dark. I didn't put the jug up too loud because I wasn't sure if they were gonna hang me from a tree for doing that when they heard it.

We tried so hard to get Roky's feedback, but he wouldn't give any. You could tell when Roky didn't like something. So, it was more like, "Roky's not digging it. He's not bringing his A game. He's distracted and in a bad mood." "Roky's really singing his face off, dialed in and happy." Honestly, maybe sixty percent of making that record was sitting around and talking to Roky while we listened to music. I had a playlist going, and would go home every day and add new songs to play for him. "What do you think of this song?" I would say. "What do you think about that song?" He'd say, "That's real good" or "They just had the one song," which means, "Yeah, I like that one song." "What do you think of Tom Petty?" "That's not meant for me." I wanted to make Roky proud. I didn't want to push him anywhere he didn't wanna go. Stuart Sullivan worked on the record *All That May Do My Rhyme*. Roky didn't want to do that record. He wasn't engaged, didn't enjoy the process. It was just Austin friends of his saying,

"We need to do a record." They steamrolled Roky. Stuart made me feel better. "This is miles different from that," he would tell me. "Roky was completely checked out and this is a far different experience."

There was a song called "The Singing Grandfather" [that didn't make the album], which was more a horror rock song. We did a creepier nightmare version, and one called "And Now We Fly," which was really just Roky saying, "And now we fly" over and over, which came out really good. We did one live take on the vocal. That one has been banging around for a while. Maybe somebody will do something with those, but that was what we did. I wanted to make a second record with Roky and brought up the idea to Darren, but we took such a financial bath on that first record. I didn't make a dime, but I hope Roky made some money. I didn't take payment because whatever payment was coming down the line for that I just couldn't have my cup out to catch any. Everyone was skeptical about making a second record because of how expensive that first one was, but I had a vision. Roky would start improvising vocals when we were rehearsing for the live shows, which he wasn't before. He also played a fifteen-minute guitar solo one time on "Goodbye Sweet Dreams," and then he kicked over the amp. He was like, "I'm sorry I did that." "No, no," we said, "that was awesome."

I had a vision of setting up a four-piece band, cranking the amps, and doing a hard rock record with improvisation. We would see what happened and maybe we could edit something cool out of it. I could suddenly see the vision of new Roky Erickson material. Maybe it would be a cowrite. In my mind, the project seemed so within my grasp. I thought it would be such a cool companion, but at the same time, it's very chaotic and frustrating working in Roky's world. Also, you start to go crazy a little when you're around schizophrenic people. That was happening to my band members. They were getting kooky. It took us almost two years to make *True Love Cast out All Evil*, and when we finished it and I came back I realized that the momentum had stalled out with my own band.

I thought I would end up being his rock and roll nurse, caring for his artistic output, a physical therapist of rock and roll if I kept working with him. I saw this world where I was no longer doing my own music ever again. That would have almost been all right if it weren't for the fact that Roky was being sabotaged by his situation and illness. I couldn't take the frustration. I love Roky—and he was such a wonderful person—

but his world was so hard to deal with. His mental and artistic health were often being undermined. I felt powerless to do anything about it and that made it really hard eventually.

For the record, I find the comparisons between Daniel Johnston and Roky convenient but also slightly insulting. Daniel and Roky were very different musicians. Daniel was not a polished musician or singer at all. Roky was a master singer with an insanely powerful trained musicianship. Roky was a veteran of the music business. Daniel was an outsider who created this crazy folk art world. Roky had an adult connection to rock and roll and playing in a band. He had a lived-in, masculine quality. Daniel had a childlike thing. Daniel had a level of sophistication in his writing that Roky didn't. Daniel had classic Beatlesque chord progressions and a sense of harmony and melody that is eons beyond Roky. Roky just played three chords. Daniel had a self-awareness and could play with the audience and subvert. Daniel and Roky are constantly compared because they struggled with mental illness and lived in Austin. There were huge differences in their work as far as music composition and lyrics.

Do you know that they're now thinking early cave paintings were done by Neanderthals and not by *Homo sapiens*? We *Homo sapiens* probably killed Neanderthals. I was looking at reconstructed pictures of Neanderthal man online, who we think of as a cave man. They were beautiful and had a friendly quality. I mean this in a beautiful, celestial way, but I think of Roky as a classic Neanderthal man doing the cave paintings and being too rare for this world. I think about this dreamy, alternate path things could have gone on. He made his mark and was mysterious and came along and accidentally created psych rock.[1]

Will Sheff leads the Austin-based indie rock band Okkervil River. The group teamed up with Roky Erickson to record his late-career high-water mark True Love Cast out All Evil. *The album led to another resurgence in Erickson's popularity and sparked renewed interest in touring.*

ALEX MAAS

Roky blew me away because the Elevators had that bubbly jug sound, insane energy, and were on a different plane than anything else. My interest was piqued when I found out they were from Austin. I found out that some members had been in Red Krayola and other psych bands, so I kept digging in and opened up this whole world that was right there. *Easter Everywhere* and later records like *May the Circle Remain Unbroken* sound completely different. I love bands that have range and can be one element, then switch and the songs still sound so believable and true. I've always felt that with the Elevators. I want to listen to music by people who sound like they're all in.

The Elevators were from the future. They were undeniable sonically. I wondered how they weren't the biggest band in the world. I know I'm not the only one who was instantly jealous when I heard the Elevators. They pushed and drove me to get better. You can have a good jealousy as a musician when you hear music like that because you strive to be like them and have a healthy admiration. Oasis said, "Why even play music if you don't wanna be bigger than the Beatles?" The Elevators had moments that were bigger than the Beatles to me. The Black Angels tried to do whatever we could to make awareness. We didn't wanna keep the Elevators in our pockets. You can wear your influences on your sleeve. The whole point is to do something fresh and say something familiar but differently. All musicians try to do that, but the Elevators pushed the envelope for us and musicians everywhere.

Roky's road manager contacted us around 2008. He knew we were in love with the Elevators. He asked if we were familiar with Roky's solo catalog as well. We knew "Two-Headed Dog," "Night of the Vampire," and "Starry Eyes," but we weren't infatuated with it like we were with the Elevators. He asked if we wanted to go on tour with Roky and be his backing band. "Yeah," we said. "Obviously." We knew the Elevators songs, and I had a couple clay whiskey jugs and knew how to play them as a percussive mouth instrument. You put the microphone up to the jug to get the resonance of your vocal. The manager said, "Let's meet in the middle and play some of the Elevators songs along with the solo ones." We agreed to the tour. The eighties stuff had more rock and roll sound like the Velvet Underground's *White Light / White Heat* when we played with him. Our guitars were jangly like theirs. We tried to play the Elevators songs to a T. We're not the caliber of musicians that they were, but we tried our damnedest with the electric jug and everything. Roky didn't remember the Elevators songs because he hadn't played them in forty, fifty years. We actually brought him to our house. The Black Angels have always lived together.

We had rehearsal sessions where we would reteach him Elevators songs. I could tell he was very unsure about doing the old songs and didn't really understand why we were doing them. I don't blame him. He was in his sixties. Relearning them seemed like work for him, but there's proof in music as therapy. Roky was difficult to work with because his attention span and memory were short, but he would start remembering things from the past when we played those old Elevators songs. We would ask him about how he came up with a song. He would say, "I don't even remember that song. Did I write that?" We would play the song, and he would go, "Oh, I was fifteen when I wrote that." Then he would tell us where he was when he wrote it and his memory got a lot clearer and lucid. Music really is therapy. His synapses were firing, his memory was working, and he was in a better mood. He was smiling.

Roky was obviously completely fucked up by the Texas Department of Corrections and electroshock therapy, which did a number on his brain. I don't know when the right time is to say, "Maybe we shouldn't put him on the tour anymore." I realized that he might not like playing live when we were on tour. He might have told everyone else something different, but that's the take I got. You don't want to have to tour the rest of your life until you're dead. You want management to figure out other ways to profit on your music. There are tons of ways, whether it's pitching your music to film or getting into sync deals. He had so much music that could have been exploited in that way so he didn't have to tour all the time. There comes a time when you look at a person and his health and ask, "Is touring gonna kill this person? Is this healthy?" Playing locally is easier to handle.

Our goal with the Levitation music festival was to get the Elevators back together for one final show. We were advancing people money in order to play the show, but we pulled it off and got the members back together. We even flew in Tommy Hall from San Francisco to play the jug. That was the pinnacle of our career. We felt a compulsion that really made us keep bugging them. You know, if you pester Radiohead to play your festival enough, they'll probably be like, "All right, man. We're gonna play it. Just leave me alone." I was superemotional watching them play. I mean, they coined the fucking term "psychedelic music." Think about how many people they've influenced. Listen to Janis Joplin yelp. She sounds just like Roky. She wanted to be in the Elevators. Nobody knows. Pretty incredible. Isn't that how the world works? The Elevators were way ahead of their time.[2]

Alex Maas is the primary singer-songwriter for the Austin, Texas–based Black Angels. The psychedelic rock band served as Roky Erickson's touring band in 2008 and helped launch the Levitation festival in their hometown. Maas helped reunite the original 13th Floor Elevators lineup for the festival in 2015.

SAM BRYANT

Our drummer and I were going to a landscape job site one day, and he asked me if I wanted to fill in on bass with Roky's band. "What?" I said. "Did you just ask me that?" We did the four California dates with Eli [Southard] on lead guitar, but we didn't have a rhythm guitar player. Our set was hard to get through without a rhythm player when we played Hardly Strictly Bluegrass in Golden Gate Park. We had a band meeting directly after the set, and I called Ryan and was like, "You wanna do this?" "Yeah, sure." Roky's voice has such a unique sound. Most songs we did were almost standards, but they sounded so different at the same time. All the guitar playing and vocals on Roky's solo albums with the Aliens and the Explosives is immaculate. The songs were very familiar but extremely unique at the same time. Roky had that subtlety in music that goes a long way.

Billy Miller was upstairs in the green room at Roky's last show in San Francisco before we were gonna play *Easter Everywhere* all the way through. I had no idea who he was besides he knew Roky. He was telling me about one of the songs we were gonna play. "Hey, man," he said. "You need to play the bass line like da-da-da-da-da, not like da-da-duh-duh-duh." I was like, "Wow. He really knows his shit." I was already nervous about playing like Dan Galindo played on the record. "Oh, don't worry, man," [drummer] Caleb [Dawson] said. "Nobody's paying that much attention." "Yeah," I said, "but I am and there's someone out there who is." I was extremely nervous before we played because we hadn't practiced that whole album. Ryan and I were on tour in Europe, and Eli lives in

Missouri. That record is hard enough to figure out. Billy scared the shit out of me. I knew he was important enough to be there hanging with Roky, so I wanted to do it right. "Man," he said after the show, "you nailed it." I felt such a sense of relief. That was one of the most nerve-racking shows of my life.

Roky was very surprising with the *Easter Everywhere* material live. He did have some difficulty remembering lyrics, but he hadn't played all those *Easter* songs probably since they were released fifty years before that last show. I think we played every song on the record. He remembered lyrics. We had them all typed out from the two times we practiced, but he didn't need to look most of the time. He was all feel. I don't think his illness affected that. He never lost the feeling. Those last two shows were at the Chapel, an amazing old chapel with huge ceilings. Wild. Lance Gordon, who does liquid light shows, went on that whole tour with us before in California. He did the shows in San Francisco. He's the photographer who took the photo of Roky's face for the cover of *The Evil One* record, which is insanely eerie. The whole show was very unique.

Roky treated everyone like his friend wherever we went. For instance, when people would come into the green room and say they loved this record or that, he would say, "Hey, good to see you again." He had never seen them in his entire life. He was really welcoming to everyone, but you had to be in the right place at the right time to experience conversation with him. We were in a van for a month traveling around with him, so we got that exclusive experience. We usually played late like around 11:30 p.m., so we would talk to him to keep him from dozing off. We were in Detroit one night and got into a conversation about the Elevators practicing at Stacy Sutherland's parents' place in Kerrville. I was prodding him and he would remember all these crazy details like what the barn looked like. His wife, Dana, always traveled with us.

We had about thirty DVDs in the van, and Roky chose to watch *28 Weeks Later* first. Then we watched *Halloween* over and over again. That was one of the coolest experiences I can remember, knowing his fascination with that movie and then watching him watch it five times in a row. "Oh yeah, you wanna watch it for the fifth time? That makes so much sense." There would be moments in the van where we would be dead silent. He would just bust out random, solid one-liner quotes. He was looking out the van window one time. "Screw you," he said. "We're from

Texas. Who's that?" "That's Ray Wylie Hubbard, man." "Oh yeah." He started talking about the New York Dolls another time. "Oh yeah," he said. "The New York City Dolls." He went on and on about their guitar player [Johnny Thunders] and kept calling him by name. He had spurts of hilarious one-liner quotes that would sporadically come out. Some days he would have twenty. Caleb started a list on a notepad. There must have been hundreds of them on his phone.[3]

Sam Bryant is the bass guitarist in the San Marcos, Texas–based Crypt Trip, whose 2019 full-length debut, Haze Country, *turned heads throughout Central Texas. The group served as Roky Erickson's backing live band near the end of his career as a performer.*

BONNIE BLOOMGARDEN

We played [the Southern California festival Burgerama] years ago because our dream was to see Roky play there. We went out in the back to chill out at one point, and Roky's guitar player Eli said that he liked our band. We were like, "What? Somebody in Roky's band likes us?" We were completely starstruck. Eli was amazing. He broke two strings that day and still played all those amazing sounds. I was excited he knew about Death Valley Girls. We talked for a while. Then we became friends and we asked them if they wanted to tour. They did. Then they asked our guitar player Larry [Schemel] to be in their band. All our dreams came true all of a sudden. We went up to New York and back around touring for about two weeks. We did a Halloween run and played Halloween shows the next year. There were die-hard fans in every city.

  We traveled in separate vans, but they were like family. The backstage rooms were for everyone. We all used the same gear, which was really nice and cool. We loved Roky and the band. Roky didn't do sound check, so we'd only see him a little bit every day, but those were very precious moments. Roky was hilarious. Every little thing he did was funny. He was really excited about the things he was excited about. We bought him *Creature with the Atom Brain* to watch in their van. He was so excited to get that. He talked about his favorite food, like orange-flavored sweet and sour pork. He loved hamburgers and would get several orders of French fries until he got the right one. He was super in love with Dana. Hearing the little things they said to each other was really sweet and amazing. He was a real gentleman as well.

We always watched his show. They changed the set list every night. I would never be able to do what they did in a million years. Roky didn't ever see the set list, but no one had to tell him. He knew what song it was instantly and would get into it the minute it started. His voice kept getting better every time. It was incredible. Roky was a real pro. Also, he really shaped our songwriting more toward the supernatural. Roky showed us that you don't have to just write love songs. You can write about ghosts and anything else. I didn't know you could write lyrics about the paranormal and hadn't heard songs about monsters before. Those songs are such a part of our lives. In fact, I can't remember a time when I didn't know Roky and the 13th Floor Elevators.[4]

Bonnie Bloomgarden fronts the Southern California rock outfit Death Valley Girls. The band channels influences from early ZZ Top and Black Sabbath to Led Zeppelin and the Rolling Stones. Bloomgarden and guitarist Larry Schemel occasionally performed in Roky Erickson's later solo band.

LARRY SCHEMEL

I heard "I Walked with a Zombie" for years and never realized Roky was repeating the same line the whole song. I only realized that when I was in Roky's band and was going over chords and lyrics. Maybe having a hook that immediately sticks with you makes the song feel as lyrically fleshed out as any other. I didn't really even think about where the first chorus or bridge was. I got hooked on that mantra. I've always been drawn to bands that write in that style like Lou Reed and the Velvet Underground. Lou Reed would write more complex songs, but he would also write ones with only a few lines that were just as effective. I guess the voice and the way the song is sung make it work. There's an X factor that certain artists have that can make a couple lines a classic song. Roky's songs are really cool, descriptive storytelling. Some are so simple that he didn't have to be Bob Dylan. I loved all that stuff about vampires and aliens. Roky wasn't writing [the Beatles'] "Love Me Do."

Roky played an amazing show when we met him at Burgerama. Then he stepped offstage and Bonnie and I were right there backstage. We all stopped and just looked at each other and smiled. Then Roky's guitar player Eli saw us. We introduced ourselves and said how much we loved the show. Eli asked if we were in a band, and we said we were in Death Valley Girls. He had heard our music and was a fan. We kept in touch from that day on. He called about a year and a half later and said, "Hey, Roky's gonna do a tour and wants to bring you guys out on the road." Of course we said yes. He called again maybe a week later and said, "We need another rhythm guitar player in our band." Being in Roky's [Hounds of Baskerville] band was a bit daunting. Eli sent me thirty-something Roky and Elevators songs to learn. I was already familiar with the material, but sitting down to learn the songs is different. The chords and structures with the Elevators were so interesting and bizarre. It was a challenge but really exciting to play all those songs.

The shows always had a positive energy and vibe. The audience members were all Roky fans to the core and were all glad to be in his presence. We were always walking a tightrope, with Eli changing set lists every night. Roky would veer off sometimes. Roky might skip a verse or be off in his own thing during "Slip inside This House," and we would have to follow his lead. The band had to be really connected and on the same page and groove. We were right behind Roky wherever he would go. We'd just go there if he would end the song early. It was amazing because Eli would say like, "We're gonna play 'Bermuda' tonight." "All right," Roky would say. "Let's do that." He would immediately know. The chords and lyrics were in his head. There was little practice before tours, so there was that rock and roll fun. The shows were always fun. There was never a sad or dark vibe. We were all happy to be there. Roky's son and wife were on the tour and that made the road a fun time.

There were nights when I could sense he wasn't having a good time. We would play the set and go to do the encore and Roky just didn't want to do it. He wasn't feeling it. We would be like, "All right, let's not do that." I never saw him be angry or sad. He was just in his head a lot of time, but he would talk about whatever subject you would bring up if you struck a conversation. He would remember old bands or what it was like playing with so-and-so at the Fillmore. He would remember things like that. I know there were hit-and-miss shows when he came back and hear things or see comments online about how he wasn't even there and needed to stop, but my experiences around him were positive. It was never like he didn't want to be there, though, especially with the family on the road. They helped. I never had a sense that he would rather be home, but I was only around him so much.

I'm glad I was in the band for that magical little sliver for the three years before he left us. His story is amazing. He came back and played pretty much until the end. The mental health issues sometimes overshadow how great a songwriter he was. He wrote so many memorable songs and was first and foremost a great songwriter and one of the best rock and roll singers. His scream was right up there with Little Richard. I think about the music when I think about Roky and the Elevators. The music alone is the gift that Roky shared with us. It's someone else's job to dissect the mental stuff. Each artist has a unique songwriting style and what they bring to the table, and Roky put a particular stamp on his. The influences from Buddy Holly and the Everly Brothers are in there, but he sure gave his music his own twist. You hear a song and go, "That's a Roky Erickson song."[5]

Larry Schemel serves as guitarist in the Southern California rock outfit Death Valley Girls. The band channels influences from early ZZ Top and Black Sabbath to Led Zeppelin and the Rolling Stones. Schemel and lead singer Bonnie Bloomgarden occasionally performed in Roky Erickson's band.

SCOTT H. BIRAM

Roky played Antone's with the Sexton brothers backing him one night when I was twenty years old. Roky's mom was there and read some weird poetry. The Sextons kept playing the intro to "Two-Headed Dog" over and over, and Roky had his arms crossed until Charlie and Will started getting mad from playing that intro over and over again. The show was free to get in, but you got a little door prize if you donated the suggested three dollars. I did and got measuring cups. I had Roky sign them. This was before Sumner got him back on his meds, and Roky had big dread-locks on the back of his head. He was looking pretty rough. "Roky," I said, "will you sign this?" His handler said, "Sign whatever you want, Roky." He said, "What the hell's this?" I said, "It's a door prize." Roky wrote R-A-Y in all caps. I don't think he knew what that meant either.

I had been listening to him for a couple years by then since I discovered the [*Where the*] *Pyramid Meets the Eye* tribute album. I particularly liked "Stand for the Fire Demon." His voice really hooked me in my twenties. I loved the Aliens' *The Evil One*, which is all classic rock–sounding with production like the Cars. His vocals sounded gravelly like Bob Seger. I liked his vocal styling, but I also liked the way he rambled the lines together. He would reel syllables off real fast even though there wasn't necessarily enough room for all of them. He would fit the words in anyway and ramble them off at the end. I also tend to say the words anyway if I have an idea I want to fit even though they don't in my song.

I played with Roky one Halloween and again on his seventieth birthday when I got to sit in on two or three songs, which was pretty cool. I didn't know what to do. I'm a one-man band and don't know how to play along with anyone, but it was a huge honor. We were upstairs where the show was, and I was standing there with Rok. They had a two-headed dog cake for his seventieth birthday. I said, "That's a pretty cool cake, Rok." He said, "Yep." "I don't know if you can eat that, it's so pretty." "I don't know how we're gonna transport it," he said. I went to a birthday and Christmas party over at Jegar's house with Roky one day. I'm good friends with Jegar. It was pretty cool watching Christmas cartoons with Roky. The dogs were going nuts. "Be careful of those dogs," he said. "They're crazy."

Roky's definitely been an influence on me. I have other influences, but he's one I have really held close to my heart. I think he was an angel put on earth. I know he sang about evil and all, but you can hear his heart coming out when he sings. He's a wonderful singer and was into sci-fi and horror movies, which isn't any different than the early Misfits. All those songs and titles were about singing about old B horror movies. Going back to that rambling thing, that's been a big influence. I was thinking of that last night as if I was giving advice to someone to not completely adhere to form as much as feeling and getting your idea out there. It makes the music itself have to change and have extra parts when you don't adhere to the form and you put in extra stuff, which makes the songs more unique and less stagnant.

I took psychedelics when I was in high school and college, and Roky's imagery and state of mind when he was writing or singing helped me connect. I write a lot of my songs in a half-dream state when I wake up in the middle of the night. I write stuff down real fast. It's not about following rules and rhymes as much as getting it out there, like watercolor splotches and not an oil painting. I feel like that's how it was with Roky. Songs don't need exact one-four-five chords with verse, chorus, bridge. They can lean toward that but not follow the rule. "I Walked with a Zombie" is just one line, but it's entertaining the whole way through. It's not really obvious that it's just one line unless someone tells you. You cover up the repetition with some spices.

The last time I saw Roky was backstage at the show he did with the Austin symphony last year. I talked to him for a minute and am glad I did. It was such a huge honor to say that I have played onstage with him multiple times and got to be around him in intimate settings. It was my wife and me, Jegar and his son, and Roky and his wife. "This is pretty cool, man," I said. "I'm looking forward to the show." "Yeah," he said. "It was pretty cool, wasn't it?" "Well," I said, "we haven't seen it yet." He was talking about the rehearsal the day before as if we were there, but he was right. It was pretty cool. The last thing he said to me is "This is my wife," even though I had met her a few times.[6]

Scott H. Biram's unique one-man band approach matches folk ("Wreck My Car") against fright ("Blood, Sweat, and Murder") as he combines influences including Doc Watson, Lightnin' Hopkins, and Mance Lipscomb with a punk rock attitude. His songs have been covered by Nashville Pussy ("Raisin' Hell Again") and Hank III ("Truckdriver").

CHRIS FULLERTON

I discovered Roky Erickson through the Okkervil River record *True Love Cast out All Evil*. I immediately gravitated toward songs like "Ain't Blues Too Sad" and "Goodbye Sweet Dreams" with those weird noises tucked into the back. I like effects like feedback, loop on a delay pedal, and sounds running backward. I always like something textural in the background. I don't picture studio recordings being played live because I know we can put as many tracks on a song with Pro Tools and overdubbing. I think sticking to the basics can be detrimental to some people. Songs stay boring. *True Love Cast out All Evil* is out there, well produced, and has many different textures from lo-fi to hi-fi. I was experimenting with songwriting in many different ways and wasn't sure which direction I wanted to go. *True Love Cast out All Evil* and Roky's different styles provided a good place for me to see that you can take songwriting in any direction you want.

Producers throughout his catalog really had control and knew what they were doing. I love the guitar sounds, microphones, preamps, and compression his producers used to give his recordings a different sound. Everything has a purpose and was mixed well. Nothing is abrasive unless it was on purpose. The bad feelings are pulled out unless they're pulled in on purpose. The shadows are exposed like they're supposed to be. Someone clearly knew what they were doing throughout his whole discography. I didn't know Roky, but he seemed to have that big personality that Austin and Texas thrive on. I feel like even before the dust settled here people were celebrating the uncanny. We have a strange and awesome place here in Austin.

Roky was a guidepost for our songwriting even when he was writing about supposedly silly shit like monsters. I'm not speaking for those like Roky who have schizophrenia, but I have epilepsy and think we who have neurological disorders all deal with those things. We see the world through a different lens. We're never gonna see things in a nine-to-five way, and we know we'll never be that even if we try. We have to worry all the time. We better know where we can go if we start going crazy in a restaurant so we don't affect the children in there. My wife framed it this way: you're part of an elite club that's been around for a long time with people like Joan of Arc who are mythologized and considered great artists. I see it as a gift. I think we owe a debt to Roky. Any musician worth their salt knows who Roky is and sees what he has done.

I relate and believe Roky really saw those ghosts. You can have hallucinations and bad headaches coming out of a seizure for about twenty-four hours. I was in the shower one time and saw the Virgin Mary. She was in the bathroom with me saying evil shit. I know that was not real. I knew it at the time, but I also draw on those experiences with my music with references related to the hallucinations in my songs. I can't help but think that there are references in Roky's songs, too. "Ain't Blues Too Sad" talks about his shock therapy. Nobody who didn't live through that knows the way to say, "Electricity hammers me through my head / Until nothing at all is backward instead."

I have no idea how Lil Wayne goes out there with epilepsy to the max. I really respect him. He has seizures in hotel rooms all the time. I tried to go up to a gig in Nashville last year and ended up pissing myself and throwing up all over my friend's car when I had a seizure. You have to psych yourself up. You start having delusions of grandeur. I start to ramp up. "I'm the shit," I say. "Nobody can outwrite me." I wasn't always that way. It's bred into me from being epileptic. I was writing shitty country songs until I wrote [Fullerton's 2017 album *Epilepsy Blues*]. Now, I can just freestyle. I can say anything anytime. I feel like that makes me a kindred spirit with Roky.[7]

Chris Fullerton sings country music bold ("Epilepsy Blues") and brave ("Seven Roman Candles"). The current Austin resident immediately turned heads with his debut, Epilepsy Blues *(2017). That record and his follow-up* Consider the Shoebill *were both released by Austin-based Eight 30 Records.*

WILL CULLEN HART

Roky was a major big deal who super influenced me. He had an incredible rock and roll voice and really sold the songs as the lead singer [of the Elevators] even though he didn't write the lyrics. They were the first true psych band to show up in San Francisco. I like the jug band thing, which is a psychedelic effect on the listener, but you don't have to be high for it to sound really cool. The Echoplex guitar was badass. They were making interesting sounds that trip your head. You get reverberations when the jugs came on like an earthquake. I've done tons of LSD, and it's very disorienting and does clear your head. You're like, "Oh, wow. That's what I've reached into."

"Two-Headed Dog" is obviously awesome. I worked at a radio station in Louisiana with a pretty good library. We had a Roky solo album there, and I played a couple tracks. Roky being from Texas is beautiful. He had an incredible charisma. I love the Elevators songs "You're Gonna Miss Me" and "Rollercoaster." He obviously grew up listening to good blues with writing lines as a teenager like: "You're gonna wake up one morning as the sun greets the dawn . . ." Also, Daniel Johnston had that song "I Met Roky Erickson": "[This guy came to McDonald's, said he wanted to do a video] / He said, 'I worked with Roky Erickson,' I said, 'Let's make a horror movie.'" They both were really sick.[8]

Will Cullen Hart cofounded the Elephant 6 Recording Company as well as the rock bands The Olivia Tremor Control and Circulatory System. Additionally, Cullen is a visual artist who has created nearly all the artwork for both bands.

EMILY NOKES

My bandmate [guitarist] Eric [Randall] made a mix tape with the clean-cut, cute Buddy Holly–sounding "Starry Eyes." I didn't know anything about Roky Erickson, but we would listen to him all the time on tour when we started in 2007. I didn't really get a load of Roky until I watched the documentary *You're Gonna Miss Me*. Whoa. He clearly was way more interesting than that one song that I've heard over and over and thought was a one-hit wonder. Also, we couldn't really be at a party around that time without hearing the 13th Floor Elevators. So, I connected the dots. His story was pretty intense. *The Evil One* was the first proper album I heard and is still my ultimate favorite. *The Evil One* is so good and the most perfect representation of Roky and his songs. Lyrics were such a huge part of Roky. His cadence and delivery are both so wild and such an interesting trip.

I almost thought the Elevators—and "You're Gonna Miss Me" specifically—were overplayed. That was when psych music in general was resonating with everyone at parties I was going to. Bands coming through town had that garage or psych sound. I remember looking into the 13th Floor Elevators and finding the Spades. I really had a time with that song "We Sell Soul," which I think was repurposed for the Elevators song called "Don't Fall Down." So good. So spooky and weird. I can never find a good recording of it, but I listen to the YouTube version. I really genuinely appreciate Roky. I wouldn't say Roky is a big influence here in Seattle right now, though.

I have never heard anyone who was able to cram so many words and sentences into a song while still singing and being in complete control of the melody. I have Roky's book *Openers II*, which has all those wild lyrics. His love songs are cute, but I think *The Evil One* specifically is the right kind of rock music to really hold those lyrics together. The way his brain works is so wild. I was in a Roky Erickson cover band for a while. Covering any song is tough for me because there's a way I like to write lyrics. Learning another style is difficult, but learning his was such a pleasure. The best feeling in the world is learning how to sing "The Wind and More" without your notes. That song doesn't make linear sense and the music is screaming along.

My Seattle musician friend Corey Brewer said he was considering putting together a Roky Erickson tribute band for Halloween one year. Seattle loves a cover band for Halloween. We got some other friends like [Pretty Girls Make Graves bassist and singer] Derek Fudesco and other friends in local bands. We played three or four shows around Halloween. Then we got it back together for other shows later on, but then people moved away. We always wanted to do it again. So fun. We were called the Unlimited Horrors. You really believe that Roky believes his lyrics. He wasn't writing horror rock for the sake of aesthetics or being cool—even though he was so cool. You can tell that he didn't really care whether you like it. He needed to get the lyrics and music out like a sermon. He was like, "These are all the ghosts, and we're gonna talk about them really quickly."

I have great respect for Roky's ability to be verbose. People are pretty minimalistic with lyrics and vocals, but I like him having it all in the front as if the music has to catch up to him. I have wrestled with how many words to be in a song or how clear or vague your message needs to be. I have listened to Roky so much that I'm sure it's seeped into how I understand and write music. He wasn't writing shock horror rock like Alice Cooper. There's an interview where he's on the radio, and he says, "I'm really at home with horror." Horror is comfortable for him and not scary. You get this sense that he's advocating for these characters who are friends. He's saying you have everything if you have ghosts. What a sweet thing to say. That's not scary.

He says the devil is innocent in "Bermuda." Everything is fine. The devil is protecting them. Roky's very genuine. He's at home in his home with the six televisions playing static. That doesn't bother him. He's just wired differently. Some of [his lyrical references] are esoteric like

Sputnik and the Cold War. "Creature with the Atom Brain" seems like a comic book or an old movie that's not scary but are maybe trying to be. I have never heard anyone like him. He's such a good singer. He can go through all those mouthfuls of lyrics and still have a good sense of melody and being the focal point. He was so good at that. That's what I love about that Spades song. I love the weird melody. It's just so weird. That's what makes *The Evil One* so good. The melodies are so good. *Don't Slander Me* is good, but *The Evil One* is better for melody's sake and better song quality.[9]

Emily Nokes is the singer-songwriter behind the Seattle-based indie rock band Tacocat. The band has released four full-length albums, from Shame Spiral *(2010) to* This Mess Is a Place *(2019).*

KASSIE CARLSON

I discovered Roky Erickson through an old boyfriend showing me his album *Never Say Goodbye,* which was recorded at Rusk State Hospital when he was institutionalized in Texas in the early seventies. I really liked his delivery and singing, especially on "Unforced Peace." What a beautiful song. Then I went down the hole of the Elevators and electric jug, which was really cool. Roky's story was really sad as it went on. There was a time in my life when I was reading everything about him I possibly could. He got busted for a single joint in Texas and pleaded insanity. He would have had a ten-year sentence in prison if he didn't. Messed up. One joint. Talk about the story of the failed drug war. I'm sure Roky had underlying mental illnesses, but I think being institutionalized pushed him over the edge in a really bad way.

Thorazine in the fifties, sixties, and seventies was really different. People were given twenty times the amount of psychiatric medications like Thorazine back then. Horrifying. I listened to *Never Say Goodbye* a lot when I was really into downer folk. Roky's lyrics were so cryptic but also really deep. I was wondering if his interest in aliens had to do with being completely isolated in the state hospital and whatever horrible experiences he had inside there. Thorazine can cause a blue pigmentation on the face and arms. I wonder if being in the hospital and seeing these effects on himself had anything to do with the alien influence. People were being experimented on in the fifties, sixties, and seventies in mental hospitals. Thorazine was described as a chemical lobotomy.

Roky's lyrics are so weird and not as straightforward as most songwriters are today. I like how they're like poetic lyrical mazes. I don't think that was purely from taking psychedelics. He had a beautiful mind. I feel like people think psychedelic music means that the person making it had to take hallucinogenic drugs. Psychedelic music is much more complicated. I don't think psychedelics should be used as a crutch to describe the music. The psychedelic mind is even more interesting than taking a drug and having an idea. I think Roky's mind was psychedelic without drugs. Psychedelic music today is driving music with weird sounds that rock. Also, Roky gets classified as rock, but he really was more like psychedelic folk with the weird lyrics he wrote.

I have a hard time listening to stuff after Rusk. The music is so sad and upsets me. Roky was thrown away by these people in the mental institution filling him with drugs and shocking him. They were depatterning and deprogramming him as well as criminalizing his mental illness. He had one joint. I'm happy for the music he left behind, but what a horrible, sad story. The songs from Rusk were just coming from such a deep, deep place of despair and pain, but they're so beautiful. He had so much to write about in there. I'm sure he was losing his mind on the medication in there. I can't imagine any of that stuff was easy to get off. People didn't understand schizophrenia then. We still don't now even though there's a better grasp. Everything was a shot in the dark then. Thorazine was just numbing. Everyone became like rubber shuffling around. So fucked.[10]

Kassie Carlson has been the lead singer for Guerilla Toss since forming in Boston in 2012. The band has released four full-length studio albums from the debut, Gay Disco (2013), *through* Twisted Crystal (2018). Rolling Stone *magazine named Guerilla Toss one of the top ten punk bands working today.*

DOM FLEMONS

I was drawn to fifties regional music and early sixties garage rock when I was starting to play guitar. I was deeply interested in that music before I got deep into traditional old-time music. I was going through the record store one day and found an original pressing of the 13th Floor Elevators' *Psychedelic Sounds of the 13th Floor Elevators* used around 1998. I thought the cover looked great. Then I looked at the back and saw the writing. The liner notes really intrigued me. Then I started listening and the songs were great blues-based music. I also heard an earlier version of what would become heavy metal. The Elevators were very different from the Beatles or the Zombies. They had a hard bluesy edge with links to Lightnin' Hopkins and Albert King. I thought the whole record was just so very intriguing. The blues base initially drew me in but then that huge sound did.

We take that for granted now, but such a huge sound coming from a record like *Psychedelic Sounds of the 13th Floor Elevators* was mind blowing. I heard more mainstream and well-known influences in bands like Led Zeppelin. The Elevators were totally different. I grew up in the mid to late nineties with noise rock and grunge bands like Nirvana. Hearing the Elevators gave me a window into some more experimental noise music that was currently out at that time like Sonic Youth. The effects on the guitars were fantastic. That experience led me into lots of sixties rock. People were much more conscious that records were an entire experience and not just a collection of hit songs. I got a little into Roky's solo music, but the Elevators really drew me. I later became interested in jug band music, which caused me to look into the Elevators again and in ways I originally didn't.

I realized that this particular rock band had a sideline influence on more contemporary jug band music the more I got into that scene. The Elevators had an influence in getting jug band music to evolve past the jug music from the twenties and thirties and the Jim Kweskin Jug Band in the fifties and sixties and into other similar bands like the Grateful Dead and the Charlatans in San Francisco. The Elevators made me see a very interesting evolution of folk and rock music and the areas in which they came together. Of course, the philosophies that were in the written materials with the music is interesting when you think about the *Anthology of American Folk Music* by Harry Smith. You can see that influence in the way Roky and the Elevators were thinking about the symbolic nature of things and the way music can create waves between people on a much deeper level than physical.

The electric jug is such a rarity. You can't buy that in a store. My music is all about rhythmic attack, and the Elevators had that the whole time. They didn't let you sit lackadaisically. Their music draws you in and gets you out of your seat and possibly to your spiritual plane. The jug is both a percussion instrument and a lower melodic instrument. You can do tuba-type sound and also play more like a saxophone or trumpet. There's an interesting connection between people listening to the Jim Kweskin Jug Band and the influence in the 13th Floor Elevators. The Kweskin band took a sound from New England and brought it to San Francisco. Also, the Elevators and Janis Joplin are definitely connected. Roky had a definite influence on her vocal style—especially when you hear a song like "Tell Mama."[11]

The years leading up to the psychedelic rock era from 1955 to 1965 are so interesting. You have the Kingston Trio doing "Tom Dooley" all the way to *Bringing It All Back Home* by Bob Dylan. You also have rhythm and blues. The strict segregation between popular musics began to break down. You have rock and roll innovators like Elvis Presley, Ray Charles, and Fats Domino. Then you have the British Invasion and Motown coming into play. Then there was Jimi Hendrix and the guitar hero culture of the late sixties. The Elevators aren't the first ones to come up in conversation, but people recognize a very familiar sound when they hear them. I think of music as a quilt or patchwork, and the Elevators are coming in at a time when you see the seams come together with different music. You can see the roots in the early stuff really clearly. Then it evolves.

I've always watched the evolution of bands. They very often start out as folk practitioners, but the mind begins to expand and grow. Most people think about Stevie Ray Vaughan or ZZ Top when it comes to Texas blues-rock. I wouldn't call the Elevators that, but you could hear where the music would evolve later in their songs. Creating their own sound made them a very innovative band. I have always looked at music in a multifaceted way. I generally look at an artist's catalog and then trace contemporaries and then who their influences were and then what came after. You'll find a line connecting many trees of different types of music. For example, the Beatles were influenced by Buddy Holly, Jerry Lee Lewis, Carl Perkins, and Little Richard. Those things become very clear when you get deep into their catalog.

You really had to sit and figure things out before the twenty-first century, especially with a band like the 13th Floor Elevators. That first record didn't really give me anything concrete. I had to figure out who they were before the internet, but that led me down many different journeys and pathways. I've always tried to be comprehensive in my own music. I have a good sense of what came before and after so I do something three dimensional—at least in my mind. Two dimensional can seem put-on or leaning into stereotypes when performing. However, my ears are really open to anything when it comes to listening. The ears can be very interesting with what they like. The Elevators had the same quality as early seventy-eight recordings just because of the nature of the way they put the record together, very lo-fi, plus Roky sings in a way that's so uninhibited. He was just so distinctive.[12]

Former Carolina Chocolate Drops lead singer and banjoist and two-time Grammy winner Dom Flemons has adopted the nickname The American Songster. He has released several albums as a solo artist, from 2014's Prospect Hill *through 2019's* Black Cowboy.

DEAN WAREHAM

My English friend had *Easter Everywhere* and played it for me around 1989. I came of age in the punk years musically but never really warmed to the whole flower power and positivity ethos with the San Francisco psychedelic bands. Then the 13th Floor Elevators came along and hit me as being a much darker band like the Velvet Underground. They weren't hippie bullshit. My friend [guitarist and vocalist] Derek [See] plays with the Chocolate Watchband and the Rain Parade now. He's way younger, but he alerted me to the fact that all the stereo mixes of *Easter Everywhere* are all from a later remix. The original two-track master was lost. I got into a few Roky solo songs like "Starry Eyes" and "Don't Slander Me," which are pretty phenomenal, but I would just hear his songs here and there. They're great pop songs. You hear the Buddy Holly in them.

We saw Roky perform about eight years ago at Southpaw in Brooklyn on December 30. It was great to see him onstage, but I didn't really enjoy his band. They were too good. He had a guitar player who definitely was too good. I came to see Roky play. I didn't come to hear someone shred guitar solos throughout all his songs, but his performance was fine. He wasn't stumbling or anything. I also saw Glen Campbell late in life and that was too much. I see Roky and the Elevators' influence is in the paisley underground bands like Jesus and Mary Chain and Primal Scream. They got really into that stuff in England in the late eighties, but then there were bands like Spacemen 3, the Brian Jonestown Massacre, and now Mercury Rev. Bands like Rain Parade synthesize the late sixties psychedelia with punk, which was already there with Roky and the 13th Floor Elevators.[13]

Dean Wareham founded the band Galaxie 500 in 1987 but left to form Luna in 1991. He has released albums with Britta Phillips as Britta and Dean since Luna's breakup in 2005. The duo scored the Noah Baumbach film The Squid and the Whale *in 2005.*

PETE KEMBER

I discovered the 13th Floor Elevators when I was going on seventeen years old. Finding these things was a level of hit and miss back in those days. You had to know the right people at the record stores. I found the Elevators at a record shop that looked pretty cool. I loved them. A friend had the *Nuggets* collection with "You're Gonna Miss Me" on it. I eventually bought *The Psychedelic Sounds of the 13th Floor Elevators*. I think it was a bootleg. The tags had been taken off the back, and it was messed around. I was blown away by the whole thing. I loved the sound. The jug was the most genius element. They reissued the album on compact disc with a decent remaster, which really made a strong impression. "Reverberation" and "Rollercoaster" were the real kickers for me. We started a psychedelic rock appreciation group called the Reverberation Club in the town we lived in named after that track. The song was such an electric, awesome, channeling vibe for the music. The song really resonated.

I think I had already done acid by then. I went on a backpacking trip around Europe when I was seventeen. I didn't really go to that many places, but I spent lots of time in Amsterdam. Some dude offered acid in the park for something ridiculously cheap like forty cents a hit. I bought some. So, I recognized the territory from the time I saw the Elevators' first album sleeve. The whole psychedelic drug music from the late sixties was really interesting to me. I felt like the Elevators were mavericks with something really awesome about them, but the sleeve is really what drew me in. I would say that about most of the records I bought back then. You can only bother the dude in the store to play you so many records before you have to buy one. I had these very strong memories when I saw the Elevators' sleeve and also the Red Krayola album *The Parable of Arable Land*.

I used to wait by the record store when school came out in my home-town, Rugby [England]. The dude had really fucking good taste with new wave, psych, and punk bootlegs. I found Red Krayola there and pored over *The Parable of Arable Land* for two or three years but never purchased it that fortnight. I remember it disappearing off the shelves. "Who bought that fucking record?" I asked the guy. "It's been sitting there three years." "No one bought it," he said. "I just took it off the shelf." "Oh," I said. "I wanna buy it." "You know what?" he said. "You can have it." I feel both of those were awesome. So were all the early IA sleeves like Power Plant's. I thought they were really cool. They were the definite way into psych rock for me. Then I tried mushrooms and listened to that album, and it became a regular one for psychedelic excursions.

You understand those sleeves when you're going through the psyche-delic experience. The Elevators were this awesome myth back then. We couldn't find photos anywhere. I started to collect all the records by Radar Records, who put those records out in the UK. Very cool label. The first record they put out was "I Love the Sound of Breaking Glass" by Nick Lowe, which went to number one. They reissued the Elevators and Red Krayola. They were doing all kinda stuff like those and the *Howdy to the Lone Star State* little promo color book to introduce the UK to all this Texas psych music. I was on Silvertone Records, and that guy had been Radar Records. He gave me all the stuff I didn't have.

I was a hip enough kid that I have relied on intuition my whole life, which has never let me down. I had a feeling with those records. "Roll-ercoaster" was a really next-level song. My band Spacemen 3 covered it twice. One was seventeen-minute-long twelve-inch vinyl, which was my favorite version. I think Tommy Hall's lyrics were so dialed in and brilliantly psychedelic. I met him a few years ago when I was on Reprise Records in the nineties. Some dude who worked there said, "Oh, you know Tommy Hall? Call him up." I never did. Maybe seven years ago we had to kill three hours between sound check and the gig one night and weren't far from the Tenderloin.

I said, "You know what? I can even remember the name of the fucking hotel. We'll just walk down there for shits." We found his hotel, which is a total central-ghetto fucking hotel. We walked in. There was a dude in a little glass cage there. "Does Tommy Hall live here?" He shot us the dirtiest look you can imagine. "Yeah, he lives on the fourth floor." So, we knocked on his door. I said, "Hey, Tommy. I'm a friend of Paul Drummond's and I'm in a band called Spacemen 3. Just wanted to say hey." He went into this psychedelic sermon, which was awesome. We recorded a little of it, but I felt I might be pushing my luck.

I have every solo record Roky did, but it started getting really fucking repetitive. I have about the first twenty-five records. I love his solo career and especially the Buddy Holly stuff. He punked out in a really beautiful way. He was an original. I don't listen to it as much now, but occasionally I'll feel the need for the metal surge of Roky solo. The Elevators were a totally different thing for me, but I definitely don't hate Roky's solo material. I probably have fifteen versions of some songs. I think there's something really sublime about what he does sometimes.[14]

Pete Kember, who is better known by his stage name Sonic Boom, was a founding member, vocalist, and bassist of Spacemen 3 from 1982 through the band's dissolution in 1991. He has recorded under the names Spectrum and Experimental Audio Research as a solo artist.

JONATHAN DONAHUE

I came to Roky Erickson through people who were bathed in cosmic radiation like Wayne Coyne and Michael Ivins from the Flaming Lips. Then I traveled to Austin and Dallas and lived in Oklahoma City and realized that Roky was really one of the first cosmic American eggs to hatch. He wasn't my Big Bang, but he certainly seemed to be in that area. I grew up in the woods in the Catskills [in New York State] so I wouldn't have discovered him on the radio. It took a while to hear the high voltage, but then I pieced the words together. They hit me like some are hit with opera. Roky was leaning into this other world. I couldn't tell if he was trying to get in or get back out, but what he was grasping for—or repulsed by—in the world and its mystery resonated pretty deeply with me. I only later understood the challenges and the depths that he was facing mentally.

Roky's lyrics took a while to penetrate deeper into me, but I could see myself in the painting on the wall in songs like "If You Have Ghosts." I could cut out a shape and fit my own likeness into these word paintings Roky was singing about. Roky and Daniel both had to use many different ways to express themselves. I don't know if it was an explosion of inner talent or perhaps desperation. "How do I get this out so the common tongue can grasp it?" I was in the Lips for a while in the late eighties, and people in Oklahoma City and Austin had a very common collective consciousness. The Deep Ellum scene in Dallas had a similar cosmic drifter thing. I remember seeing the drifters the first time I pulled into OKC on a Greyhound. Drifting wasn't limited to people riding on freight trains.

There was an effortless cosmic floating—but without an actual guidance system—in this holy spirit with the musicians I was meeting then. Took me a while to understand how they first felt this heat. I learned through the Butthole Surfers and others in the early psychedelic explosion in Austin like Roky. I learned to cut to the chase as a songwriter from Roky and even say something that may seem awkward or vague on paper. It's the best and most direct way to describe something in your mind. You find yourself going toward that challenge in the lyrics instead of a cleverness, a flourish of the pen, or a double entendre. Daniel had that root Sanskrit lyricism emotionally coded in so deep in a way that maybe even surpassed Roky.

Roky taught me to follow desperation down to the root. I learned not be fettered by trying to make it fit into this outside puzzle piece. Just say it like you see it. Stand back without needing or looking for a result. You don't need the audience to go bonkers because they understand you completely and psychologically. I understood over time that he had to face such a resistance mentally. He had the Beethovenness. My god, the things he had to overcome in his daily life—let alone putting together a three-minute song or going on tour and lasting more than an hour onstage. The heartstrings connect when you hear more about him from people who knew him in Austin. What he had to navigate and overcome connected with me most powerfully.

I think people will have to dig for Roky and the root [of psychedelic rock] in forty, fifty years. Soil swallows the root over time, but I was glad I was around during his time. I wasn't twenty in 1966, but I can say I was around while those roots were growing. Maybe after another ten years all that will be left are the upper branches. The roots will be buried. I wouldn't worry myself about it as much as I am grateful to be around something that would spiral around in an upward way. I think over time people will be able to see the magnitude of his cosmic radiation spectrum, which wasn't limited to weirdness, psychosis, a period of time, or a fuzz box. Roky was something much more expansive with radio waves way up to gamma. There was a larger dial to tune in to with Roky and his music.

Everything in Austin came down to Roky in the sixties. He was the early archetype that set Austin off on the trajectory to the moon in the eighties and early nineties when everyone in the world wanted to move there and be a part of this Texas psychedelia goulash. You have to embrace weirdness and the fragile people. You can tell when a town has had its fill of weird. I am talking to you here today from Woodstock, New York, literally in the parking lot where they say Bob Dylan met Van Morrison. Woodstock is no longer weird. Woodstock is living on something that's long decayed because it didn't support the weirdness. Woodstock sought to push weird out on the fringe because they couldn't capitalize on it financially. There are weird people left in Austin even after Daniel and Roky. How well the city supports them will determine the nature of the town going forward.[15]

Jonathan Donahue has served as singer and chief songwriter for indie rockers Mercury Rev since the band formed in 1989. The Buffalo, New York–bred band's albums span from Yerself Is Steam *(1989) through* Bobbie Gentry's the Delta Sweete Revisited *(2019).*

ISAIAH MITCHELL

I lived in Boerne, Texas, until I was eight and took my dad's *The Psychedelic Sounds of the 13th Floor Elevators* record when I got older. I liked the cover, the weird jug sounds in the background, and Roky's screaming and stream-of-consciousness vocal delivery. His voice was hypnotic and out of the box. "Step inside This House" is a dark, deep, spooky masterpiece. So, I was into the Elevators, but I was more massively into Roky's solo music. *Casting the Runes* was the record that changed everything and made me see music differently. I had never heard anyone sing about vampires and zombies. I had heard the Misfits, but solo songs like "The Wind and More" were on a different level because of how he crams all these words with his delivery. Also, his singing was so spot on. You don't hear many people singing like that. It really is an art.

I played in a few Roky cover bands in my twenties. Songs like "The Wind and More" and "Bloody Hammer" are hard to sing, but I love dark and spooky music and horror films. I think of even numbers as light and odd ones as dark, and I prefer odd numbers. They're more real and honest. I don't like peppermint, incense, and bubble gum. Light music often sounds really tame and bland. I think when you get someone who's tapping into the darker side of expression and music maybe you're seeing more inside them. Darkness is a more genuine way of expressing. When people say they're happy, I always think, Are you really that happy? I guess you could say the same about dark, but when people tap into it you're able to see what's really going on.

Roky's songs aren't all dark. "I Walked with a Zombie" is a really fun, upbeat fifties pop song. He's walking with a zombie and saying, "Let's have a good time." The music helps carry those words. "Bloody Hammer" might seem cartoonish because he's talking about comic books and horror movies, but it's not campy at all. The Misfits are more cartoonish to me. Also, the Explosives are on fire on that recording, so everything sounds real. They were kicking serious ass. I think Roky sometimes was a little tongue-in-cheek, but he had a pretty far-off look in his eye and long fingernails in interviews. He was living in the land of what he was writing about like worshiping the devil. You can tell when someone's faking it. Roky was out there and believed what he was singing.

I appreciate his style. I like getting rhythmic with my vocal delivery, but I don't think I could write like him. "Bloody Hammer" is an impressive, gifted vocal delivery. I don't think I have ever heard someone give it up like that. The cadence and flow fit perfectly with him cramming the lyrics in. He's impressive and insane and not stuttering or going over the measure, which is extremely hard—and especially when you're playing guitar and focusing on a completely different rhythm. I see his influence big-time on the psych rock world today. Look at the Levitation festival in Austin, which is the Elevators and Roky. Any psych band will cite the Elevators as an influence. They did something different than other bands with the fuzz and jugs. There was something really genuine about them, too. They were doing what came naturally and not being impersonators.

I saw Roky with the Explosives right when the movie *You're Gonna Miss Me* came out. Amazing. The band was insane. I still have the Roky T-shirt from that show and the psychedelic peace necklace they handed out when you went to see them. I went by myself and saw Roky's brother out in the crowd being his manager. The show was fierce, but I've seen him since then when it wasn't as good. He was looking around during the songs and wasn't on his game. I didn't stay the whole show and felt bad. The show was a bummer, but at least I was very lucky to see him that first time with my favorite incarnation of his solo band. That show was a game changer for me. Listen to any psych band nowadays. You can go, "Oh, the Elevators did that first." I listen to Roky more than almost anyone. I was probably influenced without it even being intentional because I listen to his records so much.

His legacy will be being left of center. He wrote "You're Gonna Miss Me" when he was fifteen. What a great, classic song. A fifteen-year-old writing that song is something. Roky will influence the Rob Zombies of the world. The Elevators' work was a cut above all else in that genre. They were doing it first and didn't even know what they were doing. They were still doing rhythm and blues, but they had acid involved. They made a specific sound. The Elevators will always be regarded as the first psychedelic band. They were at the top of the pyramid for sure. Their music will constantly be discovered by young people forever. They will get the respect they deserve. Their music gets spread by word of mouth and that has more weight. Underground people sharing has more weight. Roky was a pioneer and a pilgrim.[16]

Isaiah Mitchell serves as guitarist in the San Diego–based instrumental psychedelic rock group Earthless. The band's studio albums, including the debut, Sonic Prayer *(2005), and* Black Heaven *(2018), display a deep classic rock influence from bands like Black Sabbath and Led Zeppelin.*

PARKER GRIGGS

I got into sixties garage rock music when I was in high school and got the *Nuggets* psychedelic box set. The Elevators and the Seeds were the first ones I really got into. *Easter Everywhere* is in my top ten favorite albums ever. The Elevators had such a creative style. I liked everything about it. *Easter Everywhere* is solid the whole way through, but their "Baby Blue" cover and "I Had to Tell You" stick out. "I Had to Tell You" has lots of emotion. Their songs influenced me as a songwriter when I started doing Radio Moscow. My song called "She's Mine" definitely was inspired by the riff in "Fire Engine." I wrote that [almost twenty years ago], and the riff was like the Yardbirds with a really sixties garage-blues sound. *Easter Everywhere* was very inspirational even though we have different styles. I like how they made the album flow in one piece with a real psychedelic feel. It takes you right back to that time.[17]

Parker Griggs is a singer-songwriter and multi-instrumentalist for the psychedelic rock band Radio Moscow. Griggs cites Blue Cheer, Cream, and Led Zeppelin as major influences.

CHARLES MICHAEL PARKS JR.

I know Roky Erickson's "Two-Headed Dog," but I mostly know about his mental health issues and addiction problems. I have been playing shows and touring since I was sixteen and have seen both in a big way in this business. You're gonna see a whole host of mental illness in any business where you're trying to make people like you. You see it all the time in very famous people who are gods onstage and then are total wrecks when they go offstage. Mental health issues can develop over time with cultural pressure and societal norms on top of the obvious chemical imbalances you're born with and need to medicate. We revere actors and musicians in the public eye so much because they give us a dopamine jump that we associate with music.

People with mental illnesses are more likely to step outside their comfort zones to perform and be creative. People with mental illnesses were revered for different reasons before institutionalized medicine. They

were considered shamans who can tap into subconscious things we can't
see. We still associate musicians as somebody who can break through the
firmament and dive into the other world that people don't understand.
Then people telling you that you can see things no one else can layers
on more illness. You see that throughout all rock and roll. Look at early
Fleetwood Mac. [Original Fleetwood vocalist and guitarist] Peter Green
went absolutely nuts. He just left mentally.

You get anything from inflated egos, becoming completely neurotic,
agoraphobic, or not being able to relate to society. Healthy diet and ex-
ercise are the best ways to stop [mental illness from further declining].
I can't say I'm on that one hundred percent of the time or even half the
time. I have friends that take pharmaceutical medicines or natural anti-
depressants like St.-John's-wort because the tour hangover is a really big
thing. We'll be out for a month and play twenty-eight shows in a row.
You're going, going, going, never stopping, always getting back into the
van. Then you get home and you have three months off. What the fuck
do you do with yourself? You have no job. I don't really have any friends
to hang out with at home to see how depression might creep in. Some
people can't get away from that lifestyle when they're not playing. They
feel unimportant.

[Whether the performing high] is worth the coming down depends
on how much you believe in your own art. There's a whole spectrum:
people who write their songs and perform them, people who are good
performers who have their songs written for them, etcetera. I think the
completely vapid people who go out and have nothing to say in their
music but are there to do drugs and chase tail [feel empty offstage]. Going onstage is a high if you perform well and feel good about the songs.
You have just wasted your whole day if you go onstage and put on a shitty
show. That tacks on lots to mental stress, but it's worth it if you get onstage and get that church feeling that everyone's connected and you're
doing really well.

Not many people can tap into that feeling outside of the creative and
performing arts. I would say it's worth it about eighty percent of the time.
Having the conviction to say what you want to say as a person who is alive
on the planet today in this one section of time [is fulfilling]. That doesn't
always coincide with what people want at the time. I get messages from
fans trashing us all the time a year later because we don't have a keyboard

player anymore. Hearing that's hard, but I'm not writing songs for anyone but myself and my friends. The rest comes along with it. I have to believe in this or I can't do it. There's no part of me that wants to get up there and sing pop songs that somebody else wrote.

I can't imagine Roky in the sixties. My dad [actor and hit sixties singer Michael Parks] was touring then. He and the band would get together and put a demo together on a reel-to-reel machine. Then they would cut the best parts of their songs onto the reel. Then they would drive to every venue they wanted to play across the country. They would sit the bar manager down for five minutes if they could catch him. They would play the reel and get the show. They did that for the whole tour route. Then they would get all the way back home and do the tour all again with shows. They're going all the way up to Colorado playing their reels for people and not getting paid. I can't imagine for someone like Roky with mental illness and the way music was promoted back then. Nobody had ever heard raw, exciting music like the 13th Floor Elevators, but imagine what problems would go along with it.[18]

Charles Michael Parks Jr. serves as lead singer and multi-instrumentalist in the Nashville-based All Them Witches. The band has released several studio albums including the debut, Our Mother Electricity, *through ATW. Parks's late father, Michael Parks, starred in movies directed by Robert Rodriguez, Kevin Smith, and Quentin Tarantino.*

AMBROSE KENNY-SMITH

I was introduced to the 13th Floor Elevators by a good friend when I was about fourteen. Their unworldly, raw music was on repeat constantly throughout my teenage years. The lyrics are like an open-ended book at times and seem to adapt to a different way of processing the existential world. [Roky's album *Gremlins Have Pictures*] is a classic. Roky's "Heroin" is the best version ever done, but "The Interpreter" is my favorite. My songs are influenced by him in a way. I'm always giving myself headaches from trying to wail like Roky. I only got to see him perform once in Australia at the Golden Plains Festival in 2012, but it was so great to see a band that were really backing him so well throughout the whole show. The crowd was with them all the way. I am so grateful that I got to see him live. The way all the songs are recorded live gives it such an amazing and distinctive driving power.

The 13th Floor Elevators are still one of my favorite bands. They were a massive influence on us—especially me—when King Gizzard and the Lizard Wizard and The Murlocs started. I have made many friends over the years through sharing the love of his music and have seen it open up a lot of sheltered minds. Sometimes I might overthink an idea too much. You're better off taking a chance rather than being afraid of what people might think and or how it might be perceived by the public. You can hear how Roky can nail a moment in its true form at times. The best songs are the more honest ones that capture that high energy without trying too hard.[19]

Vocalist and keyboard player Ambrose Kenny-Smith founded influential Australian psychedelic rock band King Gizzard and the Lizard Wizard with lead singer Stu Mackenzie in 2010. The band has released more than a dozen records from the debut, 12 Bar Bruise *(2012), through* L. W. *(2021).*

STUART BRAITHWAITE

The 13th Floor Elevators were really a cornerstone band when I was getting into music in the late eighties. The Elevators were really influential and were name checked a lot. There was a band called Splash 1 named after the Elevators song. I have been a fan ever since, and we got to collaborate with Roky once on a Mogwai song. I hadn't heard his solo work in the eighties, but I got to hear pretty much everything over the years. Roky had a real unique way of putting words to music. I don't think he cared how the lines worked or if they fit into the song. He would just say something and make it fit somehow, which is almost impossible to do. I get completely confused if the words don't have a beat when I write a song, but there's a line in "If You Have Ghosts" that's like three in one.

Roky wrote so many more like that. He also went for really strange harmonies in his songs. He's the least contrived musician of all time. He just wanted to express himself. His songs aren't about anything else. There's no external factor. He was really unique in that way. There's a real innocence and poetry to his life. I have also been a horror film fan my whole life. The two biggest influences on my life have been psychedelic music and horror films. The fact that one of my favorite singers is totally happy to bring those two things together is something I've really adored. He followed the punk rock ideal from the decade before. I think Roky was totally punk to the core. "I Had to Tell You" from *Easter Everywhere* is one of my favorite songs. "Rollercoaster" is too. "You Don't Love Me Yet" is amazing. "Two-Headed Dog." I really love the *True Love Cast out All Evil* album. Incredible. Wonderful.

I pretty much love every Roky Erickson song I have heard. I think his unique chord progressions and melodies are a true sign of being an original. He didn't seem like he was trying to sound like someone else. He puts something in his songs that no one else says and with that twinkle in his eye. What an amazing dude. Getting to work with him was really awesome too. I didn't know him well, but we were so lucky to have his music. I found that he exuded that special something the few times I met him. He was a special guy. His brother was looking after his affairs around then. We recorded the song "Devil Rides" remotely and then came to Austin and went into the studio with him. We really just recorded his vocal in the studio since we'd recorded the song. The experience was really cool. We went to this local ice cream store [called Amy's Ice Cream] in Austin that had invented a Roky ice cream.

The whole experience with him was great. Roky was totally up for it. I think he was pretty excited that younger musicians were getting into his music. He was so happy to be doing the gig, a lovely guy and totally personable. Most people aren't as unique as him. Roky had it all right there on his own. Roky will be considered one of the greatest psychedelic performers and songwriters of all time when people look back at his music. I never really wrote songs copying what he did, but his legacy and how free he was musically really inspired me. We definitely feel a part of the legacy that Roky, the Velvet Underground, and the Jimi Hendrix Experience created. We write songs and perform like they did: as if there are no rules. Roky was a huge influence in that way.[20]

Stuart Braithwaite serves as guitarist in the groundbreaking Glasgow, Scotland–based space rock band Mogwai, which was named after creatures in the movie Gremlins.

GHOST TRACKS

PATRICK MCGARRIGLE

Roky was very sick in his last four years. I tried to inspire him to seek medical care by paying for tests. I got nowhere with that. I tried to convince him not to go on a European tour three Octobers ago because I was so alarmed. His heart was out of rhythm, and he was obviously having heart problems. I went backstage at Hardly Strictly [Bluegrass Festival in San Francisco's Golden Gate Park] in October 2019 and asked him point-blank, "Roky, do you want me to raise hell and get you medical attention? You need it. You're not sleeping and you're obviously water retentive and out of breath." He looked me square in the eye and said very assertively, "No, man. Don't do anything." Now I know Roky was a special-needs person so I had to battle with that statement, but still. He was no dummy.

Roky could have wound up in a nursing home if he would have sought treatment. Dana herself had her mother die on the table while undergoing angioplasty tests. So I was between a rock and a hard place—damned if I did and damned I if I did not. I did write a letter to management with my concerns saying, "Guys, he's not forgetting his lyrics. He was out of breath." This was obvious after watching videos of him that I had made. I wrote him a letter several months before he died. It was kind of an old-person-type letter requesting he seek help and talking of the world of spirit. He and Dana came over soon after, wanting to borrow fifty bucks for gas and food to get them by a day before his allowance was due. I noticed their car had close to no brakes. They said, "Yeah." I mentioned that the shop had said it would be eighteen hundred bucks to fix them. I told him and Dana to be expecting me and that I would fix them using scrapyard parts. Roky helped me bleed the brakes.

I [took] some [photos] while there. You can see how relaxed and happy he was in general. He still enjoyed doing something different from normal. Roky was driven creatively by his need to [deviate] from normal, but he bored easily and needed new stimulus. The brake job took a few days. I asked Roky to establish in writing for me who was in the original Bleib Alien band before I wrapped everything up. I planned to approach Craig and see if he might be willing to help Roky by releasing rights to enough songs so as to let Roky release an album all by himself with material we have. That would enable Roky to sign and sell them to his fans to generate some needed cash and independence from everyone involved. I was fishing for ideas to have him make some cash. He could have easily gotten a hundred bucks an album from his most devoted fans for a limited edition pressing of a thousand albums. He wrote out the names on a piece of paper and signed it. I'm now the very proud but sad owner of that paper, but then he left us. Those were the end days.[1]

Patrick McGarrigle is the younger brother of Cold Sun guitarist Tom McGarrigle and friend of Mikel Erickson. He lives in Austin.

DANA GAINES ERICKSON

Roky was writing his own music when our house burned down in 1973. We had gone somewhere to score some weed and were getting gas at a station when the police pulled up. "Roky," they said. "Your house is on fire." Where did the police come from? How did they know we were there? We didn't believe them at first. You can't trust them. We went home and sure enough, the house was on fire. Roky ran into the embers to gather up all his music. He had just written "Two-Headed Dog" and "Bloody Hammer." I was just looking at the album *True Love Cast out All Evil* and thought, My god, when did he write this? I think most stuff was in his book *Openers*. He hits an octave in the original song "True Love Cast out All Evil" that's like nothing you've ever heard. The original was when he was really young and that beautiful new melody put chills on your arm.

Roky was the kindest human being on this earth. He was so loving and a very bright star. Heavenly. His music was so brilliant and incredible. He took all the sound when he left this room. Now, it remains so quiet and still here. I miss him so much. He always would hold my hand when we were together. He would never let me walk from the car into the house without holding my hand. We had disagreements, but I got out of the car one time [after a disagreement] and remember so clearly that he grabbed my hand. "Why would you hold my hand?" I asked. "I don't deserve it. I've been angry." Roky held my hand and walked me in. "I'm sorry," I said. "I love you for doing that." We had an agreement if we were having a disagreement to say, "I love you." That would end all conversation. We had a way of not letting the world press our buttons.

Roky had this big, blue chair in the living room that he would sit in and play his music. He had the Amazon Echo set up where it can play any song he requested. I couldn't do anything right after he passed, so I crawled into that chair. I wanted to watch the film *Jesus of Nazareth*, which takes you to Nazareth for a whole day because it's a seven-hour film. So, I crawled into this chair and was watching the film, which was the only comfort I could find. Then the film stopped all of a sudden. Roky came on the Echo [unprompted] singing his song "Haunt" [with the lyric, "I wonder if she knows her own strength / I wonder if she knows what she can do / With her in my arms I'm never, ever, ever, ever blue"]. Blew my mind. *Jesus of Nazareth* came back on right after the song was over. What can I say? Thank you, Jesus.[2]

SELECTED DISCOGRAPHY FOR
THE 13TH FLOOR ELEVATORS

1. *The Psychedelic Sounds of the 13th Floor Elevators*, International Artists, 1966
2. *Easter Everywhere*, International Artists, 1967
3. *Live*, Snapper Music, Ltd., 1968
4. *Bull of the Woods*, International Artists, 1969
5. *The Best of the 13th Floor Elevators*, Reactive Records, 1995
6. *Best of the 13th Floor Elevators: Manicure Your Mind*, M.I.L. Multimedia, 1997
7. *The 13th Floor Elevators: His Eye Is on the Pyramid*, Snapper Music, Ltd., 1999
8. *The Psychedelic World of the 13th Floor Elevators*, Snapper Records, 2002
9. *Going Up: The Very Best of the 13th Floor Elevators*, Charly Records, 2004
10. *The Complete Elevators IA Singles Collection*, Acme Records, 2007
11. *Sign of the 3 Eyed Men*, International Artists / Charly Records, 2009
12. *Psychedelic Circus*, Sunset Blvd Records, 2009
13. *Music of the Spheres*, International Artists, 2011 (vinyl only)
14. *You and I and Me*, Sunset Blvd Records, 2020

SELECTED DISCOGRAPHY
FOR ROKY ERICKSON

1. *Bermuda / The Interpreter, Rhino Records, 1977*
2. *Roky Erickson and the Aliens, CBS Records, 1980*
3. *The Evil One, 415 Records, 1981*
4. *Don't Slander Me, Pink Dust Records, 1986*
5. *Gremlins Have Pictures, Pink Dust Records, 1986*
6. *Casting Runes, Five Hours Back, 1987*
7. *Holiday Inn Tapes, Fan Club, 1987*
8. *Click Your Fingers Applauding the Play, New Rose Records, 1988*
9. *Openers, Five Hours Back, 1988*
10. *Live at the Ritz 1987, Fan Club, 1988*
11. *Where the Pyramid Meets the Eye, Sire Records, 1990*
12. *Live in Dallas 1979, Fan Club, 1992*
13. *Beauty and the Beast, Sympathy for the Record Industry, 1993*
14. *All That May Do My Rhyme, Trance Syndicate, 1995*
15. *Demon Angel: A Day and a Night with Roky Erickson, Triple X Records, 1995*
16. *Roky Erickson and Evilhook Wildlife, Sympathy for the Record Industry, 1995*
17. *Never Say Goodbye, Emperor Jones, 1999*
18. *Don't Knock the Rok!, Norton Records, 2004*
19. *I Have Always Been Here Before, Shout! Factory, 2005*
20. *Halloween, Norton Records, 2008*
21. *True Love Cast out All Evil, ANTI- Records, 2010*
22. *May the Circle Remain Unbroken, Light in the Attic Records, 2021*

SELECTED VIDEOGRAPHY
FOR ROKY ERICKSON

1. *Demon Angel: A Day and Night with Roky Erickson, Halloween 1984,* Triple X
    Records, 1984
2. *You're Gonna Miss Me: A Film about Roky Erickson,* Palm Pictures, 2007

NOTES

FRONT MATTER

1. Jon Dee Graham, text message to Brian T. Atkinson, July 29, 2020.
2. Sam Dunn and Ralph Chapman, *ZZ Top: That Little Ol' Band from Texas*, IMDb, 2019, https://www.imdb.com/title/tt9015306/fullcredits.
3. Madison Bloom, "Roky Erickson Dead at 71," *Pitchfork*, June 1, 2019, accessed July 5, 2020, www.pitchfork.com.
4. Keven McAlester, *You're Gonna Miss Me: A Film about Roky Erickson*, Palm Pictures, 2007.
5. Henry Rollins, email interview with Brian T. Atkinson, September 15, 2019.

PROLOGUE: ROKY ERICKSON

1. Joe Nick Patoski, "The Roky Erickson, 1975," *Not Fade Away* 1, no. 1 (Fall 1975), June 17, 2010, accessed July 5, 2020, Joe Nick Patoski, www.joenickp.com. For more on Spades drummer John Kearney, see "An Interview with Spades' Drummer John Kearney," 1960s Texas Music, January 31, 2003, accessed August 7, 2020, scarletdukes.com/st/tm_spadesint.html.

OPENERS I: 13TH FLOOR ELEVATORS

1. King Coffey, interview with Brian T. Atkinson, September 6, 2019.
2. Ray Wylie Hubbard, interview with Brian T. Atkinson, August 21, 2019.
3. Mike "Miguel" Pankratz, interview with Brian T. Atkinson, November 1, 2019.

VERSE: YOU'RE GONNA MISS ME

1. Mike "Miguel" Pankratz, interview with Brian T. Atkinson, November 1, 2019.
2. Mikel Erickson, interview with Brian T. Atkinson, October 25, 2019.

3. Clementine Hall, interview with Brian T. Atkinson, February 11, 2020.

4. Ray Wylie Hubbard, interview with Brian T. Atkinson, August 21, 2019.

5. Bill Bentley, interview with Brian T. Atkinson, September 11, 2019.

6. "Crazy" Carl Hickerson, interview with Brian T. Atkinson, June 24, 2020.

7. Patoski, "Roky Erickson, 1975."

8. Powell St. John, interview with Brian T. Atkinson, September 29, 2019.

9. Ben Graham, *A Gathering of Promises: The Battle for Texas's Psychedelic Music, from the 13th Floor Elevators to the Black Angels and Beyond* (Winchester, UK: Zero Books, 2015), 26.

10. Powell St. John, interview with Brian T. Atkinson.

11. Graham, *Gathering of Promises*.

12. Powell St. John, interview with Brian T. Atkinson.

13. Klemen Breznikar, "Powell St. John Interview," *It's Psychedelic Baby*, July 22, 2011, accessed July 5, 2020, https://www.psychedelicbabymag.com/2018/04/powell-st-john-sultan-of-psychedelia.html.

14. Powell St. John, interview with Brian T. Atkinson.

15. Breznikar, "Powell St. John Interview."

16. Powell St. John, interview with Brian T. Atkinson.

17. Graham, *Gathering of Promises*.

18. Powell St. John, interview with Brian T. Atkinson.

19. Breznikar, "Powell St. John Interview."

"Stacy was deeply sensitive kid," Sybil Sutherland says. "Things that might not have bothered anybody else hurt cruelly and deeply. He agonized over his inner feelings and turmoil. I would find his Bible open, and he would say, 'What does it mean when it says so-and-so?' He was a happy little boy who loved to fish and hunt and be outdoors, but there was a big change in his life when he was fourteen. I never knew what. He seemed depressed from then on. He was thinking his own thoughts and daydreamed a lot, which was common in adolescents. I thought that's what was happening to him. I thought he was growing up and having a bad time, but there were evidently things changing in his life then. He had a sad look in his pictures from that point on. He wasn't too talkative in most groups. The kids at the Jade Room called him the Dark Angel. He was in another world.

"Roky had gone to Rusk [state psychiatric hospital in Rusk, Texas]. Stacy had gone to prison. I think he turned to drinking. I don't guess anyone will know really what happened [when he was killed] and what [his partner] knows about it in her own heart. She called me three times in the fifteen months they were married. It was always at three-thirty in the morning. She told me she was gonna kill him. This would throw me into a panic. I tried to tell him what she told me on the phone. He kept saying, 'She doesn't mean it. She's a gentle, sweet girl. She would never do anything like that.' 'Why does she call me?' I'd say. 'She was like a different person.' She was afraid of him. He had bought a twenty-two gun and had shown her how to use it. He bought hollow point shells."

Sybil Sutherland, from "A Psychedelic Reprise of the 13th Floor Elevators," YouTube, October 13, 2012, accessed July 5, 2020, www.youtube.com. Sybil

Sutherland was a longtime teacher in Kerrville, Texas, and the mother of 13th Floor Elevators guitarist Stacy Sutherland.

20. Powell St. John, interview with Brian T. Atkinson.

21. Breznikar, "Powell St. John Interview."

22. Clementine Hall, interview with Brian T. Atkinson, May 9, 2020.

23. "Psychedelic Reprise of the 13th Floor Elevators."

24. "Psychedelic Reprise of the 13th Floor Elevators."

25. "Red Krayola started in July 1966," bandleader Mayo Thompson says. "[International Artists Records owner] Leland Rogers had heard us playing one night while buying a parakeet for his wife at the Gulfgate shopping mall. Leland thought we were funny. He said we could barely play and felt like we were putting the audience on, but they really enjoyed it. We were loud, crazy enough, and looked funny. Leland asked if we wanted to make a record for International Artists. We ended up signing with him because we knew who the Elevators were. 'What's the deal with Roky's music?' I asked my friend Bonnie Emerson once. 'He's charismatic,' Bruce said. 'He sweats onstage and people want to lick it off.' They were quite a band. John Ike [Walton] was such a powerful drummer and kicked so hard that he had to chain his drums to his stool. International put us in the studio to record our first album [1967's *The Parable of Arable Land*] at Walt Andrus's studio in Houston. We went in and recorded two 'freak outs' the first night, which lasted thirty-five minutes on a one-inch tape. You can hear people having a strange time.

"Leland wanted Roky to play on a couple songs once we had the band tracks recorded. We thought, Cool. Roky was obviously a good musician. He and Tommy came to the studio. There already was lore about how much acid they did, but Roky and I got along just fine. He heard the tune and got the song in two takes. He understood the spirit in which we were making that music very well. [His] keyboard parts on 'Hurricane Fighter Plane' are quite lovely and really add something. His harp part on 'Transparent Radiation' lives on. He was an interesting harp player. They all talked about Roky and the Elevators when we played the Berkeley Folk Festival in California in 1967. They were trying to get the Elevators out of Texas, but couldn't because they had gotten into trouble."

Mayo Thompson, interview with Brian T. Atkinson, October 19, 2019. Thompson was a founding member of influential Texas psychedelic rockers Red Krayola and has been a celebrated visual artist for decades. He lives in Southern California.

26. Rex "Wrecks" Bell and Mickey White, "Frank Davis Interview," courtesy of Norie Guthrie, special collections library, Woodson Research Center, Rice University, Houston, Texas.

27. McAlester, *You're Gonna Miss Me.*

28. Roky Erickson, interview with Joe Nick Patoski, Doug Hanners, Kirby McDaniel, and Deron Bissett, 1975.

29. "Psychedelic Reprise of the 13th Floor Elevators."

30. Billy Miller, interview with Brian T. Atkinson, November 19, 2020.

CHORUS: GOODBYE SWEET DREAMS

1. Roky Erickson, interview with Patoski et al., 1975.

2. McAlester, *You're Gonna Miss Me.*

"I was in Austin, Texas, for South by Southwest around 1993, when a guy from *USA Today* took a picture of me walking down the street," tongue-in-cheek rocker Mojo Nixon says. "I might've been on some [drugs]. I had this full beard and crazy jacket. They ran the picture in the newspaper the next day but confused me with Roky. The headline said, 'Texas legend Roky Erickson walks the streets of South by Southwest.' I'm not sure if that says I'm crazy or Roky's crazy. Who's supposed to be offended here? The guys from my band made a T-shirt they sold with the picture: 'Mojo Nixon Mistaken for Roky Erickson.' The shirt looked like the front page of the *USA Today* with the photo of me looking like I was pretending to be Roky. I mean, I was proud to be mistaken for Roky, but it does say something about how fucking high I was."

Mojo Nixon, interview with Brian T. Atkinson, January 17, 2020.

3. Roky Erickson, interview with Patoski et al., 1975.

OPENERS II: ROKY ERICKSON'S SOLO CAREER

1. McAlester, *You're Gonna Miss Me.*

2. Will Sheff, interview with Brian T. Atkinson, September 18, 2019.

3. Stu Cook, interview with Brian T. Atkinson, June 17, 2019.

4. Michael Hann, "Roky Erickson: The Visionary Who Took a Trip to the Edge of Rock 'n' Roll: Psychedelic Rocker's Overindulgences with Acid Left a Narrow but Deep Musical Legacy," *The Guardian*, June 1, 2019, accessed July 5, 2020, www.theguardian.com.

5. McAlester, *You're Gonna Miss Me.*

6. Jad Fair, interview with Brian T. Atkinson, November 6, 2019.

7. "Austin City Limits Celebrates 40 Years: 'Two Headed Dog,'" YouTube, October 5, 2014, accessed July 5, 2020, www.youtube.com.

8. Roky Erickson, "Roky Erickson Interview 1981," YouTube, January 14, 2005, accessed July 5, 2020, www.youtube.com.

9. Will Sheff, interview with Brian T. Atkinson.

VERSE: TWO-HEADED DOG

1. Mikel Erickson, interview with Brian T. Atkinson, October 25, 2019.

2. Clementine Hall, interview with Brian T. Atkinson, May 9, 2020.

3. Roky Erickson, interview with Patoski et al., 1975.

4. Joe Nick Patoski, interview with Brian T. Atkinson, February 8, 2020.

5. Joe Nick Patoski, liner notes from Roky Erickson's *Don't Slander Me* reissue on Light in the Attic Records, 2013.

6. Stu Cook, interview by Brian T. Atkinson, June 17, 2019.

7. Chris "Cosmo Topper" Knab, interview with Brian T. Atkinson, May 6, 2020.

8. Howard Thompson, interview with Brian T. Atkinson, May 1, 2020. Nick Kent's later piece on Erickson was included as "The Bewildering Universe of Roky Erickson" in *Nick Kent: The Dark Stuff* (New York: Penguin Books, 1994).

9. Joe Nick Patoski, interview with Brian T. Atkinson, February 8, 2020.

10. Billy Miller, interview with Brian T. Atkinson, November 14, 2019.

11. Dan Cook, interview with Brian T. Atkinson, June 6, 2020; email interview with Brian T. Atkinson, June 29, 2020. The following is an opening excerpt from the interview:

"I've shot the shit with my share of rock icons over a long journalism career: Alice Cooper, James Taylor, Lou Reed, Gene Clark, Roger McGuinn," Cook said. "My meeting with Roky Erickson was by far the most memorable. Our meeting started on a warm summer afternoon in Austin in 1993 and ended with Roky gently falling asleep on the sofa of his mad hatter's cottage on the outskirts of town. It was unlike any media tour before or since and solidified my love of a man who I had worshiped from afar for many years. It raised more questions that I had asked, questions that would never have occurred to me before that day.

"We followed Roky's tragi-comedic career as best we could through the rock press, but I didn't meet the man himself until 1993, when I was the editor of the *In Pittsburgh* newsweekly. We belonged to the Association of Alternative Newsweeklies, and the *Austin Chronicle* was hosting the annual meeting that year. I contacted my friend Mike Alvarez [when I got to Austin]. We had met when we both lived in Los Angeles. He used to share stories about Roky when we would hang out at his place on Sunset Boulevard. I asked if he would be able to set up an interview for me with Roky while I was in Austin. He would and did. The plan was to meet Roky at his mom's house around noon, then go have lunch and maybe spend a little time together. Mike told me Roky was kind of drugged up and might be a bit unpredictable. Was he ever right.

"My friend Cindy Barber, who was the editor of the *Cleveland Free Times* then, was along for the trip and wanted to meet Roky. I rang the bell at the Ericksons' home and was greeted by Roky's mother, Evelyn. She explained that Roky was off to a bit of a slow start that day. Roky was washing his hands over and over in the kitchen. Over and over. I waited quietly behind him for a while but finally introduced myself. Roky continued washing his hands. He acknowledged me when the hand washing ended. He was definitely in some kind of fog. I saw a guitar against the wall and asked if he would play for me. "I can't play anymore," he said without explanation. "Why not?" "My hands just don't work like they used to," he said. "Want to go get something to eat?"

12. Jon Dee Graham, interview with Brian T. Atkinson, July 29, 2020.

13. Mike Alvarez, interview with Brian T. Atkinson, May 1, 2020.

14. Mike Jensen, interview with Brian T. Atkinson, May 4, 2020.

15. Mike Haskins, interview with Brian T. Atkinson, November 12, 2019.

16. Gregg Turner, interview with Brian T. Atkinson, November 4, 2019.

17. Freddie "Steady" Krc, interview with Brian T. Atkinson, October 4, 2019.

18. Harold F. Eggers Jr., interview with Brian T. Atkinson, October 16, 2019.

19. Will Sexton, interview with Brian T. Atkinson, February 19, 2020.

20. Joe Nick Patoski, interview with Brian T. Atkinson, February 8, 2020. "I only met Roky once," iconic songwriter James McMurtry says. "We were at the old Texicalli Grille on Oltorf [Street in Austin] in the midnineties. I went in to get a burger, and Casey Monahan was sitting in there with a guy who looked homeless. I thought, Wow, Casey's feeding the homeless today. Okay. Casey motioned me over and said, 'James, I would like you to meet Roky Erickson.' 'Okay.' I shook Roky's hand, but I was still a little apprehensive about meeting him. 'Nice to meet you,' Roky says, 'but you gotta go now, right?'"

James McMurtry, conversation with Brian T. Atkinson, February 17, 2020.

BRIDGE: STARRY EYES

1. Henry Rollins, email interview with Brian T. Atkinson, September 15, 2019.

2. Casey Monahan, interview with Brian T. Atkinson, September 17, 2019.

3. Stuart Sullivan, interview with Brian T. Atkinson, October 1, 2019.

4. Shawn Sahm, interview with Brian T. Atkinson, October 21, 2019.

5. Dylan Carlson, interview with Brian T. Atkinson, November 2, 2019.

6. Mark Lanegan, interview with Brian T. Atkinson, October 14, 2019.

7. Bill Bentley, interview with Brian T. Atkinson, September 11, 2019.

8. Bruce Hughes, interview with Brian T. Atkinson, December 21, 2019.

9. John Wesley Harding, interview with Brian T. Atkinson, September 5, 2019.

10. Jeff Heiskell, interview with Brian T. Atkinson, September 20, 2019.

11. Cris Kirkwood, interview with Brian T. Atkinson, December 5, 2019.

12. Jeffrey "King" Coffey, interview with Brian T. Atkinson, September 6, 2019.

13. Jeff Smith, interview with Brian T. Atkinson, April 20, 2020.

14. Carolyn Wonderland, interview with Brian T. Atkinson, March 18, 2020.

15. Shelley King, interview with Brian T. Atkinson, February 18, 2020.

16. Troy Campbell, interview with Brian T. Atkinson, January 4, 2020.

17. Darren Hill, interview with Brian T. Atkinson, September 26, 2019.

CHORUS: TRUE LOVE CAST OUT ALL EVIL

1. Will Sheff, interview with Brian T. Atkinson, September 18, 2019.

2. Alex Maas, interview with Brian T. Atkinson, September 7, 2019.

3. Sam Bryant, interview with Brian T. Atkinson, December 11, 2019.

4. Bonnie Bloomgarden, interview with Brian T. Atkinson, October 22, 2019.

5. Larry Schemel, interview with Brian T. Atkinson, October 22, 2019.

6. Scott H. Biram, interview with Brian T. Atkinson, December 13, 2019.

7. Chris Fullerton, interview with Brian T. Atkinson, October 15, 2019.

8. Will Cullen Hart, interview with Brian T. Atkinson, September 13, 2019.

9. Emily Nokes, interview with Brian T. Atkinson, June 15, 2020.

10. Kassie Carlson, interview with Brian T. Atkinson, June 23, 2020.

11. "I knew Janis Joplin. My group the Association opened the entire weekend of the Monterey International Pop Festival [in Monterey, California, featuring Joplin's major performance debut as well as legendary sets by cultural icons such as Jimi Hendrix, the Who, Otis Redding, Ravi Shankar, the Grateful Dead, and the Mamas and the Papas in 1967]. We stayed at the same motel as Janis and Big Brother and the Holding Company and saw Pearly [Janis Joplin] interact with all the two- and three-year-old kids whose parents were from other groups. Janis was out there jiving with them. She was a really sweet gal, which was especially neat to find out after seeing her out there onstage. She blew me away. I was incredibly intimidated because I had never seen a woman sing like that. 'Holy shit,' I was saying in the audience. 'Who is this woman?' We hung out with people in the mess tent with Jimi Hendrix, Otis Redding, Paul Simon, Art Garfunkel. We really had the Summer of Love feeling.

"There really wasn't any competition or animosity during that time. We were aware of psychedelic rock, but what we were doing was pretty much the opposite direction besides 'Along Comes Mary,' which fit lyrically into that bag. Record companies would say, 'We really like you guys, but we don't know what to do with you.' We were all over the place doing country, rock, ballads, love songs, which kept us out of the main flow. It worked out in the long haul, though. We did skits and comedy bits during our shows.

"I was about fifteen feet away when Jimi Hendrix burned his guitar, which was very sexy. You would look around and see all the women going, 'Oh. Oh my god.' I thought, Hey, man, you're burning your guitar. I swear I had been in the all-army entertainment contest with Hendrix. He did 'The Star-Spangled Banner' with one hand and waved the flag with the other [in the army] and blew everybody away, so it was very far out there to see him at Monterey lighting his guitar on fire. We do a bit onstage now about trying to remember all the groups who played that weekend. The air was scented with smoke going around. 'Those hippies are so friendly,' one guy says in the bit. 'I see they're sharing a cigarette.' Mellowness really permeated everything.

"No, I don't know the 13th Floor Elevators."

Jim Yester, interview with Brian T. Atkinson, September 24, 2019. Yester serves as vocalist and rhythm guitarist for the Association. The legendary folk outfit, who produced chart toppers such as "Along Comes Mary" and "Cherish," forever made their historical mark as opening act at the pioneering Monterey Pop Festival in 1967.

12. Dom Flemons, interview with Brian T. Atkinson, May 18, 2020.

13. Dean Wareham, interview with Brian T. Atkinson, June 21, 2020.

14. Pete Kember, interview with Brian T. Atkinson, May 1, 2020.

15. Jonathan Donahue, interview with Brian T. Atkinson, September 14, 2019.

16. Isaiah Mitchell, interview with Brian T. Atkinson, January 31, 2020.

17. Parker Griggs, interview with Brian T. Atkinson, February 5, 2020.

18. Charles Michael Parks Jr., interview with Brian T. Atkinson, November 12, 2019.

19. Ambrose Kenny-Smith, interview with Brian T. Atkinson, December 13, 2019.

20. Stuart Braithwaite, email interview with Brian T. Atkinson, April 24, 2020.

GHOST TRACKS

1. Patrick McGarrigle, email exchange with Brian T. Atkinson, May 5, 2020; text message exchange with Brian T. Atkinson, June 2, 2020.

2. Dana Gaines Erickson, phone conversation with Brian T. Atkinson, May 5, 2020.

In fond memory of Papa Mike Mikan

INDEX